RARRI 2

DOWN FOR THE CROWN

ASANI BANDZ

I want to dedicate this book to both of my sons, Kevin and Nike. The love I have for the two of you is something I have never felt before. Thoughts of the three of us together is the only thing that keeps me striving and thinking positive. Nobody comes before y'all. Not in this lifetime nor the next. There's not a day that goes by that the two of you are not on my mind. My only regret is not being able to be there for y'all how I should be right now. I promise to make better choices and to never leave y'all again. Every child needs their father, but, I'm a father who needs his children. Nuk nuk I'm so proud of you for accomplishing the goals you put in front of yourself and getting your grades up. Now all you gotta do is get some dreads, because deep down inside you know You really want to 😂.
Nike I'm also proud of you for staying so strong no matter what. You remind me so much of myself when I was your age (you're smarter tho) 😂. I still can't comprehend how you understand math so well at such a young age but I'm glad you do. Knowing numbers can be applied in so many ways. Always take advantage of that, Nike.
When I look at y'all I see me. I miss y'all so much, man. I want you both to know that no matter what, there will never be a time when I am not in y'all corner. NEVER! Your dad is goin to always have your back. Nothin is worth being away from the two most important people in the world.. I love y'all and no matter how old y'all get don't ever forget that y'all will always be daddy's babies.
AKINS ARE FOREVER 💯

CONTENTS

ACKNOWLEDGMENTS

I want to thank My moms, LATACHEE, for being in my corner. None of my visions would be possible if you didn't believe in them with me. Your support is what I needed most and is another thing that keeps me going. I'm so grateful to have a mother like you to show me the characteristics to pass down to my kids. I love you so much and I'm also proud of everything you have overcome in life and how you carry the torch that granny left behind. I know I must do the same.

I want to thank my pops for being in my corner, too. I remember always thinking you was trippin about little stuff because you were institutionalized or somethin but everything you taught me is what I needed to survive in here. In every situation I think..'*What would my pops do?'* That never fails me.

I want thank Aseera for all the support AND with typing this never ending book up😅. I know it was a long process and I may be one of the most difficult people to work with, but I do appreciate everything that you have done. You are a dope author that touches so many genres that it's crazy. I can't wait to see '*The Return of the Chosen'* reach theaters and streaming on all platforms.

I really want to thank My boy Sub0zero for messin' wit me with the magazine issues. The Phat Puffs platform is what got '*Rarri'* where it is, so I will always be grateful for that. Especially for the continuous support. Phat Puffs magazines are sold all across America and

I've been lucky enough to be featured in multiple issues. Most of my readers came across my work because of Phatpuffs. What I respect about sub0zero most is that he's not just going to put anything in his shit. The story has to be good and transparent with his work. If your locked up and lookin for a promotion source I would definitely hit him up. Sub0zero is a real down to earth and solid dude..

I want to thank CA$H for the blurb of my first book. The fact that you took the time out of your day to do that means a lot because you are hands down one of the hardest working authors out there. I see books by LOCKDOWN PUBLICATIONS everywhere. You haven't forgotten where you came from and I see that all the time when you are helping people who are locked up with their work and given them shutouts and all types of Shit. If you are an incarcerated author looking to get your work out there I wouldn't hesitate to see if your work makes the cut to sign with LOCKDOWN PUBLICATIONS. Having a publisher who's been through what your goin through goes a long way.

I want to thank My friend Kenya Redd, another dope author for helping me find someone to do my cover and for helping me with the whole self-publishing thing. You didn't leave a stone unturned when giving me that game. Thanks for remaining the same person. If you're in need of a book cover reach out to her on Facebook for ebook or paperback formats.

I want to thank Pooh from up north for giving me so much game. Everything you told me was something I was actually able to apply now. I'm still seeing results just off of the conversations we used to have. Thanks for takin the time out of your day to give me somethin that will stay with me forever. If You ever need my assistance with any of your ventures don't hesitate to macc in.

I want to thank my Cambodian nigga Pepsi, Fresno Tiny Raskal Gang, for always feeding my brain with business minded shit and sliding me books that changed my way of thinking. I know when your book drops it's goin to do numbers. Fasho a must read for anyone in or coming to prison. I can't wait to see us 10 years from now. From the yard to the yatch. These million-dollar conversations and mindsets are goin to pay off.

I also want to thank everyone who read Rarri in here who took the time to read my shit so shout out to

Pork chop (PJ watts), k.d, dayday (Rollin hunnits), pop4 , pop5 & lowdown(inglewood legends), lil stay (starz), Quake & blaze (East Coast crip), phat ghost (BLOCC CRIP), A.k (Brims), solo (357um), Jay rock (the bay), D dog (Hoover), Deek & nitty (durocc), Casper & Gotti (piru), duby from anthens park, JCap grape street watts crip. my nigga king mfn peno you really pushed me to finish this mf and put it out on everything. Good looking for staying on me and inquirin about part 2. I Listened to yo music and all of them songs go crazy bro, you gotta get out and kill em with yo music soon as you touchdown P .

Also I want to thank all y'all who I don't know who have bought my book. Good lookin on the support I really appreciate that shit and the feedback.. Y'all MADE me write this one fasho So this one is for y'all. I hope y'all enjoy the read.

Rarri 2 Down For The Crown.

ONE

"Aww shit" Rarri groaned out in pain as his head throbbed out of control. "What the fuck?" he asked himself when both of his arms were tied to the chair he was sitting in as were his legs.

He could hear Carlos and Jose talking to each other in Spanish, both of them sharing laughs back and forth as if this was the normal shit they did on a daily basis, which, they did.

"So it's like that?" Rarri asked out loud interrupting their conversation. "Ya'll scary mothafuccas can't even look me in my eyes before ya'll kill me? Bitch ass niggas!!"

Jose and Carlos started laughing again. The only who was scared in that room, was Rarri, but he wasn't about to let them see that. He thought back to that day that Heaven warned him to *"Always watch a bitch"*

Thinking back:

"What about you?" Rarri asked her.

"Even me" she answered him.

Rarri could still see the look on her face when she said that. It wasn't until now that understood the degree of her expression. Never in a million years would he have thought she would be the one to cross him or cause him any harm. He trusted her more than anyone he could think of. Now, that trust was broken. He felt like a fucking fool.

Carlos removed his blindfold and stood next to Jose. Both of them smiling with that pathetic American cool guy nod they couldn't help doing so much, still, never speaking a word to him.

Now, Rarri was pissed. He couldn't believe these two Mexican muthafuccas was about to kill him and immediately started to think, '*This how juice must have felt on the yacht as everyone found it funny when he was about to die, well I ain't never bought to cry..fuck all that. Especially not in front of these niggas'* He continued to think to himself as he looked at the two menacingly. He couldn't help but wonder how they planned on killing him. Knowing these two it wasn't about to be fast or painless.

Ways to die started to run through his head. '*Are they bout to cut me up like that nigga Enzi? They gonna inject me with some other type of crazy shit? Cut my eyelids in half? FUCC!*' So many thoughts ran through his mind. Carlos and Jose smelled like death. Murder seeped from their pores relentlessly. Killing was an art to them so they did it with passion.

"Man, Tony not goin to like this shit, I kno hi-" Rarri started to speak again.

"HA! Tony?" a voice asked from behind him. A voice that seemed to make both of these killing muthafuccas nervous while taking the smile off of their faces along with the slouch in their shoulders as they stood at full attention.

He was so stunned by their change in demeanor he tried only looking from the corner of his eyes, hoping to get a glimpse of who was behind him. He could hear and feel the person storming towards him quickly, but more so angrily.

"Tony?!" The voice asked again in disbelief. "Tony what?!"

Rarri knew not to say another word and secretly wished he hadn't of to begin with. He looked at Jose and Carlos hoping they could somehow help him but the two of them scurried out of the way as their boss stormed up.

"Tony what?!" she asked louder now standing directly in front of Rarri.

"t-t-t-t" Rarri tried to get out but was at a loss for words.

The woman standing in front of him was beautiful. The most beautiful person he had ever laid eyes on. She has on so much Prada that Rarri would have bet his last dollar that's exactly what her pussy smelled like too. Her face was so close to his that he could smell the sweetness on her breath. Time stood still as he became lost in her pretty light brown eyes. Her body was so curvy that she could easily be mistaken for a porn star. Her sex appeal was at an all time high. She was hands down the most exotic woman to be this close to him and his dick grew hard as a rock as he fantasized about her, forgetting about his current situation.

In his 'mind's eye', they were on some exotic beach he had never been to before and probably couldn't pronounce right even when she wasn't on top of him grinding that phat ass passionately; Seductively sucking on his tongue while her pussy dripped uncontrollably down his dic-…

SMACK!!

"Tony What?!!!" she screamed louder after smacking the shit out of him.

'Fuck..' he swore to himself 'this bitch crazy'

"Tony this, Tony that, Tony, Tony, Tony!! Tony is nothing without me, do you understand" NOTHING!" she said, pacing back and forth. "I give him everything and for what? Just to be left at home while he spend time and 'my money' on some cheap hooker who has a nephew as a pimp? Not anymore.

"So you the connect?" Rarri asked bluntly, ear still ringing from the previous slap.

"I'm the wife" she responded with her hand extended to show off her ring, then added, "..and the connect."

"Damn, that's all bad." He chuckled to himself.

"Excuse me?" she asked in her heavy accent. "What is this, '*all bad*', you say?"

"Nothin" he replied taking the smile off of his face.

"nooo, no, no...this 'all bad' you say is not nothing. It is something and if you don't tell what it is I'll have them kill you so you can join your little friend in the bathtub, yes?" she said seriously.

Rarri laughed sarcastically. "What difference would that make to me? Ya'll bout to kill me anyway...shidd, at least Ima be with somebody I know." He threw out like it was nothing to him. "AYE, Carlos! Jose! Ya'll heard the lady, let's get this shit over with."

They just looked at each other in question but didn't budge.

"If I was going to kill you, you would have been dead. She admitted. "Now, tell me."

Rarri could see she wasn't lying. He paused for a minute, took a deep breath making her wait as one word went through his mind, *BREATHE*. "Fuck it, ima just keep it real but can I ask you somethin?"

She sighed in frustration looking elsewhere. "Go on, ask."

"What's wrong with you?" he asked bluntly, taking her by surprise.

"Nothing is wrong with *me*." She replied not believing the nerve of this young boy as she dramatically pointed to herself.

"I mean, that's what you say but something gotta be wrong with you. Why else would a nigga leave a bitch like you? You must not be doin somethin right. What you don't know how to throw that pussy back or somethin?" Rarri chuckled to himself. "No, now that I think about it, you do look like one of those type of bitches that just be laying there getting fucked all boring and shit"

She waved him off and stormed away angry, which seemed to be enough for Carlos and Jose.

"Shit, I'm just saying, ain't nobody about to leave no bitch as fine as you for nothi-"

Carlos threw a plastic bag over his head before he could get out another word. He pulled it back tightly making sure there were was no room for air as Rarri began to struggle trying his best to break free to no avail. Maria looked at herself in the mirror, , examining everything about herself trying to see if there was something actually wrong that she had not noticed before.

"What do you think, is something wrong with me?" she asked Enzi then waved him off. "What do you know anyway huh? You're dead." *'No one talks to me like that...EVER!'* she thought as she admired herself in the mirror, straightening out the unseen wrinkles in her dress. *'Silly boy. I bet he wishes he chose his words more wisely when speaking to me now. Who does he think he is, talking to me as if I am no one important? As if I...As if I were someone he not fear....as if I...were someone he did not have to lie to.'*

Maria rushed out of the bathroom. "Let him go!"

Carlos looked at her confused.

"NOW!" she ordered with authority and Carlos did as he was told.

Rarri coughed and gasped for air. This was the closest he had ever been to dying and he wasn't diggin this near death experience shit at all.

"Cut him free" she demanded. "NOW!"

Jose did unwillingly. Rarri fell to the floor in exhaustion as the room began to stop spinning while he recovered. He got up trying to adjust his clothes as best as possible, still catching his breath.

"You know, I was thinking.." she said seductively as Rarri was walking up.

SMACK!

"Me too.." he replied, smacking her to the floor.

"NO!" she yelled, putting her hand up to stop Carlos and Jose from attacking him. "Leave us.."

"But Maria..."

"LEAVE US!" she shouted louder, giving them a look they knew all too well.

"As you wish." Jose replied bowing his head in respect before leaving the room and giving Rarri a mean mug the entire way out.

When the door was closed he looked down at Maria who was looking up at him like he was a god. She, for the first time in her life, was the submissive. Never has a person been this bold. This daring. This dangerous. This real. This exciting. Nothing ever felt this good before to her.

"Get on yo knees." Rarri instructed and she did so without question. "Now open yo mouth up bitch and keep it open."

Initially, Rarri didn't know if this shit was going to work or not. He was just playing his hand as it went because wasn't too many other options, so as soon as the bitch gave him an inch, he decided to go for the mile like any other nigga would.

Maria massaged herself as she watched him slowly pull his dick out and then put it in her mouth. She moaned in excitement as she began to twirl her tongue and move her head from side to side. He grabbed a fist full of her hair to control her head. "Did I tell you to suck my shit?"

"No." she replied with him still in her mouth.

"Is you ready to listen?"

She nodded never breaking eye contact. Rarri pushed her head far enough down to keep her drooling as she played with herself, he spoke.

"You see, you got the world wrapped around yo finger but right now I got yo mouth wrapped around my dick. I don't give a fuck who you think you is bitch, I run this shit. Not *you*. ME. If you can't get with that, yo trick ass could leave cause it damn sure ain't gon make or break me, but you ain't going nowhere cause this what you want, ain't it?" Rarri drilled then pushed her head down a lil further. "Aint it!"

"Yes" she admitted as both of her lips watered.

"You know you bout to be payin me don't you? DON'T YOU?!" He asked pushing her head down further making her eyes tightin and mouth water as she gagged on him deeply.

Maria couldn't speak a word so she just nodded as tears came down her face. She came so hard on her fingers that her body shook uncontrollably and she couldn't stop moaning. Rarri pushed himself so far down her throat that her eyes grew wide and held her there for about five seconds then pulled out leaving her gasping for air, then did it again and again until he felt himself cumming. He pulled out and came on her face so hard that it took her by surprise but she loved every minute of it. So did Rarri.

The power he felt at that moment was beyond anything he'd even experienced. Maria stood, grabbed Rarri by the hand, led him to the bathroom and turned on the shower. She looked at him like prey as the thought of feeding her kitty kat made her head spin and pussy throb. Maria had never been with another man before because her loyalty and trust had always been for Tony. Lies. Maria hated lies more than anything and Tony was full of them, but, Rarri obviously wasn't. She could see Rarri would tell her the truth even if it killed him because unlike Tony and the others, he did not fear her. That's what turned her on the most.

TWO

THE TRUTH WAS, Maria had been watching Rarri long enough to know what to expect from him. She knew about the Bentley Bitches, Ms. Brown, the way he did Supreme in the bay and how he chose Betty Wap over all the other girls at the show. She respected him for that part mostly because looking at Betty Wap, Maria could see how hard life must have been and most men would probably pass her in a line up because of her eye and shit. Maria took her heels off, stepped in the shower fully clothed and rinsed her face. Rarri watched in awe as she soaked herself not worrying the slightest bit about ruining a $2500 dollar Prada dress.

She let the water rinse through her hair, turning it into a kinky curl then grabbed the complementary body wash with a face towel and cleaned herself seductively as Rarri continued watching. Maria pulled her Victoria Secret panties down, threw them out and slowly cleaned her already clean pussy under her wet dress as he eyed her in anticipation of seeing her nakedness. She waved her finger from side to side letting him know that he would have to watch only. She then pulled the top of her dress down to her waist, took off her bra exposing her voluptuous breast, light brown nipples and cleaned them slowly with the soapy washcloth.

'*Fuck..*' Rarri said to himself as he grew hard as a rock yet again. He couldn't wait another second. He got completely naked and quickly got into the shower. He hungrily took one of her breast into his mouth and grabbed two hands full of ass, making her moan in excitement.

He placed his fingers down to her pussy from the back and massaged it as he twirled his tongue around her nipples, showing them both equal amounts of attention. When he felt the warmth of her cumming down his fingers, he started to kiss her neck passionately. Maria couldn't wait another moment, she grabbed his dick and slid it inside of her slowly, both of them pausing as this new feeling of pure bliss sunk in.

Maria's pussy was the tightest he had ever felt and she never dealt with a black dick before so she did so with caution. Rarri touched places inside of her she never thought possible. He discovered things about her not even she knew until now and Maria was more than grateful. An hour later she laid next to him, out of breath, sore, exhausted and couldn't stop smiling to save her life. For the first time in a long time, Maria felt happy. Not that pretend happy she was used to either. This time she was truly happy, she felt blessed.

"My bad for putting my hands on you...I just really had to get my slap back." Rarri admitted.

"It's okay." She replied and then added "Next time, I kill you."

The both of them looked at each other and started laughing. Maria's laugh matched Rarri's a little but too long making hers seem a little suspicious and causing him to slow down. '*This bitch serious*' he thought to himself as she put her hand on his chest.

"Leave with me "Maria said in excitement, looking into his eyes with her heart."

"Where you tryna go?" he asked with that million dollar smile.

"Home, to Columbia. We can always come back here to the

states but in Columbia, I am a queen. Well, sort of, me mama is the queen so technically, it makes me the princess but *you…*you can be a kingpin..a drug *lord"* she said with so much passion that he knew she was serious.

"I mean, that sound coo and all but I ain't no drug dealer. He admitted honestly.

"Yes you are." She countered. "You no see, *I see.* Me, see everything I need to see, Rarri. Everything."

"Is that right?" he asked.

"It is." She replied seriously. "Me no lie…I *hate* lies. That's why I want you. You no lie like me, yea? We are the same, me and you."

Rarri liked Maria. There was a feeling that he felt in this time around her that he hadn't felt yet. He couldn't explain it but he knew it was real.

"So, tell me what it is that you see."

She sat up straight in the bed to get in her business mode and cleared her throat before speaking.

"Tony '*now'* give Heaven the coka for 5,000 a kilo who is pretending she's charging 8,000 for them but she is not. She then distributes them to your friend, little Dink, who spreads them throughout the cities of Compton, Long Beach, Los Angeles and recently to a city nearby called Watts. Watts very close to Compton, no? Heaven, she has been undercutting Tony's business partners using the Bentley Bitches as a tool because men are weak for beautiful women and high price *prostitutes.* Secretly, you all rob the clients after finding out their schedules and where they live, which in my opinion is smart but at the same time, not such a good idea.

After the drugs are sold the money is brought back to Heaven who cleans it by giving the dirty money to a company called Mashtrack.inc who then wires 80% of that to numerous accounts. Mostly opened in your name. So even though you may not *want* to consider yourself a drug dealer…you are."

Maria then gave him a kiss on the chest, got out of the bed and headed to the shower. She stopped in the doorway knowing Rarri was watching her perfectly shaped ass then looked back seductively.

"If you insist on breaking bitches, why not do it like you never have before, no?"

She then turned around and switched her cheeks with precision as she walked into the bathroom. Rarri smiled to himself for a few moments then went to join her for a shower and to get specific details of her idea of course. Maria let him know that she would be the head bitch in due time but for now, he could play with his little pets, (referring to his other bitches) and entertain the thought of them ever being what she *was* going to be for him.

As she scrubbed Rarri's back clean, she talked about bringing girls from Columbia back to America to work for him. Maria stressed the fact that they *will*, undoubtedly, be more loyal to him than any of the girls he had now because of the fear she would put in them. He laughed because he knew she was serious. He could just see the excitement in her eyes when she used the word '*Fear*'. He let her know that she would have to come up with another way to get them because in his world, it's by choice and not by force. She agreed but secretly began to come up with a way to persuade him to see things her way.

"*He could be so much more if he wasn't so nice.*" She thought to herself.

As she told him about Tony's role, come to find out he wasn't Cuban, he was Columbian. To Rarri, Mexicans were Mexican. Columbian, Cuban, Latin, Mexican, it was all the same shit to him. What really had him tripping though was that this whole time, Tony was *pretending* to be the man when in reality he was just the face for Maria in America while she took care of everything in Columbia.

Tony was never good at keeping up with finances but Maria said almost a year ago the money started looking *too* funny, so she sent people that Tony *assumed* were his men to keep a closer eye on things. That's when she found out about Heaven. Everything was coming together now. Rarri always wondered if he knew Heaven was secretly stealing his clientele and not saying nothing because he was pussy whipped or he honestly didn't know. I mean, the day he met Tony he knew the man obviously couldn't count correctly.

Heaven and Rarri had been plotting up that plan for about six months coming up with a fail proof idea. They went through the text messages in Chu-chu's phone which was almost enough because he never deleted his phone. He even had the first text messages he sent out from the first day he bought the mothafucka. All that along with the shit Heaven heard him talking about over the years was everything they needed.

They already knew how much Chu-chu owed him so when Tony said, *"Where's my $250,000?"* Rarri knew something was off with him because he fronted Chu-chu fifteen kilos which would mean he actually owed him $300,000. That just put an extra $50,000 for them to keep. On top of that, his trick ass tried to show out in front of Heaven and simply told Rarri to keep the money like he had it like that. So, Rarri just ended up sliding the $300,000 that was Tony's to begin with and purchased some *free kilos* of pure Columbian blend, waaay more than he intended on getting. Speeding back up to now, Tony was in too deep.

All of the people he dealt with insisted on dealing with Heaven more than him, which was something he thought he was hiding from her. Heaven knew Tony didn't *want* her riding along with him all of the time like he *pretended* he did. She knew he hated the way men looked at her. They also loved when she brought her 'sisters' along to talk business as well. That was always the icing on the cake.

These were men who never complained about prices for good companionship. Money was nothing to them because they had so much of it. Straight cash, wire transfers, it never really mattered. Wherever and however Heaven wanted the money is how she got it. Mostly with extra tips of course. Maria told Rarri every detail of the operation with Tony, leaving nothing out. She also told him that she would go back home for a little while to get her things in order before returning to the states and for now to keep their encounter a secret until the time was right.

Even though Rarri didn't like sneaking around with *no* bitch, he agreed because of the situation. Maria looked at Rarri eye to eye as she stroked his dick slowly. "One more, yeah?"

"Hell Yeah." Rarri pulled her closer palming both of her cheeks.

"Not here." She told him, pulling him by his dick and leading him out of the shower, both of them dripping wet.

"Slow down, you about to pull my shit off"

Maria laughed sexily. He was loving every minute with her. She was a lot different than what he was used to. Not only was she a boss ass bitch, she was also sexy, fun, beautiful and smart. Everything a man could ask for in a woman, but as she put her hand on the doorknob of the other bathroom door, he couldn't help but think of how crazy she was. She opened the door, sat on the sink, spread her legs and pulled Rarri close to her almost in one motion.

"What you---"

"Shhhh"

"Oh shit!" he moaned as she pulled him closer and inside of her, wrapping her legs around him so that he was locked in. Maria's shit seemed wetter and tighter than before. Rarri grew an extra inch inside of her causing her to try and run but he gripped the back of her to keep her still then rammed all the way in, making her scream out in pain.

She stopped trying to run from him and took what she had coming with teary eyes caused by the pimp stick stuck in her stomach as she watched Enzi's dead eyes envy Rarri while he fulfilled her biggest fantasy. She came even harder knowing that the scene was enough to make a dead man jealous. Rarri laid in the bed in his briefs watching Maria slide back in her wet dress. She texted in her phone as they got to know each other even more. They laughed and flirted some more without a care in the world.

KNOCK! KNOCK! KNOCK!

"It's time for me to go for now." Maria gave Rarri a kiss on the cheek, then she looked at him deeply in the eyes while rubbing the side of his face softly. "I'm going to love you" she didn't wait for him to reply before getting up to leave. Maria didn't expect Rarri to express much of himself to her so soon. She knew what the deal was with him and she loved it. *'You will love me back'* she thought with a smile as she opened the door for Carlos and Jose.

There was a lady standing there with them holding a long black coat, a brown wig, some shades and a sun hat. Maria stepped to the side letting her henchmen in as she put on her disguise to sneak out undetected, she did in. Rarri was laying back with his eyes closed and a big ass smile on his face thinking about everything that had just happened when he heard footsteps coming near him. Thinking it was Maria coming back, he started to pop some fly shit then froze when he saw it was Carlos and Jose standing there smiling at him. He eased up a bit until he saw that needle in Carlos hand again as he pushed some of the fluid out to make sure there wasn't any air in the tube, flicking it with his finger.

Rarri smiled and nodded his head at them how they always be doing causing them to return the same gesture. Then he bounced out of the bed, hoping that was enough to buy him enough time to make it to the bathroom, but, it was too far. They were on him before he was even close. He tried to fight them off, throwing punches, kicks, elbows and whatever else he could, to stop them. He even tried biting Jose drawing blood hoping that nigga ain't have AIDS or some shit.

Jose screamed out in pain. Rarri felt the sting of the needle go into his side and knew it was all over. His body went weak and his eyes quickly began to get heavy. Jose slid from under him, rubbing his back where he had been bitten. Rarri laughed sluggishly as drool came from his mouth then went back out cold...

THREE

"WHAT'S WRONG?" Heaven asked Rarri noticing him rub his back in pain for the fourth time now.

Jose and Carlos chuckled. If looks could kill Rarri's would have caught a double homicide and if it wasn't for the duffle bag full of money he had woken up next to, he would have rushed one of those mothafuckas.

"Did one of these mothafuckas touch you?" Heaven caught on quick to what was going on. She was so loud that people looked at them in question in the five star restaurant of the hotel.

Carlos and Jose were spooked. They had the same look on their faces that they did when Maria started yelling at them. They seen how cold Heaven could and often wondered who was more vicious out of her and Maria. Even though Maria was the boss the two feared Heaven just as much.

'These two cold hearted killers are scared of two bitches' Rarri thought to himself noticing how they were looking. "

"Why would they do some shit like that. Do I look the type of nigga that would let these niggas touch me?"

Rarri jumped up with a clenched fist and flinched at Jose with a serious expression.

"I would beat the shit out of this nigga.."

The three of them was trying their hardest not to laugh. Rarri felt his coming so he said, "At the same damn time." Mimicking Future's voice while he did the nay-nay. "Ima beat both they ass, at the same. Damn. Time."

"Okay" Heaven laughed pulling him back to his seat.

"I'm just saying, chill out, damn. Carlos and Jose are my niggas. I fuck with them the long way. Tough! You understand me, tough!"

"I said okay, silly."

"I'm just saying, I get it. I understand clear but you gotta apologize to my niggas though." Rarri leaned back in his chair playfully looking bored.

"Oh, my, god." Heaven whined then turned to her henchmen. "Carlos and Jose, I apologize. That was rude of me to accuse ya'll of something I know ya'll didn't do, forreal."

They didn't know what to do so they just nodded nervously, straight faced and still too scared to smile. That chuckle was a mistake that wouldn't happen again.

"Tony!" Heaven yelled happily as she stood, gave him a kiss and a hug, *pretending* to miss him.

"Hey my love" He replied between kisses. Rarri, Carlos and Jose looked at Tony with the same eyes.

"Did you miss me as much as I missed you?"

"Yes…" Heaven blushed with her beautiful I'm in love smile.

"Who's your gummi bear?"

"You are" she replied with a kiss. "Who's your pudding cup?"

"You know you are my pudding cup…speaking of pudding cup-.." tony grabbed a hand full of ass.

Rarri shook his head and blocked them the fuck out then leaned towards Jose and Carlos, straight faced.

"Ya'll seen how I just did that shit? In the midst of fear, but ya'll ain't stand up for Rarri like that though. I see how it is."

"No, no, no, we down" Jose whispered with is fist to his chest to show brotherhood.

"Man shut up nigga. I know you bit me on my back when I was sleep" he replied lowly. "I want my bite back mothafucka *and* ya'll niggas owe me something too."

Rarri got up to leave.

"Aye ya'll, I'm about to get up out of here. Ya'll need to get a room cause ya'll scaring customers talking bout 'pudding pops and 'gummi worms' and all that shit."

Heaven and Tony laughed.

"It's gummy bears and pudding cup!" They yelled after him as he walked away. He just waved them the fuck off and left.

I get to the money you know I'm mean with the chips/
  3.0.4 bad cardi b lookin bitch/
  Yo nigga ain't Rarri ain't pushin a Rari, he sorry/
  Rarri in mauri designer be smelling like marly/
  Backyard crazy remind of a safari/
  Black card shady won't spend on a nigga but Rarri/
  I'm throwing that pussy he think he fuckin a barbie/
  I look at the flick of the wrist on a trick and I mark eem/
  Game tight, flame hot, I make a roast out a leech/
  Bae got back and I arose out the street/
  I got the answers and all the codes for a cheat/
  L1, L2 im on the road with a screech/
  Back, back, x I got a home on the beach/
  Lingo crazy they can't decode how I speak/
  They say that redbone rackin I ain't been wrong all week/
  I drive the strip club crazy
  Trick come pay me
  Spend up daily
  Hickup faded

He just rainin
We just rake it
We been made it
He still slavin
We drive the stripclub crazy, strip club crazy, strip club crazy, strip
club crazy
We drive the strip club cra-

"Damn, you still in here playing with that shit jank?" Fia asked standing in the doorway in her lingerie.

Janky was stuck for an moment which caused Fia to laugh to herself. She knew Janky wanted a taste of her juice box because everybody looks too long when their *thirsty*. Fia went and sat down next to her in front of the computer screen and the machines with all the buttons only she seemed to know how to use.

Fia, I 'ma keep it real with you, this the best shit we done made so far. The other shit bang, hands down but this one right here is the one that's going to put us on Fia, I'm telling you." Janky looked around to make sure nobody could hear her even though everyone was still asleep. She placed her hand on Fia's thigh as she spoke.

"Look, I know Stacy know all the right people and everything but She tryna hold ya'll back right now. Especially *you*. You got a gift, Fia. I could really see you makin somethin out of this shit. It's like you go harder on *every, fucking, track*, Fia. Then yo accent make yo shit sound better. I know Rarri is yo nigga and all that but you shouldn't let nobody stop you from makin it in life and prosperin to become successful for you and your family. You got a chance right here to do something that most people will never be able to do, but once you start letting people control your music, you will never be free in this game Fia, never. I understand Stacey talking about wait until we have more material but I don't see nothing wrong with us putting out just *one* song, just to let people know what's comin.....Fia, I think we should leak this one."

Fia was smiling from ear to ear. "You wanna know something?" she asked seductively.

"Talk to me." Janky replied licking her lips.

Fia's smile faded. "I think you talk to fuckin talk too much. If you ain't feeling this shit you could bounce, bitch. We don't *need you*.. we just like your beats, that's it and that's all. All of us got bandz in out accounts, pushin foreign, rocking designer and all that other shit mothafuckas like *you* sellout for. WE did that shit by sticking together and being loyal. WE aint have none of this before. This *is* my family and if you think I would ever turn my back or do some shady shit just for some punk ass clout or just to be famous, you dumb as fuck."

Fia looked down and then back up at Janky. "Why is your hand still on my leg?"

"Oh my bad." She replied moving her hand quickly.

"Yea, yo bad" Fia got up to leave the room then stopped in the doorway because she had forgotten something. "Oh and Jank."

Janky didn't say nothing, she just turned around looking hurt.

"If you ever leak one of our songs or speak on papi like that again ima beat yo ass. Just keep makin beats, bitch."

Just as Fia turned around, Rarri walked in. "Papi!" she yelled in excitement as she ran and gave him a big hug.

Rarri grabbed Fia by the ass and set the duffle bag down so he could use both hands.

"What's up, you goin to let me take you out tonight or what?"

"I don't know, I'm kinda busy-Of course ima let you take me out"

Rarri loved Fia's sense of humor and her over all persona. She was really a down ass bitch. She always kept it solid and spoke her mind.

"Ight, we goin to bounce later on tonight, so be ready."

Fia was happy as fuck. It's been awhile since the two of them had some alone time.

"Don't get up now, ya'll bitches stay sleep" Fia joked when the rest of them started to look around.

"Oh papi, come hear my new song." She pulled him away from his other sleeping beauties.

"Ya'll get up and count that for me." He yelled back to Bird, Mia, Tia and Dria as he walked into the other room.

"What that shit do, Jank."

"Hey," she said sounding all sad and shit.

"What's up with you, you straight?" Rarri asked noticing something wrong. "Don't' tell me you was in here crying over yo girl and shit."

"Naw, I'm jus tired we been on one." She lied avoiding eye contact with Fia.

"Play my song for him, Jank." Fia said nicely like she didn't just check the shit out of the bitch a couple of seconds ago.

As soon as the song came on, Rarri started nodding his head to the music in approval.

FOUR

JANET STAGGERED from the uber drivers car all the way to her apartment door. The driver watched her the entire time praying she would change her mind and reconsider his offer. Seeing how drunk she must have been, he thought it would have been easier to talk her into having sex with him. It might sound crazy but you would be surprised by how many *sober* bitches give up the pussy for a free ride. Especially in a Tesla. If Janet's pussy wasn't already sore from the train she just let some niggas from rollin hundreds run on her, she would have done it to save a couple dollars too.

After she disappeared into the hallway the driver pulled off hoping something else would come through. If not he would just have to come out the pocket for some pussy later on tonight.

"Oh shit" Janet said stepping out of her shoes as she closed the front door behind her. She didn't waste no time getting to her room and into bed. She was tired and faded so her dirty ass felt a shower could wait. Janet let out a loud burp.

"You know, I was thinkin" a voice said scaring the shit out of her in mid-belch.

At first she thought it was her boyfriend but he didn't have a key to her place and he was out of town for the week spending time with his kids in paramount. Recognizing in a split second that it wasn't his voice she was relieved but when the light came on not only was she wishing it was, she also was all of a sudden more sober than a patient in a lockdown rehab center.

"You was mad with my cro started fucking wit Trina, wasn't you?" Trouble accused with a smile on his face.

"What you doing in my house?" Janet asked in fear.

"Addin shit up.. putting all the pieces to the puzzle together and tryin to figure this shit out." He lowered his hoodie. "What about you?"

"What you mean what about me? This *my* house. You gotta go nigga" she yelled through a cracked voice.

"Look, on hood, I'm tryna just find out what happened to my lil cro" Trouble then sat at the corner of bed.

"On Hood, I don't know what happened. I loved lil trouble that was my nigg-"

"You know what happened."

"I swear to god I don't Troub-"

Trouble was too busy admiring her *new* bedroom set but because he was nodding, she assumed he was listening to her. Janet was the eighth person to *say* they didn't know what happened so by now he learned to just block them out before he got upset.

Trouble didn't give a fuck how much crying, begging and bangin it on the set somebody did. To him that was just part of the act because they got caught.

"That was a Tesla that just dropped you off, huh?" He accused looking her in the eyes for first time. The look in his was so judgmental that she couldn't even think of what to say. Now matter what she said it would still sound bad to him. "Yeah, ya'll came up like a mothafucka. How many *hots* you got left?"

"In my dresser it's some money but not from that, I swear."

She knew she had just fucked up because he was lookin at her with that *I finally got caught yo ass* look.

"Yea, I know." He replied sarcastically. "Just let me get that and we gon be even, is that coo?"

"Yea, that's coo."

"Grab that shit then so I could get out of here." Trouble said putting his head down as she got out of bed and went to the dresser right in front of him. "You know what, I'm not goin to take yo money. I'm trippin."

Janet looked back as she opened the drawer and saw that his head was still down as he talked.

"Naw, it's coo. I know you going through a lot right now. I want you to have it." She assured him as she grabbed her 22. Revolver from behind all the socks, then she turned and pointed it to the crown of his head.

"My brother did say you was a dumb ass bitch."

"That's why he at where he at now." Janet stated coldly then pulled the trigger.

CLICK! CLICK! CLICK! CLICK!

She immediately began crying, pistol still pointed at him. When he looked up at her, she squeezed one more time, pathetically then swung it at him but he blocked her.

"On neighborhood crip you really is *stuuupid*, ain't you?" Trouble teased then grabbed her by the neck and slammed her against the wall as he pulled out his .357 python .

He pressed the barrel so hard against the side of her head that his entire arm shook. Janet cried out in pain but he didn't care. Trouble was tired of playing games with this bitch. He *knew* she was lying. He just caught her in a lie and she just tried to kill him while disrespecting his lil *cro* too? Fasho she was involved or so he thought.

"Who else was with you? You might as well tell me cause I'm gon find out" He promised through clenched teeth, pressing the gun into her head even harder maker her scream. " I don't knoooo-"

"BOOM!"

Blood, brain, hair and skull fragments flew everywhere. Trouble literally had to yank the long barrel out of the side of her head before letting her body drop to the floor in an awkward position. The fucked up part about it is that Janet really didn't know what had happened to lil Trouble. Only thing she knew was that it had to have been Trouble that was the one who was running around killing their homies. Nobody knew who it was and by the time they found out, it was too late. Every person who knew now was dead.

Trouble quickly wiped his face with his sleeve, tucked his gun and left out the apartment through the back door.

FIVE

"How much for this one?" Pretty me da p asked as he picked up the all black handgun that caught his eye.

"I'ma need $200 for that one, it's a-

"I know what it is." He lied tucking it in his pants before he gave dude the money.

Pretty me da p didn't want to carry a gun but niggas was getting shot for breakfast, lunch and dinner. On top of that, some nigga named Ha-Ha was running around robbing everybody and they momma. No bullshit. He really robbed some nigga *and* his momma. He was so scandalous he even took her EBT card and went and bought some shit to eat with it.

A lot of crazy shit had been goin on but pretty me da p was just happy to be free, especially after the shit Shawn had did to him. Wasn't no way in hell he was going to stay in there after that. Being raped was his breaking point and was what had ultimately lead him into making a deal to give up information on Rarri and other pimps he knew of but so far he wasn't able to hold up on his end of deal. Pretty me da p knew the chances of him being successful was slim to none but told them what they wanted to hear in order to get out.

He figured if they threatened to take him back in he would just go on the run for as long as he could. Them crooked mothafuckas knew he innocent. They just took him to jail because they seen he was a pimp and wanted to get him on anything possible. Pretty me da p got inside his car and shook his head thinking back to the day he got arrested.

———

He couldn't believe Ebony had just pushed him in the face like he wasn't out here down and around, mashing and bashin on these hoes.

Pretty me da p shook his head in total shock then looked at Amazin angrily.

"Aye, come get yo bitch!" he demanded with authority forgetting who he was dealing with, instantly swearing to himself as he remembered.

"I got yo bitch" Ebony yelled as she tried grabbing him but he quickly back stepped then turned around and broke to his car with her on his heels.

The distance wasn't much for him to work with so 10 feet was enough for Ebony to stay on him. Pretty me da p was looking like food to Ebony and the odds were on her side to get what she wanted-but-unfortunately for her, pretty me da p was a professional when it came to this running from mothafuckas shit.

Instinctively as he took each step his mind was calculating 100 times faster than he was moving. By the time he made it between his car and the one he was parked behind, pretty me da p had already added up the correct denominator towards a fail proof plan all in his mind while doing it.

'If I fake 30% to the left, then another 30% to the right and go hard on the 40% back to the left, it's 100% chance she's goin to, yup!'

Ebony dove for pretty me da p thinking she had him until she was 'somewhat' in the air wrapping her hands around the space he disappeared from. He really juked the dog shit out of her with relative ease. It looked like some shit you would see on a college football team highlight.

From his calculations, Pretty me da p, who was already opening his door before she hit the floor, knew he had time to celebrate one laugh or fat joke but-

BAM!

Just as he was about to an F150 truck smacked into her then flipped out of control.

"BAAEE!"Amazin cried out as he ran to her side to help. She looked so bad, he didn't know what to do so Amazin just kneeled down next to her, consoling Ebony as best as he could, telling her everything was goin to be alright while he dialed for help. Putting his phone to his ear, Amazin went into tears.

"Hello, yes I need help. My wife was just hit by a car!.. yeah she's breathing but she's bleeding out of her mouth and oh my god! Ebony!. Please come help us. Don't die on me Eb. Please don't die on me..Our baby needs you... I need you.

She was trying to talk but Amazin couldn't make out what it was that she was trying to say. Ebony was just mumbling out of shock and looking into the sky tryna figure out what had happened to her, then took her last breath as he was telling her everything was going to be ok.

Amazin screamed his heart out in defeat then looked at Pretty me da p who just standin there in complete shock.

"Look what you did!"

"I ain't do nothin p. I ran to get away from her" he replied honestly.

"Naw, you made her get hit on purpose, Darshawn, that's fucked up!"

"What is you talkin bout p, you trippin my nigga-"

"This ain't no fuckin pimp shit! My baby momma just died nigga! Amazin screamed with Ebony still in his hands forgetting all about the operator on the phone.

"That's her fault! Ain't nobody tell her to chase me out into the street. I asked you to get yo girl and you just-man fuck all this shit. That's yo bitch" he replied coldly then turned to his hoes who was all standing behind him. " Come on ya'll we out of here..ya'll seen that shit, right?"

"We can't just leave her here like that...that's wrong" Foxy said with tears in her eyes and by the look of it, all of them felt the same way.

Pretty me da p grabbed Foxy by the arm aggressively. "Bitch, she dead! We Ain't leavin her, she already gone, get yo ass in the car!"

Foxy pulled away from him.

"This exactly how he goin to do ya'll. If ya'll end up like this." Amazin assured them looking them in the eyes seriously and they believed him. if Pretty me da p WOULD LEAVE HIS COUSIN and his baby momma for dead than he damn sure would do the same to them.

"Bitch I said get yo ass in the car!" he yelled grabbing Foxy this time by her hair. She kicked and screamed as he dragged her towards his car until an onlooker intervened.

"Hey man, get your hands off of her!" he grabbed Pretty me da p by the wrist.

He sized the dude up quickly then let Foxy go, only because his calculations told him that this nigga ain't playing. He could also see that this save a hoe nigga obviously did a lot of working out so a fight wouldn't be the smartest idea.

"I'ma see yo ass around bitch." Save a hoe pulled his shirt off like this was the type of shit he had been waiting on all day.

"I'll fight for her."

"P, I ain't about to fight you for no bitch."

Save a hoe put both of his hands around Pretty me da p's neck and shook him as he spoke.

"You don't fucking disrespect her motherfucker, do you hear me?"

Pretty me da p was trying to pry his hands from off of him so he could breathe to no avail.

"I said do you understand me!" he asked again, choking him harder.

"yeah."

Not yet satisfied, save a hoe guided him by the neck to Foxy. "Tell her you're sorry you fucking jerk."

Pretty me da p looked at Foxy who had her mouth open, then at daphney and his snow and quickly told himself he wasn't about to say no shit like that.

Save-a-hoe took his silence as disrespect and squeezed tighter. "I'm not fucking around! I swear to god if you don't say it, I will choke the life out of you."

When Pretty me da p started tapping on Save-a hoe's arm the bitches laughed a little.

"I'm sorry."

"Say it again, I don't think she heard you!"

"I'm sorry, I said I'm sorry."

Pretty me da p collapsed on the floor as soon as he let him go.

"Now get up and get out of here before I kick your ass!" he barked lifting Pretty me da p up by the back of his shirt.

Pretty me da p staggered to his car half out of breath. You don't have to guess who got some free pussy that night. If the police didn't accidently block him in, he would have been out of there. It didn't take long for Amazin to point him out to the police blaming him for what had happened to Ebony or for Foxy to explain what he had just did to her and how she along with the girls were forced into a life of prostitution out of fear. That's all they needed to hear to haul his ass straight to jail.

"Niggas got me fucked up!" he shouted to himself in the car before pulling off into traffic, thanking God he was back out.

SIX

Now that Backpage was on some bullshit the *escorts* had to step out and get some real hoe'n goin. The blades were looking good, especially on FIG. Bitches were everywhere walking up and down the street, jumping in and out of cars, wearing some of the flyest hoe apparel.. Some even wore seductive face masks with glitter, rhinestones, feathers and all types of shit. Others were even almost butt-ass-naked and not leaving much for the trick's imagination except for how it feels inside the pussy.

Seizing the opportunity of a come up most of local businesses raised the price of condoms just so they could get a piece of some hoe doe on the low-low. Pimps were out campaigning tryna knock somebody for a bitch non-stop. Every hoe out of pocket was getting pressed until she chose up, called her folks or ran and went somewhere else for the night. Some pimps were being extorted by gang-bangers because they ain't know nobody or was just some pushover ass niggas who would go for anything.

It was nothing to see some niggas hop out of a car and bang on some other nigga for pimpin in *their* set. Some of the hoes would be bangin on other hoes too, especially if it was too slow for them to make any money. Whoever wasn't from around there was to blame. Niggas was getting robbed for their shit on the daily. The main thing to watchout for is them young niggas because they don't give a fuck about nothing you got going, where you from, where you been, who you know or what you talking about.

They just tryna get what you got and get on so they could party all at your expense. You never really know what to expect out here but this is the life we love so dearly.

"On babies the game been good to a nigga cuh." Macky boasted to Rarri as he counted some hoe doe that was just dropped on him.

"On P's this shit been lovely lately, I can't even lie" Rarri admitted from the passenger seat. "But, it still ain't enough tho… I been tryna think of some more shit to do, I just ain't figure out what yet."

"Cuhh.." Macky swore in frustration as he stopped counting and looked at Rarri like he was crazy. "Look, we got bitches *and* bricks in the streets. On top of that we some fly ass crip'n, what else could a nigga want, YAAH?"

Even though Macky wasn't from Parc village, he always called Rarri 'YAAH' like a lot of other people who had homies Parc village did. Parc village niggas are known to say 'YAAH' so much that it kinda sticks to the people they hang around also.

"Man it's a lot of shit a nigga need, Macky. A nigga ain't made it yet. It's niggas out here with way more bitches and money than we go '*p*', so what is you talking bout"

Macky put one hand on his head in disbelief. "On babies, you got five bitches on Western, Sepulveda, Harbor, Holt and Five here. what the fuck is the problem? And that's just me knowin you keep bird and them watchin a stable *each..each*, my nigga. And that's not includin what them bitches bringin when they be out fuckin wit yo aunty or the bitches you got runnin around on some solo shit… cuh!" Macky looked at Rarri. "How many toes you got?"

"What you mean?"

"Nigga, don't beat around the bush." He said seriously. "How many toes you got? Mackey asked again with a hand full of money hitting the middle console almost after every word he said.

Rarri thought to himself for a minute. "Really, I ain't even been countin no more." He answered honestly which seemed to frustrate Macky even more. He was looking like he wanted to slap the shit out of Rarri.

"You ain't countin no more? Cuuuuh, I feel like smackin you with this money, talkin bout you ain't countin no mo. Nigga, we still out here countin and you complanin-fuck all that, I'm poppin the trunk on you, dumb ass." Macky pressed to open his trunk then jumped out quick.

"*Damn*" Rarri said to himself then got out and ran to his car to grab his motion board and light saber. He learned from previous times to keep all his shit in the front seat when around Macky because he always found a reason to pop his trunk.

As they battled and chased each other around the parking lot, Rarri thought he was having déjà vu but then remembered the dream he had a couple of weeks ago. He hopped off of his motion board then looked around seriously. Everything looked normal but he had a bad feeling. *Something just didn't feel right.*

"YAAH, come on. Let's go post somewhere else foo" He said then went and jumped in his car immediately not givin Macky time to protest.

Macky seen the way Rarri was **lookin** around clutching on his 9mm with the parabellums ready to fuck a nigga over and couldn't help but start laughing.

"What?" Rarri asked looking around paranoid.

"Cuh, that nigga Tana jay got you *spooked.*"

Rarri looked at him in pure shock then elsewhere not wanting Macky to know he was really right.

"Hell haw I ain't worried bout, cuh" he lied.

Macky laughed because he knew he was lyin. Rarri looked at him with an attitude.

"My nigga, *you* the one got me out here getting into it wit mothafuckas over the shit *you* been doing. I'm not bout to get caught slippin nigga"

"Whatever nigga just stop wavin that burner at me tho" he replied getting out of the way of the barrel and went to his car.

"My bad, YAAH" Rarri lowered his pistol not even noticing he had been pointing and waving it around recklessly as he spoke. *'Damn! Do this nigga got me spooked?'* he asked himself. *'I gotta end this shit with cuh soon'*

Rarri turned up the song " (same ole nigga by da bully) and drove off out of the parking lot with Macky behind him.

———

"FUCK!"

"What happened?"

"Them niggas just left" Tana Jay responded as he tucked his pistol and stood up straight from behind the car he was crouching behind then looked over at his partner in crime who was now standing also.

"I thought you said they be posted right here all night cuh" he said angrily.

"They usually do" Kill-Kill looked at his watch. "Something probably came up.

Tana jay was steamin, he was not even 30 seconds away from creeping up on Rarri and filling him up with something hot. The parking lot was the perfect spot to do it at. No cameras, no witnesses, no nothing but two dead bodies and a smooth getaway. Tana jay had enough bodies to know how to commit a murder and not get caught. He was tired of playing with Rarri young ass. Especially after he had shot his bottom bitch in the ass a couple of weeks ago. Now none of his bitches felt safe on the blades no more.

It was like that one incident had all the rest of his hoes traumatized. It had gotten to the point where all his bitches had to do was bring up Rarri's name to get out of some shit.

'Daddy, I'm scared. Daddy, Rarri out here creepin again. Daddy, Rarri hopped out on me. Daddy, Rarri took all my money. Rarri, Rarri, Rarri, Rarri, Rarri.'

Tana jay didn't know if these bitches was telling him the truth or not. It was starting to just seem like the thing to say now to be lazy. Regardless he was tired of hearing this nigga name almost every fuckin night and from smacking bitches for even saying his name in his presence. There were to refer to him only as *'ole boy'* from now on.

Tana jay's phone started to vibrate. "Yeah, what's up?"

"Daddy, ole boy out here trippin again. He just took—"

He hung up the phone before she could even finish with that bullshit. Now he *knew* them bitches was lying because the one that had just called wasn't even on FIG right now. They was doing that shit to tuck on him or really out of fear but either way, none of this shit started happening until Rarri came back from the bay. So, killing *him* is the solution to *his* problem.

"I'ma fuck this bitch up, cuh"

"Who was that?"

Tana jay didn't even wanna talk about it, especially not with him.

"Look my nigga, get this shit situated so we could end it. I'm not no attempted murderer, nigga I kill shit, cuh..I finish the job, *'everytime'*

"My name ain't Kill-kill for nothin, cuh"

"I can't tell" Tana jay said cutting him off not noticing how close he was to being killed for doing so.

Kill-kill exhaled deeply to calm himself. He wasn't good at doing a lot of talking and explaining shit when he felt pressured.

"Look, I'ma say this one time cause I don't care about you being all hostile. I know you got shit going on, we both do. I'm tryna handle this shit just as much as you is, if not *more.* With that being said, don't play wit my kill game again cuh. I don't even joke like that, on the set"

Tana jay had to admit to himself that he liked this young nigga. Kill-kill didn't give a fuck about how mad he was or how many niggas he done killed before. Kill-kill demanded his respect, especially when it involved his killing. That was what he took pride in more than anything. Unknown to Tana jay, playing with his kill game is just *one* of the reasons he wanted Macky dead so badly.

"You know what, I respect that my young nigga" he said with his hand extended. The two shook then went to the g-ride.

"You know what, I think I got a plan. You tryna come up on some dollaz?"

"Hell yea" Tana replied excitedly letting him know he was with it.

"Ight, let's go scope this shit out" Kill-kill said as he got in the car. "It's probably goin to take a couple of days but trust me, it's worth it"

"Say no more" Tana jay started the car and sagged out.

SEVEN

RARRI SEEN a lot of familiar faces in the parking lot he and Mackey switched to, so he decided to hop out and fuck with some of the p's.

"What up p?" he asked as he p-shook with divine, lavish, money hungry and cashout.

The four of them are what you call 'Famous pimps'. Everybody knew them or of them and whoever didn't more than likely wasn't into the same lifestyle. Even though they grew up in gang areas, none of them claimed a gang. They were strictly some pimpin. Being down there for years gave them certain advantages new niggas didn't have. Like not worrying too much about being robbed or constantly banged on by mothafuckas because everybody knew them and they were related to some of the niggas around.

Macky just nodded and gave the thumbs up which was the sign that represented his hood and continued to the next circle of niggas that were *like him*, while Rarri conversed with the *only pimpin parade*. It's not like Macky didn't like them, but, he did feel like they didn't fuck with him because he was always bangin more than pimpin. They liked Macky but it was just always some unnecessary drama with him, so they chose to keep their distance and fuck with him from afar.

What they did do was respect his pimpin and that's what mattered most around there. The hardest nigga in the world wouldn't be accepted in none of the circles if he wasn't pimpin correctly. No matter the differences, if somebody came around there tripping, or mispimpin, everybody there would be on that person's head no questions asked. It didn't matter where you was from as long as you were some pimpin, niggas would embrace you as such. It's crazy because you might see crips and bloods come together in pimpin more than anywhere else.

"Fuck that bitch. On my pimpin she's a high power faggot 'p'. The bitch couldn't keep up with my program so she fagged off to fuck with you." Pacman said to Persuasive then looked at Macky who walked up with perfect timing.

"Tell this nigga about Lacy, p"

Macky grabbed the blunt that was in rotation, hit it twice then passed it.

"I *thought* I had knocked her from some nigga named Choice. So I serve cuh, not on no gang bangin shit, all p's. So the niggas tell me that the bitch stole his money and all that. Then he like 'where can we meet?' so he can get his bread back and *discipline* the bitch.

Everybody laughed.

"I'm like, *nigga*, once she left *you* and came to *me* with some money *she's* no longer *your* bitch, she's now *mine* and *I'm* not about to let *no nigga* put hands on *my work*. So cuh like, '*Can we meet up so that I can get my bread back?*"

"What you say, p?" No love asked.

Macky looked at him like he was stupid. "Nigga, I said hell naw"

They all started crying laughing knowing Macky crazy ass wasn't about to give a nigga some money back or let him beat on a bitch he head down. Letting another man beat yo bitch is some real bitch shit. Ain't no explaining that unless she a snitch or something putting p's in jail.

"What happened after that?" Persuasive wanted to know.

"Cuh started talkin bout puttin me in a circle, taken me to court on charges of mispimpin by harborin hoes who stealin and shit and how I ain't conductin myself out here properly. He sayin so much shit making it sound cold, On babies I can't even keep up wit cuh, he so smooth wit it. While he talkin I'm still stuck on the *harborin hoes who stealin* part. So now I'm thinkin to myself, '*Damn, I might just give cuh this money back*'

Everybody started bustin up laughing again.

"Wait, hold up p" Pacman said trying to calm the crowd as Rarri walked up "Tell them what happened after that."

"Ya'll niggas is stupid" Rarri laughed as he lit the blunt no love handed him.

"I think when I got quiet, he took that as a sign of weakness cause he got hard and started talkin some high power shit, like *he 'got big choppas'*, he '*from the bay*' and how '*niggas get killed for shit like this everyday.*' That was all I needed to hear. I'm like nigga, shut up and come through so I could show you what a choppa *feel* like, nigga. Now he got me out of my character cuh wanna switch it up like he wasn't sayin it like that and he was just tellin me how it was where he was from and all that bullshit. I'm still callin him all types of bitches and he still keep tryna explain hisself like a straight bitch. So I hang up on cuh. The nigga just kept callin me back, blowin my shit up like a straight hoe. I ain't even answer cuh calls so he send some long as text talkin bout how Lacey ran off from some other nigga then chose up on him. Now that she took his shit and got on, he don't know how he goin to get back home....I send him a text that said '*pimp yo way back*'

They all laughed at the weak nigga.

"So P could have been lyin because the bitch chose up, plus he lettin you talk to him like that? That say a lot about the type of nigga he is" Persuasive told Macky, tryna justify something for the bitch on the low.

"That's exactly what the bitch told me when I asked. I honestly didn't give a fuck what she had going, I just wanted to break on the bitch. I cashed out on her for about a good week then she just started getting lazy. Complainin, askin too many square ass questions, turnin in short and all types of shit. So, I go hard on the bitch, no hands all IZM. I'm so deep in the bitch mind she feelin the fuck out of every word I'm saying. I'm telling ya'll the bitch lookin at me like I'm God comin down from the heavens P. Soon as I get done, she instantly get to apologizin, praisin my pimpin and all that."

Macky hit the blunt two hard times and exhaled as he shook his head.

"Then what?" No love asked, all the way tuned in.

"Then she just jumped out of the car and ran up and hugged this nigga Rarri when she seen cuh" Macky admitted.

"You lyin, P " Persuasive said in disbelief, eyes wide as hell.

Macky looked at Rarri. "Am I lyin, cuh?"

Rarri had one of those 'On the spot' smirks on his face. "Nah, he ain't lyin"

"DAMN!!!" The all said in unison.

"I hopped out the car so *quick.* The bitch talkin bout she came out here looking for cuh, tellin him she miss him and take her back and how I won't leave her alone. How she been tryna get away from me, all the cap. When I got close enough she go stand behind cuh with her head down tryna hold her smile on some crafty shit. Cuh, that's on everything blue I wanted to knock that bitch head off for lyin like that."

He was mad even talking bout the shit again.

"Now, I'm on Rarri like, 'you know this bitch?' On God that's why this my nigga, cuh kept it all the way pimpin on her faggot ass. He like, 'Yea, I know this faggot ass bitch. I turned her punk ass out.' Then he pulled out his phone and started recordin this bitch, he like '*Let the world know you a faggot ass, nothin ass, punk ass bitch.*

Tell them what I said to you the last time I talked to you on the phone, hoe. Tell em how I did you at the chop shop, bitch.' On babies the bitch repeated everything he told her to to say word for word and added extras for the gram."

"Blood on p's I saw that video" No love said remembering the light skinned bitch Rarri was going hard on, on his Instagram. He especially liked the part when he kicked her in the ass and told her to get the hell on and she limped away cryin.

"Yea p, I had to go hard on that bitch. Especially tryna play the homie like a sucka or somethin. That bitch stole from me the first time I let her touch some money, not knowin I was testing her. Then she started fuckin with one of my cousins not knowin that's exactly what I was hopin she did so I could get everybody bitch lookin at me at 'The Show' without they folks trippin on em for being out of pocket. Mothafuckas be so quick to try and shit on a nigga when they think he down that I was able to use that to my advantage P. Real shit, niggas was basically encouraging they bitches to record me *'live'* not knowin what seemed to be my downfall was only smoke, mirrors and an illusion of what I wanted them to see. So, when I got my crowd and pulled that rabbit out of the hat it *'looked'* like magic." Rarri finished then pulled a blunt from behind No love's ear that was never there to begin with, trippin no love the fuck out. He just handed it to him to light then looked at Persuasive.

"Yea P, her name not Lacy, it's Lae-Lae. And lil dumb Lae-Lae always doin some dumb shit. I can't tell a nigga how to run his program and I damn sure ain't bout to try and persuade a nigga who name is Persuasive."

They chuckled.

"But, I am going to let you know to watch that bitch at all times if you fuckin with her because dumb bitches do dumb shit, p" Rarri added.

Persuasive pulled out his phone after thinkin about it for a second then called Lae-Lae as he walked off.

"Ima get wit ya'll in a minute." He said then he was back to his call, "Yea, hello, you still at the house?"

"You readin the book I gave you, cuh?Macky asked.

"Yea, the James Bird book."

"Nigga, it's Jim Crow! The new Jim Crow!"

"I know that it's called, I was just fuckin with you" Rarri laughed.

"What part you at?" Macky asked, not believing him.

"I'm readin it on p's"

"Well what part you at then?" Macky asked not caring what he put it on. "Niggas blow shit up all the time."

"Now I gotta be blowin my shit up?"

"I ain't caught you yet, but you done did it. Everybody done did it. But fuck all that, why you can't just tell me what part you at?"

"I'm at the part where they talking bout President Bush and all that shit-"

"Nigga, that's still at the beginning damn near."

"Mothafucka, that's progress. I got other shit to be readin" Rarri countered.

"Like what?" Macky asked, folding his arms and turned his ear towards him waiting for Rarri to say some bullshit like Ashley and Jaquavis, K'wan, Ca$h or ASANI BANDZ weird ass.

Macky couldn't stand Urban books because they all talked abut the same shit anybody could write about...RIGHT?"

"Exactly! Macky said once Rarri didn't respond in a two second time frame. Then he turned back to lecture everybody else. "Ya'll need to wake the fuck up cause ya'll niggas is sleep right now and we at war! War wit them, war with ourselves, and everybody else. We almost extinct and the black man-"

"Come on, p. Ain't nobody tryna join yo revolution tonight." Pacman said in frustration, cutting Macky off from his routine ritual of black panther speeches.

"I'm just giving ya'll a keen insight into the Psychology of-"

"Ain't nobody tryna hear your Psychiatrist schemes tonight P, that's all I'm sayin."

Everybody laughed as they p-shook in agreement. When Rarri shook with them on that, Macky shook his head in disappointment with a sour expression. Knowing he wouldn't win a dispute, he just waved them off. "You niggas is lost."

That was probably the worst thing to say because they all knew Macky was steaming. What Macky didn't get was that nobody disagreed with him. He was really a smart nigga but they would rather hear what he be saying from anybody but *him*.

"Man, is we pop'n or what? No love asked holding up a bag of e-pills in front of Macky puttin a big ass smile on his face. "See, that's the Macky I know. Big Smile Macky, not sad lookin mad Mack."

"Fuck you, nigga." Macky tried to grab the bag but No love blocked his hand.

"Alright, look blood, these them ones foo. Fasho, fasho..I got em from V.B. They going to have you rollin '*HARD*' on p's. You goin to be feeling bomb and wantin to talk and out of everybody right here, I understand that the most p. No love got love for Macky but *don't , I repeat dont* turn into Malcom X tonight. I swear Ima put my finger down yo throat and make you throw them mothafuckas back up, Macolm...I mean Macky"

Everybody was in tears. Macky snatched the bag with an attitude but he was laughing too. They always joked by calling him Malcolm. They all popped two pills each then waited for them to kick in as more cars filled the lot. The scene was lit and so many p's were there that mothafuckas had to park down the street and walk up. Everybody was jeweled up and designered down dressed to impress. Niggas had powder, weed, drank and pills all in rotation. Nothing for sale. Pimps sell bitches, not drugs. Well at least that's what most of them say. Rarri never understood that part of the game and probably never would. Especially after how Maria had broken it down to him.

Rarri was under the impression that just because he wasn't personally passing out bricks by hand, he wasn't a drug dealer, just merely an investor, investing in a certain product. He hadn't touched a brick since he got out of juvy because Heaven and his Bentley Bitches handled everything dealing with drugs. Reading how his pops had his moms and Heaven helped Rarri to mold them better than he ever would have on his own.

"Who can beat the KING playin chess with all Queens?" was a question out of the book, 'Breathe'

That question made him look at life like from a different angle. It made him focus on routes most people around him would bypass. Rarri felt more connected to his father than ever and was more than grateful to be blessed with the game he left behind for him. It taught him to be greater than he ever was. He accepted the fact that his father was actually living his life through him and it felt damn good. He thought about the question one more time and the answer was simple.

'Nobody' he said to himself.

He was feeling the pills he had taken but he had, had better and of course an *idea*.

EIGHT

IT WAS POPPIN like a mothafucka and some real pimpin was going on. Niggas was getting served left and right, bitches were dropping off money constantly. None of them ever walked into the lot though, that was a rule and if a bitch broke that, she fasho was going to be on the choppin block as fair game.

"What up 'p', I see you out here shinnin and all that. Them different colored diamonds got you lookin like a Christmas tree" Rasheed said excitedly then held up two bottles of lean. "I came barrin gifts and all that, on pimpin"

"Im tryna catch up to you p. You shinnin harder than me..my diamonds ain't neva dancin like them mothafuckas you got on.. I can't even see if that's really you over there. Them chains blindin the fuck out of a nigga" Rarri shaded his eyes with his hand.

"Take one of them mothafuckas off for a nigga so I could at least make it back to the car"

They both laughed p-shook then embraced each other with a hug. Macky shook his head. He hated how Rasheed always came around Rarri fishing for a compliment but he really hated how Rasheed knocked him for his bottom bitch right there on FIG a couple of weeks ago then turned around and knocked him for one more the next day.

Macky came back immediately with some badder bitches who stayed in pocket so he wasn't really tripping too much off of that, that was just part of the game. These bitches ain't forever. Macky also didn't like Rasheed because he felt like he was trying too hard to be in *their* circle and Rarri wasn't noticing that shit. On top of that Rasheed called himself getting a light saber and a motion board but Macky cut that shit dumb short. As soon as Rasheed pulled it out Macky snatched the light saber out of his hands and threw it in the middle of the street where it was quickly run over beyond repair by the cars in traffic.

He didn't give a fuck if Rasheed wanted to fight or how Rarri felt. He wasn't about to let him get in on *their* thing. He probably didn't even know shit about star wars, just tryna do something because they were doing it. He waited on Rasheed to trip but he was calm. Irritatingly calm. Macky knew that Rasheed wasn't scared of him. That's another thing he didn't like. He even seemed to have more of everything than Macky. More bitches, cars, chains, swag and money. He stayed flexin on Macky like it was the easiest thing to do.

Rarri respected Rasheed's pimpin and he liked stepping out with him because everybody always assumed they were related.. Every time they went somewhere Rarri busted a bitch with Rasheed. Different types of bitches too. College bitches and bitches who had shit going for themselves. Rasheed fucked with square bitches openly just as much as Rarri did. All the other pimps were too pimped out and to them that was against the rules of the game.

Rarri didn't give a fuck about some of those rules. He was breaking on *all* the bitches he fucked with, not *some of them* and he damn sure wasn't about to limit the ways of breakin on a bitch based off of another man's philosophy that wasn't his fathers.

Rasheed handed Rarri one of the lean bottles. "That's you right there p..oh yea here" He reached in his Versace hoody and pulled out a wad of bills then handed it to him also.

"What's this for?"

"I heard one of yo close boys had passed a few days ago. I ain't know him or nothin but that's $5,000 to go to his moms, kids or whatever ya'll need cause any friend of Rarri's is a friend of Sheed's on p's" He replied seriously.

'This nigga a fuckin joke' Macky thought to himself. "Aye, Ima get with ya'll later, I gotta go handle some shit" he said giving them both a dap before rushing off.

"That's some real shit, p. I appreciate that. Ima slide this to his moms asap."

"I was bout to hit Saks tomorrow, you tryna slide?"

Rasheed looked at Rarri like he should already know wassup. The two of them been on one, fuckin saks fifth the fuck over and leaving the cashiers astounded since they met.

"My bad" Rarri laughed as they headed to the store to grab two strawberry Fantas to mix the lean with.

Once out of the store the two mixed half of their bottles and saved the rest for later. Rarri was already rollin from the pills he popped. "Good lookin on that bread for the homie, that's some real shit."

"Don't tell me that pill got you sentimental already. Just tell me you love me so we can get it over with right now"

He almost spit his drink out.

"Fuck you"

"What up nigga!"

Rarri turned around to see Bird riding in the passenger seat of a black Mercedes Benz full of bitches following slowly behind him as he walked, like some tricks tryna get a date.

"How much for a quicky? A bitch tryna buy some dick" she said hanging out the window flossing a wad of money. All the bitches in the car with her laughed and giggled excitedly.

"More than what you got in yo hand fasho." He replied still walking like he wasn't interested.

"Whatever, let me just suck on it then." Everybody laughed.

Rarri walked to the car to Bird then looked inside and said 'wassup' to some of the bitches he had selling pussy for him. After small talk with them for a minute he turned his attention back to Bird. He really didn't talk to his 'probation period' hoes until they lasted past the probation period. The bitches Bird was with just made it past that point a few days ago so he would start to converse with them more now. That small gesture meant a lot to them because they had been working hard to get his attention. Real hard.

Rarri grabbed the money and tucked it in his pocket. Bird told him it was 10 BANDZ and they were about to go back out.

"You still takin that bitch Fia out tonight?"

"Yea, why, wassup, you jealous?"

"Please, me? Bird? Jealous? Yea okay, keep tellin yoself that." Bird replied lookin straight ahead with a straight face. "The dick ain't that good"

She could feel Shaneece looking at her from the side with a 'yea right' expression. Bird tried to hold her laugh but couldn't.

"Naw, it's that good" she admitted, and slapped fives with Shaneece.

Bird had shown them videos of him fuckin her and the Bentley bitches so they all already knew what was up.

"Naw daddy, I was just askin cause if ya'll going to be out, I was goin to push out there with her crew so she could relax and enjoy herself without worrying about nothin but her Rarri." Bird laughed. "She deserve a break and some alone time with you. She been on one like a mothafucka.. Really, I was thinkin ya'll should just get a room for a couple of days and do ya'll."

"On everything, yea, that's what Ima do." Rarri replied thinkin deeply into Bird's brilliant idea and at the same time peepin her cold game.

You see, by Bird breaking it down like that to him, in front of his hoes, it let *them* see that *he* liked certain types of bitches. Bitches who weren't envious over one another and who worked as a team instead of playing against each other like most hoes be doing. It let them see that not only did the Bentley Bitches love Rarri, but they also loved each other and the bond they had was not pretend. It was genuine..

Fia was the one going the hardest so it was only right that she be the first one to kick back with him for a couple of days. Bird mentioning they should spend a couple of days together instead of 'one night' is something bitches don't do and is a foreign language in hoe talk. Mentally, every bitch in the car noted they would have to step their game up all ways around to continue fuckin with him.

His program wasn't the same as everyone else's. Rarri went about things differently than what some of his girls were accustomed to. To some of the pimps, that's what made Rarri not a *'real pimp'* but to the hoes, that's what made him standout. To him, when niggas go above and beyond to impress other niggas their one step closer towards homosexuality. It's only a matter of time before they start circle jerkin while moaning each other's names and all types of other weird shit being sashayed around.

He was in the middle of telling Bird where was going to take Fia with so much enthusiasm, he didn't see the aggravated expression on her face.

"Hold on, daddy." Bird said looking past Rarri. "Do you know me or somethin?"

Rasheed stepped forward, licking his lips tryna look cute and shit. "I mean, I see you reckless eye ballin on some pimpin and all that out of pocket shit"

Bird looked at Shaneece, What color shirt this nigga got on?"

"I don't know." She answered with her head in her lap.

Bird looked to the back. "Do any of ya'll bitches know what color shirt this nigga got on?"

"Nope" the four said in tandem.

Bird looked back to Rasheed who was now standing next to Rarri.

"He got on a Versace hoody-shirt with True Religion shorts, a Rolex watch and like four chains on."

Rasheed smiled and rubbed his hands together as he bent down to get a better look at what was about to be some new toes.

"Bird looked him right in the eyes while talking. "What did I forget?"

"The red shoes" they said together.

"What else?"

"The nose and the wig!"

Bird laughed to herself then asked, "What is this nigga?"

"A Clown!" The all yelled out.

"He a what!" she asked louder.

"He A CLOWN!!" They answered again altogether.

He stood up straight next to Rarri who was cryin laughing.

"Yea, ya'll real cute" he told them feeling played.

"You lucky this my boy"

Bird drew down on him aiming her .38 revolver at his chest. "Naw nigga, *you* lucky he don't want yo heart." She told him referring to Rasheed's chains. "Those would look good with his collection."

Bird looked greedily at his pieces. "Daddy, you sure you don't want this nigga shit? They would look better on you anyway."

"Naw, chill out" he told her stepping forward making Bird lower her weapon. "What I tell you about pointin them mothafuckas and not using them?"

"Alright, move out the way, Ima pop cuh then" Bird said opening the door to get out, but Rarri quickly closed it back shut.

"Bird, calm down before you make me slap the shit out of yo crazy ass out here" he warned.

"You the one actin like I'm scared to pop the nigga, talkin bout don't pull out unless I pop a nigga and shit. What you want me to do daddy, pop the nigga or not? Cause on V's I will pop cuh if that's what you want me to do." Bird argued angrily, talking about Rasheed as if he wasn't even standing there.

He was contemplating running, seeing how serious she was but his pride got the best of him. Rarri leaned in the car so only Bird and the rest of the bitches could hear him then looked back, making sure Rasheed was out of ear's reach.

"Look, I know you would pop cuh." He said. "It's not about that Bird. Anybody can shoot a nigga, that shit ain't hard. You in a car full of bad bitches and I expect you to lead by example when you around *my* toes cause at the end of the day, all you bitches is under *my* instructions. I'm still getting into it with mothafuckas over the last nigga you shot but he was in the wrong so it is what it is. You know ima slide for you at the end of the day because I don't gotta question yo loyalty... I would lay my life down for you without even thinkin twice bout it, and you know that shit. You gotta move more smarter, Bird."

He wiped the tears from her face. He could always make Bird cry without even trying to do so. She didn't even know why she was crying, she just was because Rarri was talking to her so seriously.

"Stop cryin, you ain't do nothin wrong. Yo heart was in the right place." He stood up and stretched out. "But right now, you need to worry about running me my money, bitch."

She tried to hit him playfully in the stomach but he dodged her, laughing.

"I love yo hoe ass."

"I love you too, nigga." Bird replied with a smile then rolled her eyes at Rasheed and told Shaneece to pull off.

"I ain't tryna be all in your business, but why you be lettin yo hoes get out of pocket like that?" Rasheed asked Rarri as he walked up and the two continued back to the lot.

"Ima give you a lil insight. Bird not my hoe, she's my bitch." Rarri answered bluntly.

"So that give her the right to be reckless eyeballin pimps?" He asked in disgust.

"Hell naw!" Rarri answered quickly and with the same tone.

"But that's what she did though P!" Rasheed stated.

"Naw, what she did was get at you how she should have for lookin too long at *her*, plus, Bird from the hood." Rarri corrected. "You see in her *world*, you was the one out of pocket and reckless eyeballin"

"HER WORLD?!" Rasheed asked in disbelief. "Nigga, that's a *bitch*, she don't got no world, P"

"That's the sill shit you and the rest of these niggas could feed to ya'll *hoes*, but to me , it's a difference between my bitch and my hoe. But see, my bitch could still be my hoe and vice versa. It all depends on where I wanna place the bitch, not where the *next nigga* feel she should be. The bitches I really fuck with I lace differently than the bitches I got out here just on some hoe shit. That's why none of those other bitches looked at you. *Those are my hoes.* My bitches don't gotta fear you niggas and they damn sure don't gotta put they head down when you around. I teach mine to walk with their heads held high cause ain't shit on the ground but old bubble gum, concrete and trash and ain't none of that shit going in my pocket so why would I instruct them to focus on things that are of no value to me?"

Rarri didn't wait for him to answer. "You see, in they world-"

"P, stop sayin '*they world!*' you givin these bitches *too* much room. They don't got no fuckin world nigga. These bitches are hoes. I don't care how you try to put it or rephrase it. They was put here to sell pussy for a '*pimp*'. They don't get no world or none of that shit you talkin bout." Rasheed defended angrily.

Rarri shook his head in disappointment. "You'sa walkin contradiction type of nigga, that's why I'm glad I'm me."

"How is that?"

""To keep it real, you insufficiently girded like a lot of these niggas but ima pass that part. The part I don't get is how '*you*' could talk all that *'super pimp'* shit, but you out here playing with square bitches. Holding hands, kickin cans and givin them a boyfriend experience when BFE is against the rules of you super pimps." Rarri explained.

"I don't know about all that *super pimp* shit, but yea, I fuck wit square bitches...who payin tho" Rasheed replied rubbing his index and middle finger to this thumb for Rarri to see. "Last time I checked, you fucked on squares too."

"Proudly, but I look at this shit different. I'm makin a whole new lane not only for me but also for the bitches I really fuck with."

"What about givin the game a black eye?" Rasheed questioned seriously.

"I'm not givin the game no more of a black than niggas been givin it. Really, I don't think I'm givin it one at all but it's always goin to be somebody to say otherwise and to be honest., I really don't give a fuck what another nigga think. That's hoe shit. If I thought like everybody else there would be no difference between us and I wouldn't be where I'm at right now, mentally or financially. Last time I checked, I done passed a lot of niggas who been in the game waay before me so obviously I'm doin somethin right. I'm not sayin *all* of the rules don't matter but in my personal opinion 'some' of them will hold a nigga back from becomin somethin more. Niggas be quick to say you ain't a pimp if you sellin drugs or got any other hustles outside of pimpin but me, I believe that I can use pimpin in other areas as a way to put me ahead. What if I wanted to pimp and go to school, am I now supposed to stop goin and say fuck getting an education which is somethin that is priceless just because other mothafuckas say that ain't what pimps do? Hell naw, fuck all that. I'm not a school nigga tho, I was just usin that as an anology but ima do whatever it is that makes me happy. Not somethin that will satisfy the next nigga and benefit him more than me, look at that nigga super natural."

Rarri pointed to an older pimp who was having the time of his life telling stories with his p-partners.

"Do you really believe that, That Niggas dream is to be on FIG every night waitin on a bitch to bring him some money? If that's his dream, it's not only sad, but it's also a gotdamn shame for any nigga to want so little for himself. I don't wanna be 50 years old still out here stuck in the same spot doin the same shit around the same niggas. This shit fun but 'we' could afford to do this shit right now because we still young. Eventually, this shit goin to get old my nigga, sheed. A lot of these niggas goin to be standin here stuck in this same parkin lot. not me though. That's why I treat my bitches good because I know they are goin to be somethin big. The crazy part is tho, I don't even care if I couldn't fall back on them. I just wanna see them at their best doin some shit that won't put them in jail or in a fucked up situation. Just seeing them successful would make me feel successful, even if I wasn't."

Rasheed could see Rarri's smile was one that came from being proud of his team. He couldn't help but notice how much faith he had in his way of thinkin and the words he chose to speak. That made him kind of believe in them too. Never has he heard a nigga talk so confidently about some bitches. Especially not on some long-term shit because bitches aren't here to stay. Outside of pimpin, He didn't know what else Rarri had going on, but he planned to find out.

Not only did Rarri have game but he could tell he also had something else that he wanted. As much as he liked Rarri and wanted to know him on a more personal level, he couldn't because he damn sure ain't come this far for nothing.

"On p's that's some real shit." Rasheed agreed and continued to listen....

NINE

"DID HE TAKE THE MONEY?"

"Yea, mom, he took the money." Rasheed replied as he flopped on the sofa.

""YES! YES! YES!" Rasheed's mom almost yelled out but covered her mouth hoping not to wake her grumpy husband. She took one deep breath to calm herself, something she found herself doing a lot of these days. "So you're in?" she asked anxiously Biting her fingernail in anticipation.

"That's what it look like." He answered, boredly as he picked up the remote and turned the television.

His mother lost control and jumped on sofa, silently screaming to herself while giving him kisses all over his face and telling him he did it and how proud she was of him. That cheered Rasheed up. Sometimes she put too much pressure on him and some of the plans she came up with would backfire on him. Like her going out of her way to buy the motion board and light saber thinking that would help him fit in with Rarri more. To be honest, he was happy when Macky threw that mothafucka in the street.

"He fuckin with me tough now." He assured his mom who put

her hand over her heart to stop it from beating out of her chest. "I don't see why I can't just talk to him ma."

"We're so close Rasheed, don't mess this up for us, not now. Please not now son, I will be so upset with you, *so upset...*" His mom begged him, instantly winning him over.

All he really ever cared about was what his mother wanted and getting her attention and approval, so if she said no, he wouldn't argue with it. Even if she was wrong. Whenever she would be upset with him, even if it was the smallest thing, he would feel as if his world had shattered.

"Ok ma, I won't say anything." He assured her before she panicked. "I need to use the credit card cause we goin shoppin at Saks tomorrow."

She jumped up almost running to her purse. "Here, take both of these this time."

"MARY!" her husband yelled from his room.

"Yes hunny!" she replied oh-so lovingly for her darling before pretending to stick her finger down her throat indicating how sick of him, she was to her son.

He hated that his mom had to put up with his stepdad, Frank, for so many years. Frank was an old, retired yet successful Geophysical Oceanographer who was somehow too rich to care who didn't like his grumpy attitude or demanding ways. Frank liked to control everything and everyone that he possibly could. He kept Mary on a foreign car drivin, designer wearin, credit card swipin, diamond crusted, 24 karat gold collar leash. He spoiled her rotten but never hesitated in threatening to take away the perks of her lavish lifestyle.

One that he felt her bastard son was also taking advantage of. The only reason he put up with him was because of his beautiful mother. In fact, Frank tried his hardest to have Mary get an abortion when she was pregnant with Rasheed but she wasn't having it. The two of them was all he really had and he loved them wholeheartedly. Frank was just a mean person on the outside and tough love was the only love he knew to show sometimes.

His father was a rich, mean and grumpy old fart who genetically passed his ways down to his one and only son, who would later inherit his fortune. He went out of his way to impress his wife and now years later, though he wasn't broke, he was starting to feel the dents in his wallet. Not sure if she would stay around if he had nothing, he started managing his money more properly. Something that didn't sit right with her. He didn't give a fuck about how she felt about it. Frank *needed her* to stay by his side and this was the way he knew to do it.

"Stop spending my fucking money!" He yelled almost into a heart attack.

"Your money?" she screamed, dropping the credit cards on the table as she stormed towards their bedroom to chew his ass the fuck out. "This is *our* money!"

Rasheed shook his head, grabbed the credit cards and bounced. He was getting tired of his moms arguing with that nigga. That shit was getting old and he was getting money of his own now. He couldn't wait for him to fall over and die already so they could make off with a fat check.

TEN

BETTY WAP never felt this good in her life. Not only did Heaven get her as and titties done, she also got her eye fixed. In awe of her own body, Betty Wap could barely recognize herself in the mirror lately. Which is something that will always bring a joyful tear to her eye. She loved Heaven for not only the transformation but also for opening her eyes (I mean eye) up to a who new world. No matter what, Betty Wap wanted to hoe. In a strange way, she felt like their connection grew stronger because of that exact reason.

To Heaven, if Betty Wap wanted to still hoe while having the option not to meant that she had problems, deeper than most bitches and maybe even her own.

'She just the type of bitch Rarri needs.' Heaven thought as she watched Betty Wap staring at herself, *again*, in the mirror and couldn't help but smile.

"Feels good, don't it?'

"Yeah" she admitted never looking away from her naked body. She knew that her new look put some of the best of them to shame. She felt how not only men but all people looked at her now.

Betty Wap was never used to being noticed before and now

instead of finger combing her hair over her eye, she a habit of making sure it was still in place. Especially when people looked at her for too long. Dealing with Heaven on a daily basis for the last three months changed her dramatically. She didn't earn no bachelors degree but she damn sure wasn't the same naïve Betty Wap mothafuckas was used to.

"Why me? Out of all the bitches out there, why did he pick me?"

"What you mean, *why you*? Look at you. Heaven countered as she walked over to stand next to her. "You're a bad bitch." She added genuinely.

"Yea, *now*. But I wasn't *then*." Betty Wap replied sadly before walking away to put some clothes on.

"Oh my god" Heaven cried out in frustration while clenching her fist to the sky.

Getting Betty Wap *mentally* where she needed to be was proving to be the hardest part of it all. One moment her confidence would be at an all time high and then, that along with her self-esteem would just fall straight to the floor. Heaven was starting to wonder if she was better off leaving Betty Wap the way she was.

"A bad bitch isn't what's on the outside, it's in here." She explained to her while pointing to her heart. " And ain't this what you wanted? All this shit?" she added waving her hand around the lavish bedroom that was now hers.

"No, YES! I mean" She sighed in frustration and sat on her bed. "I don't know what I want.

"Well what did you want before all this then? I'm talkin bout before you met Rarri, what did you want Marque-"

Betty Wap looked up sharply cutting Heaven off before she could finish. Heaven rolled her eyes and sat down next to her. Changing her name wasn't even up for discussion. She didn't care that it was a name that was meant to make fun of her, she was keeping it.

"I mean, what did you want, *Betty Wap*?"

Betty Wap looked at her sharply again and rolled her good eye causing both of them to chuckle. Heave taught her when to notice people being sarcastic and all the tell-tale signs she needed to be aware of. "For real though, Wap, what did you want?" she asked again.

"Nothin to be proud of" she admitted thinking back on all the silly shit she used to do to fit in with people or hopefully get chose by a pimp nigga."

"It had to be something that you wanted *then* that you still want *now*." She said as she put Betty wap's hands in hers.

"Naw, not really."

"So what did you magically start wantin once Rarri came around?" she asked her with a hint of attitude.

"The only thing I still want now."

"And, what's that?"

Betty Wap looked Heaven directly in the eyes and simply said, "him.."

That touched Heaven deeply and gave her that tingling feeling in her chest.

"Well" she replied, clutching her hand tightly as she stood. "The question is, are you goin to do what it takes to get him?"

"What I gotta do?" Betty Wap asked anxiously.

"Get in, wap. All you gotta do is get in." Heaven said sarcastically imitating Rarri at the show making both of them laugh.

Since then, she had only seen Rarri a few times and he still hadn't noticed her. Well, he noticed her just not who she was, yet. Not being able to talk to him was killing her on the inside but Heaven made her promise to keep her mouth shut while they around him.

"Na, but For real all you gotta do is keep doin you and remember all the shit that I taught you. That's what's goin to get you ahead, so just focus on getting to that bag and stackin that shit up right now" Heaven schooled.

"mmk…" Wap nodded. "So.....what we doing today?"

"I think it's time we get you back goin. You seem ready."

Betty Wap paraded around like a happy housewife. She had been ready to hit the streets and get back hoe'n since the first day she came but now she *knew* she was really ready after everything Heaven had taught her.

"So what's the name of the street ima be workin?" she asked happily.

Heaven laughed. "Naw, you not bout to workin on no streets or corners no more. That's not goin to be the best thing to do right now, so we bout to get you crackin on the net."

"Noooo!" she whined. "I'm not tryna be no internet hoe, ain't that for lazy hoes anyway?"

"A lazy hoe is a lazy hoe. Some mothafuckas just lazy, Wap. It don't matter what they doing or where they at. That's just them but one thing I know fasho is that, that ain't you so stop with all that shit. You bout to have these trick ass niggas goin crazy, watch."

Heaven slapped Betty Wap on the ass before leaving the room. A couple of minutes later, she returned with her laptop, sat next to her and flipped the screen up.

"What's this?"

"Remember when you took all of those pictures the other day?" She asked her then continued, not waiting for a response.

"Well, this is yo profile and *this* is what's goin to step yo game up"

Betty Wap had her stank face on as Heaven scrolled through all of the pictures, knowing damn well she liked them. She looked like one of those Straight Stuntin magazine models. She was trying her hardest to hold back her smile, her happy grin let Heaven know she was secretly impressed.

"You see if you go and stand on the corner any nigga with a couple of dollars know he got action at you, like any other bitch out there but this makes you look more sophisticated. This is how you advertise yoself to the tricks who are willing to pay the most. I'm talkin about thousands a date, wap, not that little shit you would get on the blade. Not to metion all the men I already deal with who I know will want to spend some time with you. You in a different league now." Heaven closed the laptop. "It's bout time you start actin like it." She added.

She handed the computer to Betty wap then left out of the room again. This time, closing the door behind her. Wap didn't waste no time opening the laptop and staring at the pictures in awe. She never thought about having her own website before but she had to admit, it did feel good. The layout made her look professional, important, elegant and desirable even.

"Mmhhmmm" Heaven said startling Betty Wap. she was so glued to the screen that she didn't hear the door open. Heaven knew Wap liked it, she just wanted to peek back in and make sure.

Wap smiled to herself while smelling her lip. She was about to get this money for her nigga like never before. Fasho, Rarri was going to recognize who his bottom bitch was…

ELEVEN

"WHAT THE FUCK you mean you can't see him?" Lil Dink asked angrily. "I say we just go over there and snatch cuz up. On the set that shit got me hot YAAH"

"It got me hot too foo but ain't nothin I can really do about it now. That bitch spooked and her pops talkin bout goin to the police if I go anywhere near them." Trigg hit the blunt deeply thinking about his situation. "Maybe it's better this way."

"Cuh, how you gon say some dumb ass shit like that?" Lil Dink asked as he snatched the blunt from Trigg.

"My nigga is you blind? Look at the lifestyle we livin, we neck deep in this shit. You runnin around tryna be el chapo, Rarri think he majic Don Juan and I'm knockin shit down almost on a daily, on top of that, you seen how Heaven did Juice and JJ. I ain't know she was even that cold like that." Trigg shook his head sadly. "What if that was me and lil nigga?"

"I would kill that bitch" Lil Dink said seriously.

"...and Rarri?"

Lil Dink sighed deeply knowing that was something he would never be able to do. Rarri loved Heaven. She was like the mother he never had and so much more. He just wanted to hold his godson and see Trigg be the father he knew he could be. Just because Trigg was a killer didn't mean he wasn't a good person. He just didn't like certain people, from certain places and for the right price anybody who got in the way but still, he had a good heart in Lil Dinks' eyes.

"Look, Juice got what he deserved. He tired to snitch on niggas YAAH, what was she supposed to do? I would hope ya'll would do the same to me if I chose that route, if not worse. Now that shit with JJ was fucked up, but he seen what happened. She just did what none of us would have been able to do because to keep it 700, I don't know what I would have done if it was up to me."

Trigg grabbed the blunt from him and relit it then pulled hard. "To keep it 700, I think they was goin to do that shit regardless"

"Why you say that?"

"I don't know but one night me and Rarri pulled up on Balinda and cuz slid her some work."

"What that gotta do with what had happened?" Lil Dink wanted to know.

"First off, it was just crazy because we was just parked down from her house until Juice left. We was in a rental on some sneaky shit and juice kept her high. So I ain't catch on to what we was even there for until Rarri pulled out this baggy. He told her it was the best 'BOY' in town. If you would have seen the look in her eyes you woulda knew she couldn't wait to try that shit. On the hood she damn near ran back in the house. Rarri had that grin he be havin on his face when we bout to go slide on some shit" Trigg looked at him. "You know that look I'm talkin bout"

"So what, you think that's how she died?"

"Naw, nigga. I *know* that's how she died"

"Naw, he would have told you that YAAH" Lil Dink assured with a slight smile as he thought about it. "I mean why would he take you with him and not say nothin? Don't you think he would have just went by hisself if that was the case?"

"Man, I don't know what cuh on. I really don't even give a fuck about none of that shit. Fuck Balinda, Fuck Juice and JJ would have probably grew up to be just like that nigga anyway, so none of that shit don't bother me." Trig said coldly. "..and for the record, just so *you* know, I would have threw his lil ass in the water too. That's why I don't want my son apart of none of this shit. At least I know with him being raised the way they goin to raise him, he will never grow up like us and he goin to be safe, that's what's important."

That was a hard pill to swallow but Lil Dink knew that Trigg was right. The lifestyle they were into didn't guarantee a good ending. Trigg tried getting his life together and doing things the right way but his past came back in the worst way when he had to kill Spank's momma. Mentally and emotionally that fucked him up because he knew Spank was mad at him and instead of getting high on drugs again, Trigg was chasing that rush he got when playing God.

In some strange way, Trigg felt closer to Spank the moment he killed somebody but a few hours later he would feel empty and alone again, sad even. He didn't cry about it no more because growing up in Compton was everything but easy. Trigg was just another young nigga dealing with his demons the best way he knew how and that was shooting shit the fuck up.

"Yeah, I feel it. Lil Dink said as he walked over to his dresser, opened it and pulled out his glock .40. "You tryna go slide on somethin?"

Trigg's smile said it all. Honestly he was going on something regardless tonight, with or without Dink. Lately he had been going on shit with Kill Kill or Solo because Dink was always busy selling some shit or picking up money from mothafuckas. Trigg needed this tho. He was back to his usual self joking and laughing, it's been awhile since he bonded over a body with his boy.

———

"So how they get away and cuh get caught?"

"I guess baby stayed there, shid, I wouldn't have left my lil brother neither."

Kill Kill and Tana Jay ducked down low as lil Dink and Trigg walked by talking not noticing the two lurking in the car. It took everything for Tana Jay not to hop out and start squeezing on they young asses. Especially Trigg. He had been waiting to catch him too because he was the one that had been sliding through more than anybody. Even Rarri because Trigg really ain't have nothing else better to do. *This was his fun.*

"We gon get them too, don't trip." Kill Kill assured Tana Jay noticing his menacing stare.

Tana Jay was out for blood but what he really needed right now was some money.

"But on another note, it look like we bout to be able to get craccin on this lick tonight. I think both of them niggas leavin right now...probably bout to go slide on somethin to keep it real."

Tana Jay had a look of disgust on his face knowing them niggas was bout to go on one somewhere. He decided to send a text to his make sure his homies were on alert. If they went by his hood, they would be as good as dead. As soon as they drove off, Kill Kill and Tana Jay exited the car and crept up to the house.

TWELVE

RARRI AND FIA sat side by side in the lounge of the RH hotel in Hollywood. Only Fia could pull off makin MM6 Maison Margiela shorts look like the thing to wear in a business environment. Complimenting herself with a Louis Vuitton top and matching stilettos was as close to casual as she could be. Hair and nails done, none of her jewelry costume, she was really a bad bitch. Standing at 5'6 thick, caramel complexion, features so beautiful and foreign, nobody could keep their eyes off of her. Especially not in the lounge. A couple of guys even got slapped by their dates for looking too long.

Rarri loved the way she made him feel. She was really for him and only him. The chemistry between them flowed naturally. In a perfect world she would be his wife and he, her husband. From the outside looking in, the two looked like two spoiled rich kids who never had to worry about nothing their entire lives. Staring deeply into each other's eyes as they talked, Fia kept biting her lip sexily, thinking about all the things she was going to do to him. Her pussy was throbbing since they had gotten there. Rarri, still feeling the pills he had popped earlier couldn't wait neither, but, he wanted to take his time with Fia tonight. He knew her body like the back of his hand, but he wanted to learn more about her.

Seeing how much she was talking, he knew the pill he had given her had kicked in. Not that he needed her to be on one to talk but Rarri knew that while on ecstasy, one would have some of the best conversations because people are known to say exactly what' in their hearts at the time they are rollin. Fia had a special spot in his heart. She was the one he connected with the most on a more intimate level. Day in and day out she the one going the hardest for him in every way, so it was no mystery why she's the one by his side now.

"Can I ask you somethin?' He asked, cutting her ramblings off.

She put her hand on his lap under the table, "You can do more than that, papi."

"I know" he replied as he locked his hand in hers and put both of theirs back on the table. "But tonight, I wanna get to know *you*."

"What are you talkin about, you do know me, papi." She laughed.

"What I mean to say is, I wanna know you, like yo story, yo struggle, yo journey, yo mind.." he made clear, kissing the back of her hand.

"I wanna know everything about you fifi, like everything." He added, passionately and never takin his eyes off of hers to let her know how serious he was.

"It's not much to tell." She replied, unconsciously laughing nervously and by the way she looked to the left in a split second, he knew she wasn't being truthful.

"Fia...you goin to do me like that?" he asked in disappointment.

Her smile faded slightly as she thought about not keeping it real with him, which was something she wasn't used to doing. It wasn't like she wanted to in the first place, it's just that Rarri never asked these types of questions before. Nobody ever cared to ask. It's been so much that she's been through before meeting him. Just the thought of it all made her eyes water and looking back into his, she could see just how sincere he was.

"Where should I start?"

"How about from the beginnin?" He said as he stood. "Let's go back to the room.

Fia stood looking up at him all lovey dovey as can be. He really was her everything and she loved him deeply. Never did she believe a nigga so young could have so much potential. Not only did her life change after meeting him, but also the three girls she loved the most, Mia, Tia and Dria. Would the Bentley Bitches even exist without him? He was the first nigga to ever put them in position to shine and be on.

He genuinely wanted the best for them. Makin money *with* him and not just *for* him was important to Rarri. Most p's wouldn't understand that part but he didn't need them to. All he needed was for his bitches to believe in him and the sky was the limit, or so he thought. She kissed the back of his hand sweetly then the two exited the lounge. The walk to the room was quiet. Rarri sat on the couch as Fia grabbed one of the pillows, placed it on his lap and laid her head on it.

Lovingly rubbing his fingers through her hair and massaging her scalp, he didn't need to see the tears to feel her pain. He planted a kiss on the top of her head, then another on her cheek. Gently turning her face towards him, Rarri for the first time in a long time, kissed her on the lips, then more followed by another.

"Papi, I—" she started but was silenced by another one of his kisses....

"Tell me later" he said before slipping his tongue into her mouth passionately causing all of her insides to flutter.

Not wanting him to ever move, she put her hand behind his head and kissed him back. Their tongues touched and circled slowly. So slowly it felt like sex itself. She wasn't willing to wait any longer so she slipped out of her shorts. Rarri, just as eager, quickly took off his shirt. Both them, stood, still hungrily kissing, they undressed. Once naked, Fia was making her way down but Rarri stopped her and got on his knees.

"Papi, you sure?" she questioned.

He thought about it for a moment as they locked eyes. He ain't never ate pussy before and he was tired of thinking about the shit, he didn't want to think about nothing right now. So, he just did it.

"Oh shit, papiii" she moaned out as soon as his lips touched her clit.

Rarri ate her pussy the same way he kissed her. Then he sat her down on the couch, placed her legs over his shoulders and continued feasting. Instantly falling in love with the way she tasted. Fia was cumin nonstop, pussy was on super drip. Every lick was sensational and gave her body a feeling of bliss. Of course she done had niggas on their knees before but never did she think Rarri would be the type and if he was going to do it, it wouldn't be on a bitch like her. This feeling was so good that it brought tears to her eyes.

'He really loves me..' she thought as she moaned out loud "PAPI..."

She wanted him inside of her but by the looks of it, Rarri wasn't planning on stopping no time soon, so she had a better idea. She stood, pussy still in his mouth, slowly laid him on his back and rode his face from the front while he gripped both of her ass cheeks. The sight of him down there enjoying himself made her cum again as she grinded back and forth. Fia looked back and seen his dick standing straight up then turned around in a 69 position and started twerking her ass on his face as she took him in her mouth. Both of them were fucking each others faces like it was the best thing in the world to do.

Fia was sucking her dick loud as fuck, gagging, spitting, slurping and all of that just made Rarri want to eat her pussy even more so he just started going crazy. Sticking his tongue in and out of her, licking around her walls, smacking her on the ass, spreading her cheeks wide and kissing her pussy wildly. She started playing with herself while simultaneously twirling her tongue sloppily around the head of his dick then went down deep, came up, down deeper, came back up then down deeper, deeper, deeper. Her eyes tightened as she took him into her throat, causing her to cough up spit. She never had this much dick in her mouth before. The next cough made her pussy spray, hard.

"Oh Fuck, Papii" she moaned.

He thrust his dick into her mouth deeper this time and her pretty pussy sprayed again.

"Papi—" He shut her up with another pump causing her to spray again.

Every time he stuffed her face, she wet his dick, Her body went into overdrive. She squirted so hard and long and that her body began to shake dramatically as she collapsed on top of him. His dick still in her mouth, her head was spinning out of control. Rarri slapped her pussy with four of his fingers.

"Stop being stingy bitch, I know you got some more." he added and continued licking on her pussy like a cat cleans it's fur.

She couldn't escape him, he had her gripped by the waist and he was all in there, tongue showing her no mercy.

"Ah Fuuuuck!" she screamed and came repeatedly as he cleaned her sloppily.

Fia felt the build up of what she was holding in coming. Unable to hold on any longer all of her insides tightened as she exploded and came hard then passed out on top of him with cream still oozing out of her.

Fia woke up and saw Rarri next to her smoking a blunt and watching TV.

"What happened?"

"Yo nasty ass blacked out on a nigga." He replied as he hit the blunt smoothly.

"Wait, what? Fia sat up. Everything was a blur for a minute then it all started to come back to her.

"Papi, you didn't?..." she asked in a happy shock.

"I did…" he said proudly.

She put both hands over her mouth trying to hold her excitement. "But, I thought you didn't…You-me-I…"

"Gotdamn Fi, just kick back, it ain't that serious."

"What? Fia said in disbelief. "Not that serious? Hold on."

She got up, went and grabbed her phone then came back to the room, already Face Timing her bitches who she knew was waiting on her call anxiously. Dria answered on the first ring, Mia, Tia and Bird were all in place, also ready to hear every detail of their night.

"Breaking Fucking news" She said as she got back in bed so they could see him too. "Papi got *looooow* last night, got a bitch feelin *gooood*" she clowned dancing around with her tongue out.

"Watch out, cuh" Rarri took the phone out of her hand. "we just chillin"

She grabbed the phone back and gave them her '*yea, the fuck right*' expression. "Bullshit, papi hit me with the sloppy toppy" she yelled as they wrestled for the phone in laughter.

"Ayyyeeeee!" they all cheered in tandum.

Hearing them all yelling out, Rarri gave up and let her get her shine on. She instantly began giving every detail she could remember. Her happy ass even went as far as showing them the positions she was popping her ass in and everything else. Rarri wasn't really trippin on Fia telling them, these were his bitches. They weren't out there sucking and fuckin for money no more but they would have if he told them to. You could call it cuffing or anything else but he didn't give a fuck. The Bentley bitches were his and all his to himself as of now and if the music shit went right, ain't no tellin where they would end up..

All he knew was that music was something that they loved doing more than anything so that's what he pushed them to do whenever they wasn't running bricks or his hoes around. He didn't have to give them shit. The Bentley bitches earned everything they got.

"Tell them bitches we gon call them back later." Rarri said as he got out of the bed. "We bout to sag out for a minute."

"Where we goin?"

"To fuck Saks over. I told the homie to meet me up there" He replied then walked into the bathroom.

"Byeeee" Fia waved to the phone before hanging up and following him not wanting to waste any time. Plus, she wanted to get some dick before they left.

It's been a couple of weeks since she had been shopping, so, fasho she was about to go crazy but most importantly, make sure Rarri didn't have to spend none of his own money. Fia loved buying him shit but what she really loved was the looks on the cashier's faces when she did it. Priceless…

THIRTEEN

RARRI AND RASHEED walked out of Saks with their bitches behind them, bags in tow. Choppin game causally on some fly shit, this was nothing new to them. Fia and Brandy was doing the same, feeling good after breaking a decent amount on the two kings ahead. Brandy was Rasheed's bottom bitch and would be baby momma if it wasn't for the miscarriage she had a couple of years back. Even though they had lost a child she still considered him, her baby daddy. Brandy's been down with Rasheed from the jump and from the looks of things, wasn't going nowhere no time soon.

She loved his pimpin more than anything. He went hard on his hoes. To her, his game was beyond the rest of these niggas out here *so-called* pimpin. she couldn't see why he fucked with Rarri so much. Besides having money and bitches lined up, to her, he was soft on these hoes. Too soft! Brandy could never see herself payin a nigga like him. Especially seeing how loose he allowed the Bentley bitches to be. Running around out of pocket like they *unknockable* and all that. She overheard Rasheed talking about the shit that happened with Bird last night. Brandy couldn't wait to see that bitch.

She was starting to not like none of them hoes. The only reason she was actin coo with Fia wannabe high maintenance ass was because Rasheed told her to. Brandy didn't know what going on but she had been around him long enough to know when her daddy had something up his sleeves, so whatever it was, she was with it.

"Damn girl, you rockin that dress. You had all them bitches in there stank facin, must be nice." Brandy complimented with a smile.

"Me? Bitch they was on yo fine ass in them booty shorts. You the one walkin round lookin like fraud." Fia joked back while thinkin, '*this bitch fake as fuck.*'

If Brandy didn't think she saw through her like an arrowhead water bottle, she need to take a seat in a recycling bin cause she damn sure plastic. Fia didn't like bitches like Brandy and Brandy didn't like bitches like Fia. They were two completely different types of hoes. Brandy sold pussy that's it and that's all, where as Fia did all types of shit to get money. Brandy didn't have her own money or none of that shit like Fia did . She wasn't allowed to stack for herself like Fia because she was laced differently and that's where jealousy sets in.

Fia didn't look down on bitches like Brandy because she once only did the same shit and if it came down to it, she would bounce back on a trick's dick to hit Rarri's mitt if need be but it was other bitches like Brandy around for that now. She loved and respected that lifestyle to the fullest but she had been leveled up from the bitch she used to be. Yea, she kept Sugar daddy's spending on her daily but she wasn't fuckin none of them niggas. The Bentley bitches were trap stars so they could and would always bring in more than a lot of bitches that was down selling pussy just finessing tricks and talking them out of shit. They made sure they had a trick willing to pay for anything they or Rarri needed.

They stacked up for him daily and would cash out more than the bitches he had out there, so he allowed them to get it anyway they could. You see, at some point, when you're doing something for so long, one must elevate. The plug ain't standing on the corner with the pack or sitting at the traphouse bustin fades. If your plug is, that says a lot about you, (Really think about that..."

Rarri was in the middle of poppin some fly shit when his phone rang.

"What's the deal? WHAT? WHEN? I'm on my way.." he hung up the phone then looked back at Fia. "Come on, we gotta sagg out."

"What up, p, you straight? Rasheed asked sensing something was wrong.

"Yea, I'm good. Some shit just came up."

"You want me to push with you?" My work could post up with ours till we get back." Rasheed lifted up his shirt to show Rarri he was clutching. "You know how this shit go." He added.

Rarri thought about it for a moment then looking at Fia who shrugged in response. He thought for a couple of more seconds, "Fuck it, come on.." he said as they walked off.

———

Rasheed pulled his car into the spot where Rarri told him to park and killed the engine. The two sat in silence as Rarri thought deeply, takin a few moments to himself.

"So what we---"

"Look.." Rarri said cutting him off. "I don't fuck with p's outside of pimpin but me and you been rockin hard. I got a lot of other shit goin on in my lielife, my nigga. The type of shit niggas think they ready for and the ones who not, bybout time they find out, it's too late. With that bein said, you could drop me off here and we could link up later with no love lost...ain't shit gon change between us. But, if you push with me.." He looked Rasheed directly in the eyes to let him know how serious he was. "Just know ain't no turnin back from that cause I'ma rock with you on some other shit, outside of what we been on."

Rasheed had never seen this side of Rarri. He was all business, *serious business with not a drop of bullshit.* He was hesitant but he didn't waste time showing it. He just got out of the car. Rarri smiled to himself then got out as well and walked towards the house with Rasheed behind him. He could hear everybody arguing as he reached the porch.

When he opened the door it looked like a tornado had hit the inside. Heaven and Lil Dink were at each others neck in the greatest debate ever, while Trigg, Macky and the flocks had their separate arguing session going on a couple feet away. Everybody was so busy yelling nobody noticed Rarri walk in. He stood there listening and wondering what was wrong with them all. Fighting with each other wasn't going to solve anything and seeing them do so was pissing him off by the second.

"Everybody shut the fuck up!" He barked in agitation getting everyone's attention. "What the fuck happened?"

"Nigga, you shut the fuck up!" Lil Dink shouted at Rarri then everybody else joined in chewin him the fuck out too.

Heaven was too stuck looking at Rasheed to answer Rarri's question. Unlike Rarri, Rasheed had short hair with waves, a grill and seemed to be a bit older. Besides that, the similarities between the two were uncanny.

"What the fuck is *that* nigga doin here?" Macky asked in disbelief pointing at Rasheed.

"The same thing you is." Rarri shot back.

"On babies you trippin..you don't even know cuh like that, third—"

"Obviously, I don't know a lot of niggas like that"

Macky looked like he had a foul taste in his mouth. "What you tryna insinuate?"

"I ain't insinuatin shit. What you feelin guilty about somethin?"

Macky wiped down on his face aggressively, something he

always did when trying to calm himself before reacting because his anger often got the best of him.

"You know what, I'ma just go chill out in the backyard." He replied talking to Heaven. "Let me know when ya'll figure out what we goin to do" he added then looked at Rarri, "Cause I ain't with all the theatrics."

"What was all that about?" Heaven asked once he left the room.

"Ain't nobody worried about Macky right now" Rarri replied waving him off.

"Everybody, this my nigga, Rasheed. Rasheed, these the homies, Lil Dink, Trigg, Flock, Lil Flock and this lovely lady right here is my aunty Heaven."

Rasheed didn't say anything, he just greeted them with a head nod and they did the same. Nobody needed to know why Macky didn't like Rasheed to not like him neither but now wasn't the time for that.

"So what happened tho?" Rarri asked lil Dink.

"Last night we was chillin then we like fuck it, let's go slide on somethin. When we got back the house was like this" Lil Dink explained simply.

"Slide on somethin? Are you fuckin serious, Dink?" Heaven intervened angrily. "I hope it was worth it. You and Trigg runnin around here with Peter pan syndrome, scared to grow the fuck up"

Rasheed couldn't help but to chuckle at the last part but he immediately regretted it as soon as everybody looked at him all crazy and shit.

"You know what, ain't nobody got time for this" Heaven snatched her purse and headed towards the door to leave. "Ya'll two lil niggas better run me my dough by tonight"

"What if we don't?" Trigg blurted out sarcastically as Heaven opened the door. She looked back, laughed, then walked out closing the door behind her.

"YAHH, you just gon let yo aunty threaten us like that?" Lil Dink asked hysterically.

"She ain't even say nothin" Rarri replied as he sat down on the couch.

"Do she need to?" Trigg stated in a panic knowing exactly how Heaven got down which was something they had just witnessed days ago.

"Fucc all that, I'ma go holla at her real quick." He said then jetted for the door. "Aunty! aunty!" he called out tryna sound as innocent as possible now lowkey causing everybody to laugh.

Everybody but Rasheed. He didn't know what to do so he just stood there straight faced, not wanting the unwanted attention again.

"What they say about Baby Flock" Rarri asked flock

"They goin to let blood out today. I guess the lawyer Heaven hooked us up with was able to get the judge to give him a bail, so we just paid that shit this mornin" he replied.

"Who pickin him up?"

"His moms" lil flock butted in sadly.

"I don't know what she mad at us for, everybody actin like we was supposed to stay and get caught like blood did. That's out! We ain't the ones that made him—"

"Blood, *shut up*" Flock pleaded with his lil homie. He was tired of him tryna explain shit to mothafuccas when they were going to think and say what they wanted regardless anyway. On top of that lil Flock didn't know how to talk to people. Everything he said always rubbed people the wrong way.

Rarri didn't care what nobody said though cause he could see how much they were hurting. Wasn't a day that went by that he didn't hurt for Spank and for having to leave him in the vacant like that.

"Oh yea, my nigga Rasheed slid 5 bandz to give to his moms for the funeral but you know we all goin to take care of that so this just goin to go to her for whatever else she needs." Rarri told them changing the subject.

Lil Dink and the flocks looked at him for the first time in

approval. They didn't need his money but it was the thought that counted. Flock was the first to walk up and greet him with a handshake and a hug, followed by the rest of them.

Trigg came in and sat down next to Rarri looking exhausted.

"What she say?" lil Dink asked anxiously.

"Shit" Trigg replied half out of breath. "She pulled off on me...I tried to..tried to chase her down to the stop sign..but she didn't stop at the mothafucka."

"Damn!" lil Dink swore.

Trigg looked at him in disbelief. "You got it just come up off that shit, YAAH"

"What? Nigga this is yo fault"

"You asked *me* if I wanted to go slide YAAH" Trigg reminded him "that's on you" he added and started laughing.

"Yea, ight whatever. Remember she said '*ya'll*' run me, *my money. 'ya'll'* meaning both of us, not just me, nigga."

"Oh yeah she did huh" Trigg spoke to himself as Heaven's exact words sunk in on him.

"I got my half" lil Dink said with a smirk.

"yo half? Oh so now we splittin up and shit? Trigg questioned with attitude.

"You boo-boo as fuck cuh, we ain't splittin up"

Lil dink laughed as he walked out of the living room.

"That's why I'ma tell her run our shit concurrent nigga" He yelled after him then looked at Rarri. "You got me right?"

"I'm lowkey tapped right now foo" Rarri replied tryna avoid eye contact.

"tapped?" Trigg almost screamed "go'n with that bullshit Rarri stop playin. It's a pawnshop around the corner we gon have to turn one of them chains in or somethin, on the set" he added then turned to Rasheed with his handout. "And you tryna be down like Brandy and all that you might as well come up off of one of those mothafuckas too, god blessin all the trap niggas, you'a get it back."

When lil Dink walked back in everybody was in tears.

"This clown still here" Macky said looking at Rasheed as he entered the room.

Rasheed had enough of this lil disrespectful ass nigga. "Look 'p' I been tryin my hardest to be civilized wit yo lil ass cause I think you some real pimpin. Matter of fact naw, I *know* you some real pimpin, so I'm not gon assume that you trippin over them bitches I knocked you for cause the last thing I'ma ever do is smut a real nigga. But 'p' on some real shit, you ain't been conductin yoself properly this here game and it's almost bringin me out of my character with you. We supposed to be buildin each other up to be better, not tryna break each other down to be the worst...I'ma man before anything. A black man at that and im damn sure prideful of my culture, where I come from and what my people been through, so I understand why you hate me...society made us all that way my nigga in order to stop a lot of us from prosperin as a whole because we *are* a dominant race. We just been actin too stupid to notice it but Macky, we ain't gotta be like that. All of us in here are black kings."

Rasheed said with so much passion that he had everybody's attention then he extended his hand to Macky.

"I humbly extend my hand as an olive branch to form peace and a great bond between two brothers before destruction, do you accept my offer or would you rather continue this same senseless cycle and be a pawn instead of a king?"

Looking him directly in the eyes, Rasheed was putting Macky on the spot. Not only did he feel all eyes were on him, it was also so quiet that he could hear lil Dink's breathing. Rasheed was kicking some fly shit but Macky wasn't about to let him slide that easy.

"What black panther was most influential to you and why?"

"Fred Hampton because he was a young nigga who wasn't afraid to step up, lead his people and give them hope when they needed it most"

"My nigga" Macky smiled shook his hand and gave him a hug with his free arm tightly. He was happy to finally have somebody around who understood him, *too happy*. The nigga was smiling from ear to ear. "You know they say the Chicago chapter was the –"

"Macky, Macky, Macky. Please don't start with that shit right now" Rarri begged "Ya'll squashed ya'll lil beef and joined forces, *p* got you blushin we get it"

Macky took the smile off of his face, withdrew his hand from Rasheed's and sucked his teeth feeling a bit played while everybody else laughed. "Whatever"

"Do anybody know who could have done this shit."

"Naw but somebody had to been watchin this mothafucka. Probably followed one of ya'll here or somethin. I mean shit, that's what we would have did" Flock explained.

"Fuck it. We don't know who did it but what I do know is that it wasn't nobody who here right now. So, let's just wait and see Who slip up and tell the wrong person, ya'll know how niggas is. until then we goin to switch spots" Rarri instructed "Matter of fact I know the perfect place…"

FOURTEEN

Nigga, you didn't say it was going to be this good" Tana jay said excitedly pacing back and forth never takin his eyes off of the 10 bricks on the table.

"I ain't even know he had all this in there" Kill Kill admitted "But, I'm glad they did." He added, laughing as they slapped fives.

"I bet them bitches ass niggas mad as fuck right now" Tana Jay joked loving the dumbfounded look on his bitches faces as they sat quietly on the couch in awe.

Kill Kill didn't like the fact that he had his bitches around but he assured him they wouldn't say shit. Kill Kill didn't trust that shit but he wasn't willing to risk being seen running around with Tana Jay in public and damn sure not in Long Beach. Everybody knew how much Macky fucked with Rarri. Both of them niggas slid for each other no questions asked, so Kill kill was playing with the enemy. He just hoped it continued to play out right.

"You wanna just cash me out for my half?" Kill asked reluctantly. "if not it's coo, I got it" he added and proceeded to grab five of the bricks.

"Hold on! Talk to nigga" Tana jay replied placing a hand on kill kill's arm stopping him in his tracks.

"Really, I was just goin to dump all this shit to the homie from Asian boyz cause I know he got it"

"Man, them Asian mothafuckas ain't got shit." he shot back. "All they gon try and do is lowball yo ass. Look check this out, let me get em for 10 a piece. I got thirty bandz for you right now and another 20 in a couple of days" he added with a smile.

Kill kill was looking indecisive.

"Fuck with *me*, crip" Tana jay added putting emphasis on the word *me* to make Kill kill feel bad.

That shit didn't work though. Kill kill didn't feel bad for no nigga. Not in this lifetime cause wasn't nobody moping around feeling bad for him. Kill kill planned on leaving the bricks with Tana jay from the jump cause he really didn't have nobody to dump them on without having to worry about the news getting back to Macky. He killed shit, he didn't sell drugs, but Kill kill learned early on to never expose your hand to a nigga no matter what cause that's the easiest way to get takin advantage of.

"I got you cuh" he assured and shook Tana jay's hand. "After you hit me with the rest of the bread I got another one for us. I'ma put it together ASAP."

"The same niggas?"

"YUP"

"Damn cuh, you don't think it's better to leave these niggas breathin for a lil while if we able to keep on bankin on em?"

"Naw, don't nothing last forever, my nigga, and we ain't goin to be able to *keep* bankin on em like that" Kill kill explained. "They far from stupid and Rarri connected to some people"

"He ain't the only nigga who got people, nigga" Tana Jay countered defensively. "Niggas gon to cracc when I say cracc"

"I never said they ain't"

" but you actin like you *think* they won't"

"Look my nigga, what I *think* don't even matter. What we don't *need* is for them to find out who took they shit. This lil personal shoot out shit you and Rarri got goin on is funny to cuh. Trust me, I done seen cuh laughin bout this shit but when we fuckin with the drugs and shit, it's more people than just him"

Kill Kill paused knowing he had everybody in the rooms' attention.

"I know you with all the bullshit, yo name ring but a nigga don't want no unnecessary problems, especially like these, I'm tellin you.

"I'ma go grab this bread for you" Tana jay replied not wanting to hear no more of the bullshit Kill kill was kicking.

He didn't give a fuck who Rarri was connected to, he bled like everybody else. Besides that he couldn't stand none of the niggas from Rarri's hood. He returned a few moments later and handed over the money.

"I'ma hit you later" he added and walked towards the door to hurry up and let his ass out. *'cuh talk too fuckin much'* he thought angrily.

Kill kill could sense the change in his demeanor. *'Nigga nose all flared up, chest all poked out, walkin wit the extras all of a sudden. weird ass Compton nigga'*

"Did you get what I was sayin tho"

"I said I'ma holla at you later!" Tana jay snapped.

Kill Kill looked at Tana jay and his hoes and shook his head. "It's a lot of dead tough niggas" he said out loud before walking out, leaving his bitches to think about what he had just said.

Initially he wasn't gonna go that far but the last thing he needed right now was for Tana jay to get comfortable because lax niggas always got caught slippin. Kill kill knew Tana Jay wasn't mad at what he said, he was just mad that he was saying all that shit in front of his hoes. Hopefully them being scared would push him to wanna move quickly. Anything is possible but one thing was for certain, Kill kill wanted Mack dead..SOON!

"So what ya'll be pushin crystal or somethin?" Rasheed asked as he swerved through traffic.

Rarri hadn't said as much as one word since they left lil Dink's spot.

"Or somethin" he replied. "What part of the game do you love most P"

"The part when I break on a bitch" he answered proudly.

"..And what ways won't you break on a bitch?"

"I'ma break on a bitch any way I can, P. You know how Sheed get down. I'ma send her like a vender. If the bitch don't wanna sell pussy she better come up of one of those kidneys and get daddy dough that way. I'ma take it any way she bring it, P" He replied honestly. "Why, what's the deal?"

"Why you be hittin yo hoes for little silly shit? You can't just fire the bitch and get another one? I mean if they are a dime a dozen don't that make them disposable?"

"Damn, what you criticizing my pimpin now?" He asked defensively.

"Naw, nothin like that." Rarri assured him. "Just askin"

"Well since you don't know I guess I can give you a lil bit of insight." He threw back sarcastically. "These bitches gotta know who in charge at *all times*, P. The second you take yo foot off they neck, they going to think you weak. Then everybody else goin to think you weak and when everybody else think you weak, these bitches goin to eventually stop payin you and when they ain't payin you, they playin you and if you allow these bitches to play you, you can't consider yoself no pimpin P. Simple as that"

"A pimp huh?" Rarri chuckled. "Is that all you care to consider yoself? Just a pimp?"

"My nigga, you stay talkin like you better than the rest of us out here"

"That's cause I am"

"What?"

"I said, that's because I am…you might not want to admit it, but you know it" he replied like it was nothing as he looked out of the window.

Rasheed puffed in amusement. "I don't see how you figure that"

"I know you don't, but that's what I like. If I was the type of nigga to carry myself like everybody else, what would make me different? I don't mean to sound like I'm always talkin down on pimpin cause that's not what I'm doin. I love pimpin and no matter how much money I get doin different shit, don't nothin compare to the feelin of breakin on a bitch but I'll be a fool to let that feelin consume other things I could pursue in life. In my personal opinion, the game right now ain't where it was set out to be. You got niggas who *say* they some pimpin, harborin hoes who are known snitches. Why them bitches ain't poppin up dead? They need to be findin little bitty pieces of them hoe's scattered all through the mojave desert. But niggas ain't out here pressin that type of line for this shit, as long as she ain't tell on *them*, it's coo. If I find a bitch in my stable told on somebody or about to tell, either way you would never see tha bitch again. *That's on my pimpin.* Just cause I don't hit bitches don't mean I won't kill they ass for disrespectin this shit." Rarri looked at Rasheed seriously. "My feet not just in the water, Sheed, my whole body in that bitch."

Rasheed didn't see any sign of bullshit in Rarri's eyes. *'this little nigga serious'* he thought to himself as he smiled.

"It sound like you got some type of plan or somethin. By how much you pressing me, I could see you got a lot on yo mental and I could tell that you be meanin what you say. Just let me know what we on and I'm with it."

"Remember when I said, no turnin back?" Rarri asked.

"I got out, didn't I?" Rasheed countered.

"You did" he admitted with a smile as they pulled up to the hotel him and Fia was staying in.

Once in the room, Rarri rolled a blunt to smoke on and Rasheed rolled one of his own as well.

"This a cold ass view" Rasheed said, taking the view of the city in from the balcony as he pulled on his blunt.

"Yea, it's straight." He replied as he pulled on his then exhaled, "It's time we start our own way"

"You talkin bout like our own chapter? I was thinkin bout doin that one day too-"

"Naw, I'm talkin bout a new way to bring us together. A whole new foundation to build. One with more meaning and structure, somethin we could be proud of." Rarri replied with passion.

"Look, you know a lot about black history and that panther shit, I know a lot about this gang shit and we both know alot about this pimpin...at some point, somewhere down the line the three of those things went wrong because none of them are where they set out to be right now. But that's part of our history and although they didn't succeed, in doing so, they actually showed us how *not* to fail. So technically, they still winnin by us being successful"

Rasheed was stunned. He never thought about it like that before and he thought about a lot of shit.

"We goin to take in all the great ideas that inspired those movements, throw out the bad ones and constantly add new ones that are beneficial for us all to make sure everybody shines" Rarri continued. "We gotta separate ourselves from all the known establishments but still fuck with them at the same time from a close distance, you feel me?"

Rasheed nodded. "Yea but what about the P's who been in the game, who ain't for it? You know they goin to try and campaign against it"

Rarri laughed "Those who ain't for it just ain't for it. This shit ain't for everybody and if they campaign against it" he hit his blunt then shrugged. "Let em. as long as they don't attack us physically they could say whatever they want. We not hoes tryna make them niggas happy but we not tryna make them enemies neither. we just doin us, Sheed, and everybody wants to be apart of somethin..it's out job to create somethin beautiful to be apart of. somethin that's goin to be here long after we're gone. if we not living to leave a legacy behind then we're not living at all. alot of niggas walkin around breathin but they been dead P and by the conversation, you had with Macky earlier, I know you know where that statement came from.

He smiled knowing exactly what Rarri was talking about.

"Me, you and Macky and a few other P's goin to be the startin faces on this side of the game. no bigger me's or little you's to anybody accepted by us…we all equal in here. We gotta be here for each other and have morals. This pimp shit is just one lane amongst many others to come. We goin to generate revenue from every-possible-source"

Rarri jumped up with his hands in the air slightly leaning over the rail of the balcony. "We going to break the world P!!! he yelled into existence. "We Gon break the world!!!"

Rasheed laughed in approval "You picked a name?"

"Naw" he answered smoothly as he pulled on his weed. "It picked me" he added, threw the roach and lifted the back of his shirt exposing his tattoo proudly. It was a big letter 'B' with a pimp sign in the middle.

———

"What's wrong?" Mary asked in a panic, immediately rushing to her sons aid as he walked through the door looking baffled as fuck.

Rasheed sat on the couch staring at nothing, zoned out pondering to himself in deep thought. " I can't believe this shit"

"Baby, what happened? His mom asked sympathetically. "Talk to me. talk to me son, please, talk to me."

"You were right" he replied finally snapping out of his thoughts then looked at his mother. "He has the books…."

FIFTEEN

"DADDY, I can't make no money out here. These hatin ass bitches keep blockin on me, makin tricks run off and shit" Monique said with her hands on her hips. What's been going on out here? These niggas ain't respectin yo pimpin or somethin cause these hoes sho'll talkin reckless."

"Talkin reckless like what?"

"All types of shit, like my folks ain't official, you ain't no real pimpin, you be getting marked out by niggas, runnin from mothafuckas and all types of shit" She replied through judgmental eyes then smacked her lips.. "What's goin on?"

"Just get in the car" pretty me da p ordered.

"So, what you goin to let mothafuckas smut you out like that and not do nothin?" Monique asked in disbelief with a sour expression. "Uh-unh I ain't goin nowhere witchu" she added with a look of disgust.

She grew up in a house full of niggas who handled business. She had 6 brothers and was the only girl, so she was with all of the bullshit. Monique was raised in the Gardens and even thought she didn't claim a gang, she still lived by the code of the streets. Her brothers were well known in San Bernardino and she too was loyal to the soil. Wasn't no way in hell she was going to ruin their reputation by fuckin with a buster. None of them were pimps but they knew how the game went. If she was going to sell pussy, that was on her but one thing was fasho, '*it wouldn't be for a bitch nigga*' Pretty me da p knew it too. He was getting tired of this shit.

Not only was Monique broke and running her mothafuckin mouth, she also the third bitch he had to pull off on this month. This shit was getting old real quick and looking back in his rearview mirror, pretty me da p could see there would be more Moniques to come if he didn't end this shit. He was tired of all the shit he's been through and the way mothafuckas kept treating him everywhere he went.

"NIGGAS!" he shouted to himself, swerving through traffic like a mad man. "It's always these niggas fuckin with me. I don't even fuck with you niggas like that but you know what…" he laughed to himself, "maybe it's time I should, yea, that's what I'ma do" He had the power to make moves and if possible, he was going to utilize his resources to the best of his abilities in order to put himself in a better position. He reached under his seat, grabbed his pistol and clutched it in his lap feeling like the mothafuckin man.

LATER THAT DAY……..

"We gotta step this shit up! *I'm pretty me da P*! This ain't how I'm used to rockin. I control pieces with these bitches on my say so, not the other way around. I ain't frivolous simpin. I'm pretty as fuck, it's bitches who winnin feelin this pimpin. It ain't a blade in California that I ain't touched. Ask around I done opened shit up, these other niggas bogus as fuck. Actin like he ain't notice she tucked, steal from me and I'ma slow up her luck. When I went hard they ain't blow up enough. blindfolded, I could find her and design her, in designer. you need to watch cause there hoes on a timer. I'm not sellin ya'll no dream. all we need to do is build me a team of bad bitches who could-"

"NO!"

"What?" Pretty me da p asked in disbelief.

"I said, no. We're not helpin you build a team of prostitutes" Vanessa Mendez replied with authority.

She was the lead detective of the human trafficking task force in San Bernardino county, who just so happened to have enough pull with the DA to work a deal that would release him immediately as an informant once he decided to start talking. She knew that he was in a messed up situation but she didn't give a fuck about him or his situation. As far as she was concerned, he got exactly what he deserved. To her, pimps were the lowest of the low and no matter the type of pimp they all deserved the same fate. *life in prison.*

The site of his face was enough to make her stomach turn but it wasn't everyday that a pimp chose to cooperate with the police...in fact, he was the first one she had ever gotten to do it, so she was at least thrilled about that. Yet, the only thing she wanted more than putting him back in jail was to be able to throw Rarri and a lot more low life's in there right along with him. Even thought Rarri was out of her county, he still was on her radar. Mendez had seen a video of him show boating in the bay at the show and the other one of him knocking supreme.

Sometimes videos go viral in the wrong way. All she needed to do was find a way to lower him to her and everything else would fall in place. As of now Detective Mendez's plan wasn't working so well. Pretty me da p wasn't able to fulfill his part of the deal, yet.

"I ain't able to give yall Rarri, yet, but what about the other mothafuckas I been givin yall? I know that gotta count for some-thin.." he paused for a moment. "Listen, if we gonna be partners-"

"How many times do I have to tell you that we are not part-ners?!" Mendez shouted. "You're a snitch! My snitch! And if you can't do what you promised to do than neither can I"

'*She didn't even let me finish my chop*' he thought in defeat, feeling like a battered woman who had been used and abused by her ruthless boyfriend.

"If I can't look the part, how do ya'll expect me to play the part? He countered more as a plea, looking at her *'real partner'*, who was standing in the doorway.

Detective Malone was the same one who had all of the jokes when Shawn had violated him but in all he seemed to be the one who understood him the most, when it came down to the investigation.

"NO!" she replied the looking directly at him, then at Malone who didn't seem to agree with her decision.

"No" she said once more noticing his expression as she fumbled through her desk.

"Maybe he's on to something, Mendez, just hear him out. I mean, it's not like we're any closer in out investigation and we do need some sort of progress to show the men upstairs, if you know what I mean" Malone stepped all the way in, closed the door behind him, , walked over to her and leaned in close to be out of reach of Pretty me da p's greedy little ears. "Listen, I don't like this scumbag any more than you do. He's a piece of shit, just look at em"

They both looked up at him with smiles, then back down.

"Do you see what I'm saying? This guy is a clown but we need him just as much as he needs us right now. Our goal should be using him to get more jerks off of the streets"

"But not by putting more vulnerable women in them" she whispered angrily.

"You're right!" Malone admitted "That's why we just let him do it"

"We're already letting him do it, Malone, what do you say we buy him a Cadillac and one of those hats with the feathers on it?" she asked sarcastically.

"I was thinkin more of a Maserati just to start with-"

"Malone, No! I can't believe I'm even hearing this." She shouted and stood not caring about being quiet any longer. "Why don't we start him a gofundme page while we're at it, or hell what about a chain and some new clothes? oh you know what? Maybe we should get him in his own pretty little mansion, so he could wiggle his pretty little toes in his pretty little pool- and hey! Me and you could personally help him on his tutorials because the only thing this little pretty son of a bitch would be missing then is a gotdamn YouTube channel!! NO! I'm not doing it!" She stormed out of her office in disbelief with Malone on her tail.

"Fuck.." Pretty me da P swore to himself, falling back into his seat in defeat. Thinking about all he's recently been through was hard to hold in and although he put on a strong poker face, right now he could feel his eyes watering but he promised himself he wasn't going to shed no more tears, not one. If it wasn't for the thumbs up assurance and reassuring smile detective Malone just gave him before walking out of the office, this mothafucka was going to fall fasho. It was so close of a call that he had to literally blink it back in.

The mood was better when the two of them returned, not only was Mendez on board now, she also seemed excited about the whole ordeal, coming up with more ideas, asking Pretty me da P for tips and all types of shit and by the way Malone kept his hand on the small of her back as they talked, he knew she was excited about something else too.

'That's how you know I got game. I sent that nigga at that bitch knowin she was goin to eventually bite' he thought to himself proudly. Like he wasn't just about to cry a moment ago. But, all of that was irrelevant now. The only thing that mattered at the moment was the results in which he produced using the game that god blessed him with. You see, Mendez had all the resources because her dad was a fed, so that gave her connections that Malone didn't have but that didn't matter to Pretty me da P because he knew one thing. And that was that no matter what her position or status was, at the end of the day she still just a bitch and bitches are stupid as fuck when it comes to niggas.

She could have been a Rocket scientist but the bitch still wouldn't have been able to calculate a fraction of game Pretty me da p had. Well at least in his opinion. While the two of them laughed, giving googly eyes and flirtatious gestures pretty me da P pondered up another plan of his own. Sitting back rubbing his chin in deep thought, thinking about all the bitches who was going to bow down to his pimpin *now* had him feeling like a mothafuckin PLAYER! *Pimpin ain't never been easy, but its sho'll bout to be* he thought to himself.

SIXTEEN

Rarri loved the couple of days he had spent with Fia, she had never opened up to him how he wanted her to but they still had a great time talking about all types of other shit, so he did have a better insight than he had before. It could take years to learn who a person truly is. Fia always proved to be worth the wait. She was special all by herself but as Rarri sat outside pulling on his blunt, he had to admit, wasn't nothing like being around them all at the same time. All of them were unique in their own way, that's what made them the perfect team.

Bird, Mia, Tia, Fia and Dria still stayed on Stacey's head every chance they got and Rarri would laugh like it was the most funniest shit in the world. Which, in return would piss her off for letting them do so but he ain't give a fuck. He would act like he did just to shut the bitch up sometimes. Stacey obviously wasn't Bentley Bitch material because her square ass was always crying about some shit. He had to put her in her place more than enough times and if it wasn't for Heaven stressing how valuable she was for the girls, he would have been fired that bitch. For now, he would let her walk around with her head held high not knowing how close to elimination she really was.

Rarri might have been cocky but wasn't oblivious to the fact that everybody needed somebody when trying to reach a certain level in the game. Especially in the music industry which Rarri didn't know much about, but Stacey did. She not only had the knowledge of how things worked she also had connections with a few people already established in the game who wouldn't mind doing a favor for a favor. Heaven knew Stacey didn't mind fuckin her contacts in order to get 'her' nigga to the top. The two clarified that before Rarri had gotten out of juvy.

In Stacey's mind's eye, once she got Rarri's label off of the ground he would finally be able to be legit and leave the streets alone once and for all, all thanks to her. That's when he'll notice that, yea the Bentley Bitches might be down and all that but they ain't have shit on her. Regardless of how Stacey might have felt about them personally, she did have faith in their talent. The music they made was undeniable and everything about them was authentic in the studio. It was just five girls in the booth having fun. The Bentley Bitches were good at doing a lot of shit but making music is when you truly saw them at their best, which is why Heaven and Stacey called Rarri over to talk business.

"So, what ya'll sayin, I should stop everything I got goin on now?"

"What type of bitch would I be to ask you to do some shit like that?"

"Honestly, that's *exactly* what I was just thinkin" he replied looking at Stacey like she was crazy. "What type of bitch is you?"

"Rarri, be nice" Heaven intervened. "You know it ain't nowhere near like that"

"Well, why don't ya'll tell me what it's like because right now it ain't makin too much sense to me"

Stacey blew out in frustration, sat back in her seat and shut the fuck up because the look Rarri had just given her said to do so. That shit didn't intimidate Heaven none though.

"I think it's time we let them focus more on their careers now to see how that play out."

"Since when do what you think outweigh what I think?" He shot back. "Because I think they could still do both at the same time."

"But why risk it when you don't have to?"

"Because they want to.."

"*They* want to, or do *you* want them to?" Heaven countered just as hostile.

Stacey had her '*oh shit*' face on and dame sure wasn't about to get in this one

"Look at them, Rarri" Heaven started, nodding her head in their direction. "Just look at them"

Rarri looked towards the pool and as if on queue Tia looked at him, waved then jumped in the water. That put a smile on his face.

"Do you love them?"

"Of course" he replied quickly looking here directly in the eyes.

"What about me?" Stacey asked defensively.

"Would you excuse us for a minute" Heaven asked "Thank you" she added before Stacey even had time to answer or get up.

She tolled her eyes in the cut and got up with an attitude.

"Don't nobody give a fuck about you rollin yo eyes, bitch!"

"I didn't even roll my eyes" she lied.

"Whatever" Heaven replied waving her off then turned back to her nephew placin her hand on top of his. "Don't be the type to hold his bitches back from becoming somethin better in life because in the end, they will start to resent you for it...you are way better than that, that's why it's important to expand your horizons. This whole music thing was your idea" Heaven laughed. Every time I came up there to visit you in L.P all you wanted to talk about was yo boy fly boogie and how good he was at rappin"

"Fly nitty" Rarri corrected

"Fly somethin..whatever happened to him anyway?"

"He ended up going to Y.A for some shootin shit they picked up on him before he got out"

"Well don't let that stop what you had planned. Still go hard at what you want to do and I know right now what that is...you still wanna be in the game, so let me tell you somethin Rarri" Heaven said seriously. "You gon always be in the game because it's not on you, it's in you. Sendin a bitch is in yo DNA but yo daddy left you with somethin that will take you far in life. All you gotta do is follow the steps. You remind me so much of him that sometimes it hurts." Tears fell from her eyes. "But, then I think of everything he used to tell me and yo momma and now it all makes sense. That day you came and got that work from chu-chu, I knew it was time for me to get my shit together. It was time for me to do what I had promised to God..."

———

1999

"Angel, have you seen my earrings?!"Heaven yelled getting no response as she got all dolled up. "Oh my God" she whined to herself looking around the room hoping to find the earrings God had bought for her. "where the fuck is my shit?!" she yelled in frustration while looking through her drawers.

Heaven was already looking bad as fuck but the powder blue Chanel dress with the matching pumps was enough to put any bitch standing next to her to shame. Her body was bangin and the low-cut dress complimented her legs perfectly. Rocking her hair in one long ponytail braid gave her an elegant salsa dancer look. She grabbed her purse and exited the room deciding to use a pair of Angel's earrings before they left but as she got closer to her room, she heard God and Angel arguing. Which is something they never did.

Heaven being the nosey sister that she was decided to peek inside to see what was going on.

"This ain't no negotiation bitch, I ain't playin with you!" God barked holding Angel up by the neck against the wall.

He was so angry, Heaven could see the veins in his neck. Angel looked like she had been crying a river. She looked over and seen Heaven watching from the cracked door and tears fell harder as she shook her head sadly.

"I don't wanna hav—"

Smack!

God smacked her so hard, that she fell to the ground sobbing. Heaven put her hands over her mouth and backed away from the door not knowing what else to do. God had never hit Angel before. Hell, he never even raised his voice to her because she stayed in pocket.

"You stay yo ass here and get yo shit together" he ordered then walked away.

As soon as he snatched the door open he saw Heaven standing there looking scared as fuck. "Come on, we out" He said, but Heaven was frozen.

"Sis, are you okay—"

Angel stormed to the door and slammed it in her face.

"Heaven! God called out angrily."

"I'm comin" she replied making her way to him.

Heaven walked outside of the house and went to the passenger side of gods car where he was waiting for her with the door open as he always did. But the way he slammed it once she got in, she knew he was steaming. He got in not saying a single word to her after a brief moment he exhaled, started the car then out of nowhere, quickly reached for the glove compartment. She flinched dramatically and curled into a ball crying.

"Fuck" he swore to himself then killed the engine. Heaven was shaking like a rabbit in a snake tank and he ain't like that shit not one bit. "Aww. Look at the little scary bitch shakin like a puppy" he teased petting her like a poodle.

"Don't touch me!" she yelled swatting his hand away.

"..Or what? What you gon do? Yo scary ass ain't gon do shit!" he barked. "Matter of fact, take this shit off, bitch"

God stripped her out of her dress. "Swapmeet ass how. You don't even deserve to have this shit on right now. talkin bout you from Compton. Bitch, you ain't from Compton crying like that hoe. Matter of fact, fuck Compton, bitch, get yo faggot ass out of my car, hoe! He added pokin her in the side of her head with his finger. "Get out of my shit, bitch!" he said while pushing her but Heaven didn't move, she just clenched her fist angrily.

"Oh yo scary ass think I'm playin? I got somethin for yo punk ass"

He got out of the car and walked to the passenger side. As soon as he swung the door open he was looking down the barrel of his own pistol.

"FUCK YOU! WHO SCARY NOW!" Heaven cried.

God smiled. "That's what the fuck I'm talkin bout. Man the fuck up, bruh!"

"I'm not playin with you!" she yelled. The fire in her eyes was so intense her tears felt hot.

"I'm ain't either, take yo shit back." He said and held her dress up. "Or, I'ma take my gun back and beat the fuck out you wit it, on pimpin"

She had never been this scared in her life. She loved this man with her all but he was tripping right now and all the shit he was saying had her pressured up. He took step forward.

"Please, just stop, daddy" She pleaded contemplating dropping the gun, hoping that would stop him but she wasn't sure. She wished she would have just left it where it was at to begin with because he was certain to hurt her for drawing a gun on him. Heave didn't know if he was high and tripping off of the drugs or what but in that moment she wished she had never gotten involved with him and her sister because it was going to cost her, her life or his.

"I'm not yo daddy, bitch. You a scary hoe" he replied with a look of disgust and took another step. "You got two seconds to choose what you goin to do"

"Please don't do —"

"ONE!"

"Daddy, don't!"

"Two!" He lunged at her, Heaven screamed, closed her eyes and pulled the trigger.

CLICK! CLICK! CLICK! It was empty. God started laughing as he clapped his hands giving Heaven a standing ovation. He never kept that gun loaded, the bullets were in his pocket. She opened her eyes to see god standing there looking like a proud father.

"What the fuck is wrong with you!"

"I can't stand a scary bitch. if you could kill me, I know you won't hesitate to shoot the next nigga. I don't want you to fear no man. You 'my' bitch and these niggas beneath you" he held out his hand. "Come on, let's go back in the house"

She wiped the tears from her face, put the gun back, grabbed his hand and stepped out of the car in her lingerie. "Is that why you hit Angel?"

She couldn't read the sad look in his eyes but Heaven knew he was hurting inside. God pulled her to him and hugged her tightly, planting a loving kiss on the top of her head.

"I want you to promise me somethin" he said as he pulled away to look her in the eyes.

"Anything" she replied, lookin back into his.

It seemed as if he was staring deep into the depths of her soul looking for something inside of her.

"I always tell ya'll to never hoe for a nigga who ain't a son of god but I'm tellin 'you'" he said pointing at Heaven "..to promise that you will make ours greater than 'me'

"Ours?" she questioned, knowing damn sure she wasn't pregnant. "Oh my god!" she blurted out, putting a hand on her chest. "but, when-I mean-like-damn, are ya'll sure?"

"Yea, we sure" he said with a million dollar smile."

"How ya'll know if it's a boy? What if it's a girl"

"It's not gon be no girl...you got me or what?"

Heaven hugged him tightly. "Yea, I got you...I promise he gon be great" she assured."Come on, let's go back in the house, it's cold out here

and I wanna give this bitch stomach all the kisses I can tonight" Heaven
added excitedly, then ran back in the house.

"If he wanted me that bad what he hit my momma for then?" Rarri
asked. "Obviously, it's somethin else to the story that he wasn't
tellin you"

"Actually, it was somethin that your *momma* wasn't tellin me"
Heaven corrected him.

"What, she didn't wanna hoe for the nigga no more? She was
tryna do her own thing now that she had me to worry about. Or
maybe she was tryna get her life together." He stated with a
chuckle. "Naw, maybe you just ain't tryna tell me the reason she
slammed the door in yo face was because she ain't want *you* in the
picture no more"

"Yo momma was tryna get an abortion Rarri!" she yelled as she
slammed her hand on the table in anger. "She ain't want you in the
picture. So yea, you damn right yo daddy slapped the shit out of
that bitch. She lucky I didn't know that's what it was over at the
time cause I woulda slapped her ass too." Heaven admitted.

"So, the moral of this story was to let me know that my momma
ain't want me? Good for her. Now that I know, are you happy or
what?"

"No, you foul mouth ass lil nigga, the moral of the story is to let
you know that everybody gotta do shit they don't wanna do and
make sacrifices for this shit. Even when we might not understand
them, they still must be made, Rarri." She drilled. "Yo momma
loved you, but you gotta understand that all the shit that we went
through with our momma made us both scared to ever have kids
because the last thing we ever wanted to do was end up like her.
We ain't know if that shit was somethin her momma passed down
to her but we damn sure ain't never want to pass her ways down to
our kids so we always said we wouldn't have any. Look at me, I

still never had kids of my own so that should tell you somethin right there. It wasn't until meetin yo father that we knew that you would be alright. He gave us the confidence we needed in that. You are part of their legacy. You were born to lead so don't be stagnant. I made a promise that day to my nigga that I would never break. So, no matter how much I love and care for you Rarri, I will never be able to sit back or ease up because when you fail, I fail." Heaven added sincerely, then stood up knowing she finally got through to him. "One way or another they leavin so you got until the funeral" she added placing a hand on his shoulder a kiss on his head. "..after that, they out"

She walked away to give him some alone time plus she had shit to do. Rarri didn't like the thought of being without his Bentley Bitches but he couldn't deny the fact that the shit his aunty dropped on him made a lot of sense. If they wanted to pursue music fulltime, he wasn't going to be the one to try and stop them. Fame always comes with a price. Rarri just hoped it wouldn't cost them their relationship.

'Fia talkin about she a bad Cardi B lookin bitch'...her ass bet not try and leave a nigga for on of the migos' He thought as a joke to himself, then another thought came into his mind and instantly and instinctively Rarri started plotting, as usual.

SEVENTEEN

EVERYTHING BUT TIME was on Rarri's side. With the funeral only days away, he needed to figure out what bitches could replace the Bentley Bitches. The mere thought of that sounded stupid as fuck to him. He honestly didn't know a group of bitches breathing that could do that. The loyalty they had for him solidified a place in his heart not many could get near. They were the pieces that completed a portrait of him.

He had plenty of bitches, now he just had to come up with another game plan. Wasn't no way in hell he was going to stop pimpin. Pimpin was a part of him and besides, he hadn't been in the game long enough. It was still niggas he had to surpass and a gang of mothafuckas he ain't even get to knock yet. He wanted to experience everything the game had to offer. Thinking about all this shit was putting a strain on his brain. Rarri stripped down to his briefs then ran and jumped in the pool. The Bentley Bitches turned all the way up.

Tia slid off her giant pink flamingo floaty and into the pool, making her way to her papi. She wrapped her legs around his waist, arms around his neck and kissed him passionately as the rest of them waited their turn.

"damn bitch, hurry up" Mia said as she splashed Tia. "You always hoggin papi like we don't want some of him too."

The rest of them agreed cracking jokes on Tia, who was too caught up to break her kiss so she just flicked them off. They all started splashing her. Tia broke free and started swimming after Bird under water and Mia immediately took her place. Heaven had already talked to them earlier so the Bentley Bitches knew what was up. Although they wanted to still move bricks and bitches on the low to keep money coming in, Heaven didn't leave much room for them to debate with . The Bentley Bitches were like the little sisters she never had. She wanted what was best for them. Wasn't no way in hell she was going to let them waste their talent by turning a blind eye to it.

They had a gift that was undeniable and if she had to cut them off in the dope game to see them become as successful as she knew they could be, then so be it. Heaven was willing to fight tooth and nail for them and they loved her for that.

Rarri was in the middle of doing some nasty shit to Bird and Dria when he looked over and seen his aunty laughing with her little protégé she had been bringing around lately. She was looking better and better every time he had seen her but that bitch was just on some standoff-ish shit. Well at least that was the vibe he got from her. Rarri tried on numerous occasions to chop at the bitch but she seemed to wanna talk to everybody but him.

'I ain't bout to chase that—'

"Neva?" Rarri said simultaneously lifting Bird off of him and before he knew it, he was out of the pool walking towards Heaven and her company.

He stood there looking down at the girl not saying a word. He looked at Heaven who didn't say anything then back down at the girl who had also gone mute. She put her head down.

"What I tell you bout that?"

She looked back up.

"My bitches keep they head up, Wap."

Betty wap jumped up into his arms. "How'd you know?"

"I caught you smellin your lip" he pulled her back to admire all of her features. "Damn, that's crazy. You like a whole new bitch, Wap."

"Thanks.." she blushed.

He hugged her once more then sat down as did she. "So, what's been going on?"

"Shit, tryna get to it." She replied bluntly.

He looked at her awkwardly. "Why I run into that bitch Lae Lae out here." He joked. "I chopped on that bitch hard as fuck, ended up kicking her in her ass and all that" he added laughin.

"That's wassup"

Again he looked at her in question. Something wasn't right with her but he didn't wanna fuck up the moment. "You know KD and them bout to come out here in a minute."

She made a sarcastic grin, small chuckle and rolled her eye all in one motion as if Rarri had made a lame joke or something, then continued to look at him all dreamy and shit. As much as Rarri had been around Betty Wap, he had never seen her act this way. He was puzzled.

"I thought KD was big bro. What happened to all that?"

"Um, naw. I got a folks now, so I don't got time for bros and shit.. but that's yo boy so I guess he straight" She replied like it was nothing still looking more interested in him than anything else. "What's up with you though?"

He looked at Heaven then back at Betty Wap with a smile.

"Hold on, Ima be right back" He got up. "Let me holla at you real quick" he told Heaven and the two walked off out of ears reach.

"SO?" she asked excitedly.

"What happened to her?"

She was proud of herself but her head wasn't too high in the sky to miss the disappointment in his voice. "I fixed her."

"Yea, but you broke her at the same time. She all mean and shit now. That ain't Wap."

"It's the new Wap" she replied pointing at her from the distance. "That's the wap you need right now, Rarri. You should be thankin me instead of being ungrateful."

Heaven sounded hurt. He hated when it seemed as if his aunty was about to cry because he was used to her being so strong all the time. He made a mental note to start remembering a lot of shit he says had an effect on her too. Heaven was like his mom and his dad and in some awkward way, she was also like his bottom bitch.

"My bad, I ain't tryna make it seem like I'm ungrateful cause I am. it's just. it's just different. It's like everybody gotta become somebody else now and I don't wanna lose everything we had for a bag cause what we share is priceless." He faced her, then looked away. "I know that shit sound weak, but it's how I been feelin"

"That's not weak, Rarri, that's real. You got a good heart ain't nothing wrong with that but when you tryna win tomorrow, you can't value people for who they were yesterday because today, is today. That's why I'm constantly goin hard because what I've done for you in the past ain't shit. None of that mean nothin. It's about what ima do for you right now."

She pulled a cigarette from her pack then lit it. "We wouldn't be where we are if you still had the same mentality you had at 16. Sometimes you be hard headed but overall you been on yo shit... I'm more than proud of who you have became but I'm even ore proud of who you will become."

Heaven always knew the right words to say to brighten his day. She was molding him more and more. Sometimes in ways Rarri wouldn't understand at the moment but would always see later on. A lot of niggas didn't have that type of guidance to rely on like he did and despite not having his parents around, life had been pretty fair to him. How long will that last? Only time could tell.

"Thanks, that really means a lot to me" he told her honestly. Heaven smiled. "I get everything you been sayin today. I just been low-key stressed out"

"Why?"

He sighed. "Granny. The last time we went over there really fucked me up. I ain't never seen her like that." He looked at Heaven. "It gotta be something we can do"

———

Heaven didn't like seeing her mother like that neither. She and Rarri decided to stop by there. When he came back from Oakland to surprise her with a couple gifts and hopefully get things back to normal but she was pissy drunk. No bullshit the house really smelled like old piss and beer. It was filthy with empty beer cans and trash everywhere. If the T.V wasn't on one would have thought the place was abandoned.

Rarri seen his grandma halfway sprawled on couch talking to herself....one of her titties were out of her blouse, with a cigarette in one hand she continued drinking out of the same beer can she had been ashing in all morning. Around her mouth was crusted with ash and all types of other shit.

"Momma!" Heaven cried immediately rushing to her mother's side.

Barely able to see anything, she leaned forward squinting her eyes to get a better view of the person coming to her aid. "God is gon bless you, chile. God is gon bless-" as her vision came to so did he a distasteful expression.

"Momma, I'm sorr-"

Before Heaven could finish her mom spat a big glob of nasty black, sticky, stanky spit in her face.

"Get the fuck out my house, you bitch."

Heaven backed away stunned. It was so much spit in her face she couldn't even open her eyes. Rarri ran to her side takin off his shirt to use to wipe Heaven's face with. He was at a loss for words. Rarri had never seen his grandmother like this. She had been drunk before when he was younger but this was not the same woman who had raised him. Her voice didn't even sound the same. Not only that, she was also looking at him like he was nothing. like he was the scum beneath the scum. Like he was dirty and filthy. Rarri didn't know it, but she was looking at him the same way she used to look at his father.

"…and take that punk mothafucka with you, wit his sorry ass. Wanna go out there with some mothafuckas who ain't never did nothin for yo dumbass, You'sa stupid mothafucka. that's why you couldn't even finish school cause you stupid and you always go be stupid, just like the mothafuckas who had you was stupid" She slurred in a drunken rage full of contempt then spat at him too but missed due to a now dry mouth. she had gave Heaven all she had.

Heaven was so angry she was shaking, it was takin everything in her not run over and beat her drunk ass. Plus Rarri, was holding her back but he was just as mad. Not because of what she said about him but because of what she said about his parents. He wanted to tell her how stupid she was for even thinking to call his parents stupid. He wanted to tell her how stupid she looked and how weak she was compared to his other grandma. He wanted to clown her on getting stripped naked by his grandpa on the blade back in the day.

Rarri wanted to tell her about all the game his dad had and how he came up because of him and not her. He wanted so bad to argue about how smart his parents really were and throw everything he learned from his grandparents in her face. It was so much Rarri wanted to say but couldn't. And she knew it. It's like she was reading his emotions, then came that smile again that one he hated so much. Loving, serious and firm all in one this time just a little more menacing and heartless.

"I'm yo daddy"

"No the fuck you aint!" Rarri screamed…"You ain't ever gon be my pops so stop sayin that shit!"

"Who the fuck you think you talkin to!? She tried getting up but fell back on the couch spillin beer on her self.

"I'm talkin to you!" he shouted.

She dropped the rest of her cigarette in the can, took a big ass sip then

tired to throw it at him but missed. She just stared at him with hatred in
her eyes, breathing harshly because she was too drunk to do anything
else...Rarri just shook his head and walked out followed by Heaven.
   "I hate you!" She cried out then staggered to the kitchen for another
beer. "I hate both ya'll" she mumbled to herself.

———

Heaven took a pull of her cigarette threw the butt then exhaled
deeply.
   "Ight I'll tell you what. Just enjoy yo time with Wap and them
and let me worry about momma...I think I know *exactly* what will
sober her up"
   "Okay I could do that" Rarri smiled.
   Heaven kissed the back of his hand "Love you"
   "I love you too" he replied looking into her eyes, Heaven smiled
then walked off.
   Rarri went back over to chill with Betty Wap. She filled him in
on everything that she had been through with Heaven in the past
months and how she opened her eye up to a whole new world.
Betty Wap told him about her website and how she was about to
start fuckin with tricks who spent real money, so now she would be
hitting his mitt with some big shit when she broke bread. She told
him she already had 20 bandz for him and that was from two dates.
She told him how the tricks was some big time drug dealers who
wanted to see her again in couple of days and how fasho they were
going to become a regulars.
   As she talked Rarri couldn't help but smile at her dramatic
change, she was like a little mini version of Heaven now. Her entire
persona was on boss status, like she was more confident in herself.
Betty Wap was talking like she *knew* she was that bitch. By now
they Bentley Bitches had gathered around listening to what she was
saying. They all like Betty Wap...all of them except for Bird.
   Bird whispered something into Tia's ear then they both laughed.

Betty wap just ignored them but after a few more times she was irritated.

"Um, excuse me, I ain't tryna be rude or nothin" she said looking at Bird, "..but what's so funny?"

Bird rolled her eyes then whispered something to Tia again and they continued to laugh some more.

"Anyways" Betty Wap said as she flicked her hair away with attitude. "Scary ass hoe" she mumbled loud enough to be heard turning to Rarri in tandem.

"What you say?"

"I said scary ass hoe" Betty Wap repeated louder as she turn to face Bird.

"Bitch on parc village crip I will beat yo ass back here!" Bird said simultaneously taking her earrings out as did the rest of the Bentley Bitches...

Bird was from the hood so one thing she loved to do was fight. Mia, Tia, Fia, and Dria had no choice but to be aggressive since fuckin with Bird. Especially whenever they were at a club because she was quick to fire on a bitch running off at the mouth. She had got craccin on bitches for merely talking to one of them the wrong way so it was only right that they do the same for her. So just like that all of them were ready to beat the shit out of Betty wap. It wasn't nothing personal, that's just how they got down.

Rarri wasn't having none of that shit though, so he quickly intervened.

"On God ya'll ain't neva bout to jump wap" he said seriously. "Look, I don't even want ya'll fighting but if ya'll really need that and it's that serious, fuck it, ya'll can get a head up." He added looking between them both.

Betty Wap and Bird looked at one another in question. Neither of them were scared but the fact that Rarri said he didn't want them to fight was enough to kill the tension between the two instantly.

"So what's up, ya'll gon squabble up or leave that shit alone? He asked after a moment of them staring at each other.

"Ain't nobody worried about that jack sparrow as bitch." Bird clowned knowing her eye is fake. "Ole pirates of the *caribbean* ass hoe" She added and the Bently Bitches started cryin laughing.

Rarri was trying to hold his in but as soon as he looked at Betty Wap and seen her smelling her lip again he started laughing too. Betty Wap looked at them all laughing and started laughing. They was laughing at Betty Wap cause of the pirate joke and Betty Wap was laughing cause well, the shit was just funny. For some reason, seeing her laugh at herself made Bird like her. On top of that she wasn't no scary bitch and Bird couldn't stand scary bitches in her circle. Rarri noticed right then how the front seat had broken Lae Lae and Fonda up but a fuckin joke brought Betty Wap and Bird together because after that they were inseparable.

EIGHTEEN

"BRANDON WASN'T JUST my brother, he was my best friend, too. We ain't have no daddy around so we had to lean on each other and go get it when moms couldn't pay the rent or another bill got cut off. At first, it was all on me to take care of everything but ya'll know how Brandon is. He got tired of askin me for $5 here and there and wanted to get his own money"

Baby Flock wiped both of his eyes at the same time using his right hand, tried his best to hide the cracks in his voice and exhaled deeply.

"So, he started breakin in lockers at school stealin everybody stuff while they was at P.E. I ain't know what he had goin on until one day he got suspended because the principal thought he took the school fundraiser money" Baby Flock chuckled. "Brandon swore to God he didn't take it but I knew he was lyin. He wasn't dumb though. Brandon waited a whole month before he pulled any of it out his lil stash spot. I was hot because he was askin me for money. the whole time, he got more than me."

Everybody in the funeral home laughed lightly.

"I wanted to punch on him *so bad* for that, but I had to respect it.

That let me know he could get it on his own with or without me. And in out neighborhood, that's what you gotta be ready for cause ain't no tellin who might not be standin next to you tomorrow. I just wish it was me who understood that...maybe he would still be here."

Baby Flock put his head down and walked away from the microphone stand. The entire room went mute. Everybody was hurt and at a loss for words. Infant Flock was loved by so many people all over California. It wasn't too many in Compton who didn't know him or at least heard something about him at some point in time.

Baby Flock looked at his lil bro one last time laying peacefully in his all red Armani suit, UR-110 watch by URWERK and the already, all red, red bottoms. He couldn't help but smile. Infant Flock was still shinnin. Baby Flock turned to walk away.

"So, that's how you gon let me go out, blood? Without a bang?"

He turned around quickly & infant spirit was sitting up in his all white casket but his body was still laying peacefully.

"What you mean, bro?" he asked him back.

"Look at everybody all sad and shit. You get up here talkin that bullshit on *my* day. That shit ain't boo bro." Infant's spirit replied. "I don't want nobody walkin out of here like that...go ahead and tell em, blood. DAMN!" he added in frustration, then smiled before lying back down.

"Tell em what?" he asked as he walked up closer to the casket. "Tell em wha—"

He laughed to himself then kissed infant on the forehead. "You's a food blood. Stay dangerous" He then went back up to the mic, damn near pushing the Pastor out of the way.

"Aye, ya'll wanna know some funny shit?"

Heaven was right outside the door of the funeral home smoking her third cigarette. She was back to backin them mothafuckas like Drake on a Meek Mill diss. She took a big ass pull of her Newport when all of a sudden she could hear people inside erupt in laughter.

"What the fuck?" she said to herself, threw the cigarette, blew the smoke out, opened the door and seen everyone cryin laughing.

Mothafuckas was falling out of their seats into the middle aisle, holding their stomachs and running around screaming like they was crazy. She heard so many "oh shits" and "God damns" You couldn't tell her nobody wasn't going to hell.

"God forgive me!...Oh shit! Lord Forgive me, please forgive me!" she heard somebody screaming out.

Even the pastor was in tears. Everybody in the front row was on the floor. She even seen mothafuckas tryna climb back on the seats looking like they fell out a wheelchair or some shit. A Kevin Hart show ain't have nothing on this funeral. The laughing wouldn't stop and everybody was scattered all over the place.

"What's goin –" she stopped when she saw Baby Flock at the stand, smiling and the look on his face told it all causing her jaw to drop with a smile. "No you didn't" she mouthed to him, shaking her head. He turned his hands upside down as he shrugged his shoulders with a smile.

Nobody walked out of that room crying. This turned out to be the best funeral any of them had ever been to or heard of. The after ceremony was off the chain. Everybody was getting fucked up & exchanging stories about infant Flock at the mansion rental Heaven got for the occasion. A lot of people looked at Flock and lil Flock sideways for leaving infant and not staying like Baby Flock did, but he and the other people who mattered, understood.

Wasn't no point in all of them going down for some shit they could avoid. Baby should have left too cause now he was out on bail. Not only was he charged with attempted home invasion, but the bitch ass DA even charged him with his brother's murder. He didn't want that on the other Flocks because he really wished he had done what they did. No point in crying over it now. He was goin to keep doin what he did best.

"This flockin shit don't stop" he told himself, took a big sip from his bottle of Remy then pulled this lil fine bitch who was walking by closer to him and started gamin her up.

NINETEEN

Rarri, lil Dink and Trigg was talkin to Big Spank. He was cooking up a storm of some exotic shit with his crew of *"Trap Kitchen"* workers. Him and Taco Mell was goin in.

"Wassup with ya'll lil partna that got killed a while back? You know, the one that was *callin* himself Spank." Big Spank asked.

"What you mean wassup wit him? Cuh dead" Lil Dink responded seriously still chewing on his Taco looking like was ready for the bullshit.

See, Spank was only his nickname so people always assumed he was up under Big Spank. Even though everyone around knew he wasn't, Big Spank still didn't like that shit not did lil spank. It wasn't nothing personal, that's just how shit is in the hood. Muthafuckas pride themselves on their names cause sometimes that's all you got to fall back on when all else fails. Big Spank was successful with *Trap Kitchen* way before Rarri, lil Dink or Trigg started poppin so he wasn't worried about them lil niggas. He actually liked how they did business.

"Chill out, lil nigga. I was askin cause ain't nobody heard from his moms in awhile. I guess she missin or some shit." He responded as he dried his hands on a towel, looking at Lil Dink who broke his stare all of a sudden.

"Damn, that's crazy YAAH. Who told you that?" Trigg butted in trying to take the attention off of lil Dink.

He looked at Trigg with that, *Are you serious?* look as if he would really say who, sucked his teeth and threw a toothpick in his mouth.

"Ima holla at you lil niggas later YAAH" He answered as he walked off shaking his head and smirking at lil Dink.

Rarri was fuckin his plate of tacos over so he barely caught what was going on. "What cuh talkin bout?"

"Aye Rarri, let me holla at Trigg on some gang shit real quick"

He looked at them like they were crazy. "Damn, what ya'll kickin me off the team of somethin?"

"I mean, I'm saying though, YAAH, you about to be a non-affiliate soon. You need to be worried about bigger shit than what we talkin bout. Like stayin yo ass out of trouble before you hit that county." Lil Dink clowned and slapped fives wit Trigg.

"On god" Trigg laughed. "I heard they make all the non-affiliates fight on Friday nights"

"On YAAHAMPTON my nigga Rarri gon be a TUNA though" Lil Dink added as they walked off laughing.

Non of them had hit the County jail yet but they all knew a TUNA was a *"TURNT UP NON-AFFILIATE"*. Them was the ones who wasn't scared to fight back. In some units non-affiliates couldn't even go to commissary without paying taxes or getting robbed for they shit. It's so fucked up now that niggas don't give a fuck if you fight back or not. They just gon beat yo ass and take it anyway. Oh, and don't think you goin to *"win"* a fight. HELL NAW! All you gotta do is 'almost' land the right punch and fasho you getting ran by the rest of his homies there.

"FUCK YA'LL" Rarri said waving them off and started off in the other direction to go holla at Baby Flock. He wasn't feeling that non-affiliate joke at all.

It wasn't that he didn't like bangin, he was just tired of feeling boxed in and of being limited on people to fuck with on some money shit. Gang bangin is like a never ending war. Nobody wins in the end and Rarri wanted to start seeing more wins and not only for him, but for his homies too. He didn't have a clue as of how to produce those kinds of results but after all he had been learning about lately, it was worth a shot.

Lil Dink and Trigg watched as Big Spank mingled and laughed with other people there. He was like a real player type nigga. You could tell he was sure of himself by the way he moved around. They studied him briefly looking for who knows what but he was too cavalier to figure out.

"What you think?"

"I think he know."

He looked at Trigg in disbelief.

"How he gon know, YAAH?"

"I don't know.." Trigg replied, never taking his eyes off of Big Spank. "What you think?"

Lil Dink looked back up at Big Spank. "I think he know too", he admitted.

Now Trigg looked at lil Dink in disbelief and shook his head. He was about to continue observing him too but froze when Lil Dink quickly turned towards him with his head down.

"Shit!"

"What?"

"I think he saw me lookin" he whispered trying not to move his lips as much as possible.

"My nigga, we *lookin* stupid. how he goin to see *us* out of all these people out here?" Trigg asked like it didn't make sense but was still frozen also. "Cuh way over there and you whispering and shit"

"You whispering too" Lil Dink tossed back with aggression.

"I am huh?" Trigg whispered back

"YAAH, we both is.."

"Alright, look" Trigg started in his normal voice on some gangsta shit."

"I don't give a *fuck* about cuh lookin. I don't a *fuck* about him. I don't give a *fuck* about Jaheim. I don't even give a *fuck* about myself"

"Cuh, stop playin" Lil Dink replied. Knowing Trigg was actin like 2Pac in the movie 'Juice'.

"Man, fuck if cuh looking he don't know shit and I know he ain't lookin, but I'm bout to look up and make sure, just so we good though. Then we boutta finish enjoyin ourselves like everybody else. Dink, goddamn nigga." He looked up, "Damn!" He swore quickly looking back down.

"What?"

"Yea, cuh lookin" Trigg whispered not moving his lips. Looking like a ventriloquist without the dummy on his lap.

"I told you---"

"Alright, look, I got a plan." Trigg answered cuttin Dink off. "We goin to sike cuh out"

"How?"

"We goin to get up and push off. Just don't look at cuh."

"Just don't look at cuh? How is that gon sike em out?" Dink asked in disbelief.

"You got a better plan?"

"Naw" Lil Dink admitted

"Then come on, we goin to sagg out on 3" Trigg then started counting. "1"

"Hold on, what if we---"

"2!" he kept counting not wanting to hear whatever Dink was bout to say.

"Look YAAH, just wait---"

"3!"

Both of them got up and walked off quickly with their heads down to a slanted angle looking at the ground as they moved stiffly through the crowd of people, making eye contact with nobody. Zig -zaging, chin to chest all the way back inside the house.

"Why it look like Trigg and Dink just stole somebody purse?" Baby Flock pointed out.

"I don't know. Them niggas on some *GANG SHIT*" he replied sarcastically. "Talkin bout I ain't invited" Rarri laughed. "Whatever they on, I'm glad they left me out now"

"Damn Blood, so you really bout to just throw in the towel? Game over?"

"The game ain't never over" He signaled for Baby Flock to let him hit his bottle, took a drink then handed it back. "I don't know. It's deeper than what it really look like and easy to say but I really can't see myself not being from the set. It's just a lot of other shit I wanna do. Shit I be think bout *now*, that I wasn't thinkin bout *before*."

Baby Flock took a big sip then passed the bottle back to Rarri.

"You wanna know what I think?"

"Not really. But, I'm pretty sure you boutta say it anyway." He joked and took another swig.

"I think no matter what you do, everybody still going to view you as Rarri from Parc Village. *You* can't even change that because of all the shit that you done did already. I see yo heart into that pimpin shit even more though. Like, you love doin that, but don't forget it's still niggas out here ready to catch you slippin. They was talkin bout that shit in the bounty. Everybody know I fuck wit ya'll tough. They asked me more questions about *you* than about my mothafuckin self. I literally had to tell a few niggas, 'stop askin me bout blood..' Mothafuckas be fishin for all type of different reasons so I don't like talkin bout nothin to em. Everybody wanna talk about what the next nigga said he goin to do when he catch Rarri or what so and so said he gon do if you land in his tank but nobody ain't say what *they* was sayin cause on RU's I would have caught any fade on yo behalf. That's what mothafuckas do know. What I'm tryna say is that it ain't gon to make no difference, whether you like it or not, that's just who you is, my nigga. You always gon be Rarri. Ain't no way around that one, buddy."

Baby Flock pulled another bottle from his back pocket, cracked it open & downed some.

"But hey, we all got dreams, right?"

Rarri knew that Baby Flock was just being completely honest with him. Not because he was drunk but because that's just the way Baby was, regardless. He was saying what Rarri *'needed'* to hear.

"So much for wishful thinkin" Rarri killed the rest of the Remy and threw the bottle in the bushes behind him.

"Look, I be paying attention to shit, Blood. One day I found myself analyzin yo situation. Like yo status & shit."

Rarri looked at him with a playful sour ass expression causin Baby Flock to laugh.

"Not like that, my nigga. On some real shit, just hear me out cause it's simple" he got serious for a minute, grabbed him by both shoulders and looked him in the eyes.. That made Rarri think about chu-chu for a split second.

"You'sa young nigga.. You can't even walk in the store and by a pack of cigarettes yet Blood and you got yo hands in so much shit that *I* can't even keep up wit. Powda! Bitches! Gang shit! Business shit! Shid! You even getting money off licks we hittin for yo aunty—"

He looked around to make sure nobody was close enough to listen never takin his hands off of his shoulders.

"Look, I gotta ask you somethin" he looked back at Rarri. "Is you gon keep it real with me?" he asked seriously.

Rarri hesitated.

"On Infant grave, I would never tell a soul." He swore to assure him which seemed to be enough. Rarri knew he would stand by that.

"Alright, wassup?"

"Blood, is you fuckin yo aunty?" he asked with an already

shocked face like he knew the answer. He was looking at him like was disappointed and Rarri was nasty.

"HELL NAW!, Man watch out" Rarri said in disbelief as he swatted both hands off of him. "Let me hit that drink"

"Bang that" he countered as he passed the bottle.

Rarri took a big sip tryna stall as much time as he could. He knew Baby Flock was tryna get him going back on his bullshit again. He swallowed, pretending for the first time that the Remy was burning his throat, which didn't get pass Baby. Which Rarri noticed by the look on his face so he hurried and said, "on V's"

"Got em!" Baby Flock paraded around throwing up Piru in excitement. Rarri just shook his head and laughed.

Baby Flock was always tryna lowkey corrupt somebody into some gang shit. He really loved that life. You let him tell it, everybody should be from somewhere. If he could make laws fasho it would be illegal not to bang. Non affiliates would stay on the run or living life like the factionless in *Divergent*. For sure he would be among the Dauntless.

"Alright, now that you back, blood, don't tell nobody what I'm bout to tell you."

Rarri gave him that 'you already know' face. Baby Flock just hit the bottle.

"Alright, look. Lil bro was mad after that dog video went viral like that. Even though we was the only ones who knew. Blood was still TRIPPIN! Talkin bout *"everybody clownin and shit"* They both laughed.

"I was getting tired of hearin him talk about the shit on Piru. So, I get mad. I'm like, *"What you wanna do then, Blood?"* He whip out his burner like *"Take me over there"* I'm like hell naw I'm not about to take you to go bust on nobody in the circle. He like, *"Naw, take me back to the house"*

He took another sip then passed the bottle before going on.

"...So, we jump in my shit. I'm ready to take blood home by

now, so I don't gotta keep hearing him cryin all night about every-body bringin it up and all that. I'm driving, right."

"Yea"

"I'm bout to jump on the 105 cause I'm thinkin bout pickin this lil bitch up off of Bullis on the way but he grab the wheel and stop me from getting on. Now, I'm trippin. I'm on blood like a mutha-fucka. I wanted to pull over and punch his lil ass up but he had that gun on em and he was just *too* hostile at that moment, so I wasn't even gon play with him. He like *'nigga! I said take me to the house'* I'm like, "That's what I was doin, dumb ass nigga' He say, *'naw, take me to the doghouse.'* Now, I'm lost. I don't know what the fuck this nigga talkin bout, so I ask em and he like, as he starts to imitate infant's voice, *'To where the dogs at, nigga. Take me back over there so I could do my shit!'*

They both started crying laughing. Rarri couldn't even breathe.

"Hold on nigga, listen." Baby Flock said between breaths. "So, I ask em like, *'Blood, you foreal?'* He just looked at me cold, then looked back out his window not sayin nothin. I ain't neva seen blood that mad so I just kept drivin not sayin nothin else. When we get there, I park down the street…soon as the car stopped, he ain't waste no time. He just cocked his shit and hopped out. I leave my shit runnin cause I'm knowin any minute I'm bout to hear at least like two shots so I'm just waitin. on Ru's Like twenty minutes go by and blood still gone. I'm not knowin what the fuck but I get out and start creepin my way down there lowkey spooked cause of that old nigga from last time. I'm just knowin this time he going to shoot fasho to get his get back. Now I'm thinkin I shouldn't have even brung this nigga but when I get closer it ain't lookin like nothin bad happened. So I push to the side of the house and went to the back like we did before and Look over the gate and don't see nothin. *Now* I'm thinkin he done went in the damn house, got caught or probably bout to tie these mothafuckas up, kill em or make them fuck the dogs or the dogs fuck them so they could see how the shit feel too now on some weird shit I don't know. I'm just regrettin all that shit but that's lil bro though, I can't leave without em. I open the gate and push back there..."

He shook his head...

"On Piru, I take like five steps and I see the burner On the ground!"

Rarri's mouth was open in surprise. "Then what?"

"What you mean, then what? I ran over there, picked the moth-afucka up" He then took a sip and had to lean forward cause he almost spilled some on his shirt. "I'm standin there lookin around for this nigga, ready to kill some shit! Whole time, he a few feet ahead, sittin on the patio back against the wall, one dog on each side of em, layin down."

"What, he poison them mothafuckas?"

Baby Flock smacked his lips, "Hell naw! That's what I thought til one of em looked over at me" He took another sip then passed the bottle. Rarri grabbed it and took a quick drink too.

"What was he doin?"

He shook his head and looked at Rarri, "Pettin em"

"Pettin em?' Rarri laughed.

Baby Flock started laughin a bit too. "Blood was cryin talkin bout he couldn't do it."

The both of them burst out laughing. It was funny to them because Infant ain't never froze up to shoot no 'nigga', EVER! So him not being able to shoot two dogs he felt responsible for him being labeled the 'Turtle Burgler' was crazy. Rarri could see that the tears in Baby Flocks eyes weren't from laughing and the anger building inside of him rapidly as he spoke.

"I grabbed that nigga up so quick. I was so *mad* I think I *threw* his ass back in the car"

Once they were back in the car together, Infant spoke.

'They ain't know no better" Infant said, looking at his brother for approval. 'It ain't they fault I-'

"Shut yo crybaby ass up blood!" Baby Flock barked through clenched teeth looking where infant would have been. He was so mad, Rarri could see the veins in his face and neck vividly getting bigger as he grew more angry.

'But I.."

"Ain't no buts, blood. You a Mark like yo daddy, nigga!" Baby spat angrily even though they had the same father. Infant hated being compared to the man he never got to meet because of how much his brother hated him. "Brung me with you on this bullshit. On Piru I should knock yo ass out"

'My nigga, you ain't just gon knock me out!' Infant yelled back just as angry. He wasn't scared of his brother. He just wanted his respect and the love that his father wasn't around to give, he looked for in his brother.

"Oh, you hard now?" Baby walked around to the other side of the car. "Get yo crybaby ass out my shit, blood!"

"Fuck you nigga, I ain't getting out!" Infant screamed with tears in his eyes.

"What?!" Baby Flock reached for the handle but Rarri stopped him before he went any further.

"YAAH, its-"

He pushed Rarri off of him forcefully and gave him a cold stare.

"It's goin to be alright, my nigga. Everything gon be alright"

He lifted the bottle to his lips and chugged the rest of it never breakin eye contact with Rarri, then dropped the bottle on the ground in the grass and wiped his mouth with the back of his hand.

"Mothafuckin, Rarri" he said, smiling like nothing had just happened.

Rarri looked at him sadly because he understood how he was feeling. He felt like that when Spank died. He just ain't have time to grieve over it because he was caught up in tryna pay for his funeral and make sure his mom was at least straight. Right then he made a mental note to go and see what's been going on with her. Heaven ain't say nothing about her *not* picking up the money he arranged for her to get every month.

Baby Flock's smile faded and he sat back down looking at everybody else in the backyard having a good time. The scene brought more pain to his heart because so many people loved infant Flock and it showed at that very moment.

"I should have just let em leave my nigga"

"What you mean?"

He sighed deeply before answering Rarri.

"After we left the yacht we went to flock a house *we* been plottin on. I mean, the shit Heaven be puttin us on is boo but we wanted to do one on our own. Like we used to and shit. When we got to the back, blood did his lil doggy call to make sure it wasn't no dogs back there and we started laughin. I mean, he always pump fake like he gon leave when we be fuckin with em but on the set this time, I *knew* he was really about to leave. I seen it in his face. He wasn't playin "

He pulled out a cigarette, lit it and pulled on it hard, then blew the smoke out. He held the pack towards Rarri but he declined.

"I think him seein how cold Heaven is didn't scare em, but it woke his game up and after that he just wasn't in the mood for no type of playin. His whole demeanor was different like that shit aged him or some shit like that"

"So what, he came back again like he always did?" Rarri asked knowing how infant was known to be.

"If he would have left, he wasn't comin back. He would have *never* came back. I felt it"

He hit the cigarette as hard as he could. "That's why I called blood a crybaby. I knew that would *make* him go"

He just got up and walked off to go fuck with the other Flocks, leaving Rarri in his thoughts. It was no secret that Baby Flock was the most aggressive Flock out of the bunch YA had really fucked him up mentally. It was crazy though cause he was also the most laid back Flock. When he wasn't mad at some shit, that is. It made him *seem* like the coolest one.

Rarri thought back about all the stories he heard about infant shooting shit up and the few times he witnessed it firsthand then wondered if the reason he never froze up was because of his brother. If he reacted like that over him not killing the dogs, Rarri couldn't help but wonder how he would have responded if they were *people* he couldn't kill. Maybe behind the mask infant had it harder then he thought. A lot of people hide who they really are when they feel the need to be accepted.

'Damn!' Rarri said to himself as he shook his head before getting up and walking to go inside. Now it all made sense.

That's why infant was always so overprotective and territorial over everybody else. He was like one of those mean ass poodles always attacking whoever gets too close to it's owner or friends. But, he was like that because he was only protecting the ones he loved the best way he knew how, with aggression and violence. He walked into the house and went to where the older ladies were sitting at a table, drinking and talking.

"Girl, you couldn't tell Brandon you wasn't his girlfriend..." Infant's mom told Heaven loudly as they both laughed themselves into tears along with everybody else. "Yea, he loved him some Heaven"

Infant's mom sighed and her face became more sad but she still smiled. She told herself she wasn't going to cry no more. Instead, she would just smile because that's what he would have wanted. She chuckled to herself thinking about her baby.

"Yea, he loved Bird and all them too, but when he talked about *you*.." She paused, closed her eyes and shook her head like her favorite song was on. "MMMHMMMM, when he talked about *you!*" she repeated with so much passion Heaven immediately cried silently. "His face lit up like.." She sighed again and started laughing as if she were happier than ever before speaking again. "His face lit up like he was in *love*, girl!" she said then looked at her. "No you ain't. You ain't bout to do this today, not on *my* baby's day you ain't"

Heaven looked down as his mother walked to her, "Come on" she said and grabbed her out of her chair.

"Somethin was in my eye" she lied, wiping away her tears with her free hand.

"I know, that's why we goin over here" his mother answered while going over to the surround sound with Heaven still close by her side.

"*When a man loves a wom---*" she unplugged whoever phone was playing that soft shit and put the aux cord in hers.

"*Bitches, Bitches, Bitches, Bitches, Bitches, Bitches, Bitches..*" started to play causing Heaven to look at her with a smile.

"Yeeahhh Bitch! We bout to turn up" she yelled grabbing Heaven by the hand again as they went to the middle room. Everybody started pouring in quickly, singing along to Infant's favorite song, "Bitches" by Y.G and RJ.

'*I got bitches, too many bitches still it ain't enough bitches to handle my business*'

Heaven immediately felt better as she sang and danced. She even felt better than when she killed the guy who killed Infant. She understood he had the right to do what he did. Hell, she had done the same thing if not something worse but fuck all that. She wasn't tryna hear nothing besides him begging for his life followed by the sound of his body burning in a blazing fire as she sipped on her favorite martini, playing with the mini pink umbrella while the flames danced in the her eyes. One *must* remember, there will always be hell in Heaven.

TWENTY

Lɪʟ Dɪɴᴋ ʀᴀɴ and jumped up as high as he could.

"Get that shit out of here!" he yelled as he swatted the basketball out of Rarri's hand.

Everybody went crazy. The Wilmington arms was craccin like always. Bitches was out flockin as usual tryna fuck with some fly crip'N. To you it may have looked like a party but to everybody else it was just a normal day in the hood. Everybody was there.

JMacc, Punchout, lil Greebo, Tcash, Mike dog, Chewy, Clues, burger, Rocc, lil Jay, Pap, suspect, happs, sunshine, yaah boy, Crip face, 7 slim, heavy, gleek , folsum, Lil Jay, 81, bam, coo coo, Danger, Bird , claybo , Killbo, elbo, Shank, AD, bo wacc, Jigga, Banccer, The twins, Veezy, Ant, DC, Steve O and the list goes on and on.

"foul" Rarri said half out of breath.

"What you mean, foul?" Lil Dink asked then turned to the niggas on the sideline, "Ya'll hear this nigga talkin bout foul?"

JMacc tossed the ball back in the court to lil Dink who then bounced it to Rarri as he walked to half,

"Check up weird nigga. Ain't no fouls."

Rarri was hot. He was fouling him the whole game and he was

tired of it. He had already busted his lip in the first game now he just elbowed him in the face during the third and had the nerve to act like it wasn't shit. Lowkey this was all Rarri's fault to begin with because don't nobody like playing basketball with lil Dink except for other big rough niggas.

Lil Dink loved playing basketball a little *too* much. He played every game like a million dollars was on the line. He ain't give a fuck who you was. He was a real bully on the court. Known to throw his weight around. The only way he knew to play the game was aggressively. Rarri knew the reason he was going extra hard was because he was losing and he hated losing, especially in front of a gang of mothafuckas *ooh'n & aw'n*.

Rarri ain't give a fuck, though. He wanted to play rough so Rarri was going to give him what he wanted.

"CHECK!" he said and as soon as lil dink turned around the ball smacked him in the face.

Rarri busted out laughing as did a lot of others from the court-side. Lil Dink wasn't phased by it but when he touched his lips, looked at his fingers and seen the blood on them, he got hot. Rarri was his nigga though, so he wasn't trippin.

"Aye Myesha" he called to his sister who was watching from the upstairs balcony.

"Wassup?"

"Throw the gloves down"

Wanting to see some action, she ain't waste no time running inside to grab the two pairs of boxing gloves he loved so much.

Everybody went crazy. They already knew what it meant when he called for the gloves. Rarri stopped laughing.

"Fuck..." he swore to himself.

The last thing he felt like doing right now was boxing but turning down *any* fade is a NO NO. Especially in the hood because mothafuckas would never let you live that shit down. Punchout was already waiting at the bottom with open hands when she came back out with the gloves. He fasho wanted to see some shit, if not get in it. His name wasn't Punchout for nothing. He anxiously gave both pair to lil Dink.

"Which ones you want, cuh?" he asked holding the gloves up.

"Man ain't nobody bout to be out here playing with you, YAAH." Rarri replied as he grabbed the ball then bounced it to him *nicely* now, "Check"

Lil Dink kicked that shit over the gate then tossed a pair to Rarri before sliding his on.

"Ight.. I tried to give you yo chance foo. I'm bout to do my shit regardless, you already know." He said as Punchout quickly tied his gloves for him.

His scandalous ass was assisting in anyway possible *with* a big ass smile on his face cause like everybody else laughing, he too already knew what was up. Rarri was either going to put the gloves on and get craccin, get chased around the hood by lil Dink until he caught the fade or just sit there and get punched on. You would be surprised by how many niggas he done ran out the hood by playing. Rarri wasn't never bout to go out like that though and if he thought he was, he had him all the way fucked up. Rarri was a real one. His name rang bells in the streets. On top of that, his pimpin was on another level. He almost had a bitch on every blade in L.A. What the fuck he look like running from a nigga?

Rarri picked the gloves up like a muthafuckin loc and got craccin.

———

Pinks was texting back and forth with some trick nigga she had bust on seeking arrangements a couple days ago. He was talking bout spending some big money on her and usually she would be smiling from ear to ear but the tension in the room was thick. Even though she was one of them blue-eyed, blonde white barbie doll lookin bitches she was far from dumb and the bitches she hoe'd wit had laced her fully to the top.

Pinks stayed in pocket because she knew her place but something was really on he mind and as time passed she finally built up enough courage to look up from the phone and ask the million dollar question.

"Daddy what happened to your eye?"

Rarri gave her a cold stare. This another part of the game that ain't been taught. What do you tell yo bitch after you just got beat up by a nigga you know you can't see?

"SHUT THE FUCK UP!"

"I don't know what you mad at her for" Lil Dink chuckled

"Cuh, let me holla at you outside" he said in frustration. Lil Dink sighed loudly just as aggravated and followed him out.

Soon as he closed the door Rarri went in. "Cuh, how many times I gotta tell you to stop speakin up in front of my bitches like that? You keep on doin that shit"

"Nigga, you the one got the bitch sittin in *my* sister house like this the spot or somethin. Everytime these bitches be around you want a nigga to walk on *eggshells* and talk to you all sweet and shit. I ain't one of yo hoes cuh" he shot back. "That pimpin shit got you trippin on V's" he added shakin his head.

"You just don't get it cuh" Rarri replied shaking his head as well."Fucc that bitch! It ain't about her foo. Matter of fact never mind, I don't even know why I'm talkin bout this shit with yo game green ass."

"Whatever nigga. That's why yo eye like that now. Always runnin yo mouth" lil Dink countered.

"I ain't trippin, watch, that's why Ima knock Monica stanky pussy ass from you"

"Stop *playin* with me cuh" lil Dink said aggressively knowing if Rarri pushed up on her she was fasho gone.

"Ain't nobody *playin* cuh" he laughed. "Watch, next time I see that bitch I'm knockin her"

"Ight, I'ma just keep makin you throw the gloves on every time I see you then"

Rarri chuckled once and gave him that *I don't give a fuck look*.

"*In front* of yo bitches" he warned takin the smile off of his face.

"You a nasty ass nigga cuh" Rarri shot back with a sour expression. "Her pussy be stankin and you *still* fuccin on that bitch"

"Cuh, you actin like you ain't never fucked no stank"

"I fucked some stank but I ain't keep fuckin it after that" they both laughed.

They was always arguing about something only to end up laughing about some other shit in the end. No matter how many times Rarri told him about not talking crazy in front of his bitches. Fasho lil Dink was going to do it again. That's just how we was and no matter who Rarri was to everybody else, he's always goin to be the same lil nigga to Dink. They was family.

"Hey babe" Monica said as she walked up the stairs greeting her knight in shining armor with a kiss.

Lil dink wrapped his hands around her waist as they locked lips. The small booty shorts she had on made her ass look good but Rarri was looking at it like it was the nastiest thing in the world. Still he decided to fuck with lil Dink.

"Damn" Rarri swore, licking his lips seductively. "What that shit do?" he asked never takin his eyes off of her ass.

"Hey Rarri" she blushed still in lil Dink's arms, instantly making him mad as fuck.

It wasn't because she said '*hey*' to him. Lil Dink didn't like the *way* she said his name. Monica said it the same was all the other bitches be running around saying it. With that look in her eye all lustful and shit.

"Take yo ass in the house!" he ordered as he '*strongly*' guided her towards the door.

"I don't know what you mad at her for" Rarri intervened loudly making sure Monica heard him. Lil dink gave him a cold look, opened the door, pushed her in and slammed it back shut quickly before Monica could say anything.

He looked at Rarri seriously, ""YAAH! On the hood stop playin with my bitch cuh"

"Man, what is you talkin bout? All I said was *what that shit do*'

"CUH!" he swore as he literally stopped himself from swinging on Rarri. "You know what you doin" he added angrily, smashing his fist into his palm.

Rarri busted up laughing, getting his friend mad was always one of the funniest things to do because he didn't like doing too much talking or explaining himself to mothafuckas. He wasn't a good debater, so most of his problems he solved through violence, but no matter how made he got, he could never see himself really hurting one of his closest friends and vice versa. That's why it's always the homies that will get on yo nerves the most. Them niggas just don't know when to stop playing.

"Cuh, you can't tell me not to talk to Monica. I knew that bitch way before you did my nigga." He replied seriously. "Besides, sometimes these hoes want a *gentleman* in they life"

Lil dink lost it. He had enough of this shit for one day so he started bodying Rarri the fuck up. Both of them laughing as he did though.

"What that nigga trippin on now?" Trigg asked as he walked up the stairs smoking a blunt.

"Cuh don't want me talkin to Monica no more" He blurted out before lil Dink tried to lie and say some other shit.

Trigg looked at him strangely then passed the blunt to Rarri.

"Don't let cuh hit my shit" he told Rarri then looked at lil Dink shaking his head in disgust. "Nasty ass"

"Fuck yo blunt" lil Dink replied waving Trigg off like he didn't care.

Rarri took a couple more puffs then tried to pass it back to Trigg but lil Dink smacked it out of his hand and picked it up from the ground quickly.

"Come on cuh, stop playin" Trigg cried as he ran up but lil Dink held him back with one hand then hit it with the other and as soon as his lips touched it, Trigg gave up. "Yup, you could gon and keep that mothafucka, I'm coo."

"Naw, I'm good" Rarri said when he tried to pass it to him.

"Fuck ya'll"

They both started laughing. Myesha came out of the house all dolled up looking good and shit. She was one of those bitches that always kept a lot of gold around her neck, nails and feet on fleek, hair done and sexy tattoos on her body. She learned to always have her own shit at a young age because she had no other choice but to do so.

When her mother decided crack and her weird ass boyfriend was more important than the welfare of her own kids. She grabbed her little brother and left. Afraid of being spilt up in the system, they took their chances being raised by the grimy streets of Compton, bouncing from house to house sometimes even sleeping in the hallways of the apartment complex when there was nowhere else to go.

They ended up squatting in a vacant apartment in the Parc village apartments also known as the Darc side long enough to save enough money to rent a room from somebody in the Wilmington Arms. She got so good at doing hair that she ended up getting her own spot quickly but it was in somebody else's name because she wasn't old enough to technically rent yet. Turnin that place into an in-house beauty salon was the best thing she could have ever done because now her *clientele* was on point.

When Rarri put lil Dink on, the first thing he did was buy his sister her own shop. That was the least he could do after everything they had been through. She could have moved out of the hood but wasn't no other place like it. Right now her only concern was stacking as much as she could and to keep gettin it while the gettin was good.

"Bro ima be back later. Don't forget to lock up when you leave cause last time y'all niggas just left my shit open" she said with a hint of attitude as she walked past lil Dink and Rarri.

She took a couple steps down the stairs, dug in her purse, pulled out a .40 then handed it to Trigg. He tucked it in the waist of his pants.

"Ight, ya'll we'a be bacc" He said then proceeded to follow Myesha down the stairs.

"We?!" her brother asked in disbelief, "Hell naw! Where ya'll think ya'll goin?"

"To the movies" they both replied still walking down the stairs.

"Hell naw, fucc all that!"

"Boy, I'm grown"

"Well shit, he technically ain't yet!"

"He bought to be" Myesha laughed. Trigg turned around and threw up V.L at him then grabbed her by the hand as they walked to the car.

Lil dink ran down the stairs and watched them leave in complete shock. Rarri started crying laughing.

"Cuh, how you let Trigg knock yo *big* sister?"

He looked up at him looking defeated, "Rarri, please, just shut. The. Fuck. Up. Gotdamn YAAH" he said shaking his head then sat down at the bottom of the stairs.

Rarri couldn't help himself. He damn near ran down the stairs and squeezed a seat by him placing a brotherly arm around his shoulder.

"Gon let it out, cuh, I know you wanna cry"

Lil Dink just shook his head and exhaled deeply. He didn't see this shit coming but now as he thought about the situation, Myesha has always been *extra* nice to Trigg and went more out of her way for him than she did for Spank or Rarri. He couldn't recall a time she ever turned Trigg down for anything and now he knew why. She always liked him because out of all his friends, he was the one that was there for them when they were younger.

He couldn't count all the whooping's Trigg got for sneaking them in his room after they out stayed their welcome. Or how many times he stole snacks from Miracle market for them to eat on because they were hungry. Trigg would take food out of his aunty fridge to make sure they both ate. One time he pulled up to the Vaco pushing a basket full of groceries.

Only 11 at the time, he came up with the brilliant idea of waiting until his aunty went to sleep to steal her EBT card and go on a shopping spree. The electricity didn't work so the refrigerator wasn't running but they still put everything in there. They were in there fuckin that food up. For the first time in a long time nothing else mattered to them. They laughed and joked as they happily stuffed their faces until their stomachs was full. He didn't eat nothing but a few chips cause he knew they needed it more than him. Plus he had plenty of food at home.

He was just enjoying seeing them happy, *especially* her. He knew why she was always sad, so he tried to make smile as much as he could. Everything was going perfectly. Until the front door flew open and the manager stormed in with Trigg's angry aunty behind him. She whopped his ass, took her EBT card and the groceries back. Myesha and Lil Dink were back on the streets.

His aunty felt bad for them but as far as she was concerned, Myesha was 15 and should know better than to have Trigg stealing for them. Speeding back up to now, Trigg was going though so much shit that lil Dink knew he needed somebody like her to keep him balanced.

'It's better him than any other nigga' Dink thought to himself. Rarri was his boy too but he damn sure was glad his sister ain't like him like that. Ain't no telling what he would have her out there doing. Which brought him back to a question he'd been wanting to ask.

"Aye cuh, you gon teach me how to be a pimp?"

"Hell naw!" Rarri said immediately takin his arm from around him.

"Why not?" he asked him as he stood up. "You know how many bitches done asked me to be they pimp?"

"Naw, how many?"

"Alot...I just ain't have time to do the shit."

"YAAH, you playin cuh"

"On the hood I'm serious"

"Ight, you gon let *Monica* go slide out with Pink's tonight?" Rarri asked seriously.

He got quiet and Rarri looked at him and shook his head.

"Exactly! You ain't got the heart for this shit"

Lil Dink waved him off. "That shit weak…so what you bout to do cuh? I'm bout to bounce."

"All of a sudden" Rarri replied as he stood. "Tell that bitch I said come on we gon sagg out too then."

"YAAH" he said as he gave Rarri a hood shake then went upstairs.

"Tell yo bitch I said what that shit do too" he joked. Lil Dink flicked him off then went inside.

As he waited on Pinks', Rarri found himself entertaining the thought of lil Dink pimpin. It would be fun to be able to swang with him in that type of lane but he already knew that he was just too aggressive for that shit. He could see Lil Dink knockin a nigga who knocked him for a bitch the fuck out. Just thinking bout that shit had him laughing.

Pinks came down the stairs looking at him like he was crazy but knew not to ask any more questions. She just wanted to make enough money today to make him happy. Rarri's hoes was tryna step it up a notch now that the Bentley Bitches were gone. Even though it's only been a couple of days, he had to admit, shit was looking good.

TWENTY-ONE

UNABLE TO GET the answers he had been looking for Trouble grew tired of this shit and apart of him started to feel bad because of all the people he killed after his lil bro got shot. He didn't give a fuck about Trina, as far as he was concerned, if that bitch didn't die that day, he damn sure was going to kill her later on. Somebody had to know something and if it wasn't none of his homies, that only meant one thing. Maybe it was one of Rarri's

'On hood' Trouble said to himself as he tucked his burner then rushed out of the house. 45 minutes later he was walking into an apartment complex. The same ones he seen Lil Dink and Trigg walk into months after his lil brother's shooting. At the time, Trouble didn't think they had nothing to do with it but you could never put nothing past nobody. So he followed them anyway.

When he saw Lil Dink clutching his pistol behind his back as Trigg knocked on the door, Trouble 'thought' he knew what was about to go down. Especially when they walked in. On top of that, when he crept up and put his ear to the door, he could hear them arguing about something but couldn't make out what they were saying. Just as he crept back off to get a better layout of the complex, lil Dink walked out, without Trigg.

He ain't give a fuck about none of that though. That was their business. He was just tryna find out what happened to his brother. He didn't know what they had going on but it damn sure looked shady. He thought Lil Dink bodied Trigg but Trouble had been hearing stories about Trigg young ass shooting shit up so he know he wasn't dead.

'But if he ain't dead, then what happened that day?' That's the question that's been troubling Trouble right now. He doubted it had anything to do with his brother but curiosity got the best of him. Trouble reasoned with himself that it's better to never leave a stone unturned. He contemplated knocking on the door but giving the circumstances of his visit he quickly discarded that idea.

He looked around one more time to make sure no one was watching then pulled out his lock pick and went to work. He picked the lock with such skill that within seconds he was in the apartment with the door closed behind him. *'YOUTUBE is a mothafucka.* he congratulated himself quietly for a nanosecond as he stood still and scanned the room. To his surprise it still seemed to be renovated but it didn't feel occupied. It didn't smell occupied either.

'These niggas need to take the mothafuckin trash out' he mumbled to himself as he removed his hand from the grip of his gun then walked to the kitchen counter where he seen a bunch of mail. He put his hand through the sleeve of his hoody again making sure not to leave any prints and scanned through the papers.

"Rachel Benitt" He said to himself but the name didn't sound familiar. "Gotdamn cuh" Trouble covered his nose with his hand as a foul smell smacked him in the face.

He knew it had to be the refrigerator but his nosey ass had to open it up and see for himself. All the food in there had gone bad just as he thought. Trouble was about to finish looking around the house but as soon as he closed the refrigerator door he found himself lookin down the barrel of a big ass gun.....

"FUCK!!"

TWENTY-TWO

As usual, Pretty me da P was back poppin. His new *partners* had him plugged all the way in. They hit him with the 2019 Maserati, mini mansion in Rancho Cucamonga , fly chain, new clothes and a couple dollars to keep in his pocket. Pretty me da P had bitches but he ain't never had all this shit. Now, his pimpin was about to be on a whole new level. This time, when he hit the blade mothafuckas was gon recognize his pimpin. He ain't give a fuck what niggas was talking bout. Is he hard now? FUCK NO!" But, the police *just so happened* to have been scoopin up all the p's who was saying shit about him. That's on them though.

He was feeling good and as he turned on G street banging 'Bounce Back' by Big Sean with the windows down, bitches was breaking necks. He drove a couple blocks and pulled up on a lil light bright bitch who was reckless eyeballin from a far. He put the car in park then hopped out like a boss.

"Aye, say bitch I see you, seem me, so you must got my fee, am I correct or what?"

She was frozen. Which was bad for her but good for him. He then walked right up on her.

"What you doin walkin around in those? He wanted to know looking down at her no name shoes.

"A bitch like you need to be hoppin out in nothin but the best of everything now that you on *my* team"

"Hold on, who said I was on yo team?" she asked.

He gave her that *bitch please* look then walked off.

"Just hit my mitt before you jump in my shit bitch. You know what it is" He added over his shoulder not needing to look back to see is she was coming. He *knew* she was. That bitch was ready to jump in before he even stopped the car.

Hoes always chose up on him quick, that's never been a problem. Bitches will fuck a nigga just cause he got the new Jordans on, so when you pull up like he just did, them hoes go crazy. Speaking of hoes, two onlookers bent the corner just as out of pocket as that bitch, standing around staring and shit. He got in the driver's side and turned down his radio.

"Hold on, wait up" He said as she opened the passenger side door.

"Close my door and hit my mitt like I instructed, hoe. purse first."

She tolled her eyes (Out of his sight, of course), closed the door, reached in her bra, pulled out a wad of bills and handed it to him through the window.

When he fingered through the money his smile turned upside down. The hundred was wrapped around all ones.

"How much is this?"

"Like $130" She replied proudly.

"Never mind" he said and threw the money back out at her. Then he looked at the two bitches behind her as she chased for the bills. "Say bitch, ya'll hoes spread the word around. Pretty me da P will never put a short hoe down. If they ask why I didn't empty the bitch who tried to itty bitty my mitt, Tell em I'm fly, high and way too Pretty for that shit!" He added overly animated then scurred off, Leaving them pointing and laughing at the hoe he just rejected.

If this was any other time he would have put that right in his pocket and had some new toes but this wasn't any other time. This is now and now he was on. Bitches was gon have to come all the way correct tryna fuck with his pimpin. The only thing he regretted was not asking her name because he was bad with remembering faces but he, for some reason always remembered names. The last thing he wanted was to have that bitch double back on him later on someday. One of his main rules for himself was to never back track on no bitch for any reason at all. That shit was just bad luck for him.

Only a couple blocks away from the previous crime scene and another light-skinned bitch was breaking her neck from the other side of the street. He made a hard U-turn not giving a fuck about getting a ticket. Thanks to his *partners* he had a get out of jail free card. He was now feeling untouchable.

"Say hoe, is you choosin or ghost followin cause I see you logged in!?" he yelled to her from the car. "I ain't gotta mention pimpin Bitch you see it. don't try to not look now hoe, you busted. I'm Pretty me da P, the professional hoe bussa, by the way.

She looked away tryna hide her smile but her eyes were still cuttin from the side. She was short, thick had long hair, green eyes with nice full lips, A pretty face and some booty shorts so small her cheeks hung out.

"I know you thinkin bout it baby but don't overdue it. He should've thought about that before he put you down while I'm in town. Stop feelin sorry for that nigga, he gone pimp again just not as good as me. I know you ain't wake up with leavin on yo mind but you could do it now and save us both some time"

She again looked away, hoping her folks wasn't looking. She was feeling Pretty me da P, he was fly, cocky had word play but the craziest part was that he really just named exactly what she was actually thinking bout. He had her feeling like shit because she just swore to herself that she wasn't going to blowup on this one, This time because the pimp she had now really treated her good, cared for her and made her his bottom. He was fly but not like the nigga in the mazi fly. No matter how good he was, she instantly started making up reasons in her mind why he wasn't, just to justify her being out of pocket.

Pretty me da P knew she was weighing out her options and thinking deeply. This was really his full time job so he knew not to give her too much time to think on her own.

"I'll tell you what. As soon as you get in, Ima give him a courtesy call and serve him properly. I'm still a gentleman baby, the least we can do is let him know that everything is alright cause you in good hands *now*. So he ain't out her worried lookin for you all night thinkin somethin bad happened"

She tightened her lips trying to break her smile.

"I literally just stepped out, so I don't got no fee"

He was about to hit the gas but something about the bitch wouldn't let him. "Look, I usually don't even do this but Ima let you make it up to me if you choose up, right now."

She nervously bit her bottom lip and anxiously as she looked around for a moment then built up enough courage to power walk to the car and hop in.

"Call that nigga and put it on speaker" he told her as soon as she closed the door. She did as instructed then leaned the phone towards him as it rang. "My bad, beautiful, what's your name?"

"Laelani, but everybody call me Lae Lae"

TWENTY-THREE

'Man, I can't wait to get rid of this nigga' Kill Kill thought to himself as he passed the blunt to Macky who was in deep conversation about some weird shit with Rasheed. He wasn't feeling how they been all buddy buddy lately. Rasheed was a mark in his eyes cause he let Macky throw his shit in the middle of the street in front of a parking lot full of people and ain't do nothing.

Now Macky wanna kick it with the nigga like he coo? Naw, Kill Kill wasn't feeling it but for now, he could play his part be coo. Macky pulled on the blunt a couple times then passed it to Rasheed.

"Aye, you heard about that ranch Mike Tyson supposed to be building?"

"Yeah, that shit gon be in Palm springs. Niggas gon have to hit that shit up when it opens." He said before hitting the blunt, hard."

"They talkin bout it's gon have the longest lazy river in the world P, and you could smoke wherever. I know I'm taking my own weed though. I heard a nigga be smokin frogs and shit now. I ain't wit all that"

Rasheed started crying laughing. "Naw P, they not smokin the frog. This doctor dude discovered how to milk the venom that the frogs use to throw off mothafuckas that be tryna get him and shit. It's like a hallucinate they using in a smokable form." He added. "That nigga said it took him on like a spiritual journey that changed his life P."

"Man, cuh just tryna sell that shit" Macky replied, waving imaginary Mike off.

"I don't know. Shit, what you think?" Rasheed asked, passing the blunt to Kill Kill.

He looked at the both of them niggas like they were crazy.

"Man, you niggas is high, cuh." He said as they all started laughing.

"Damn, I thought niggas said we was playing fig" Rarri said as he pulled up on the trio.

"We *was* playing fig" Macky replied as he grabbed the blunt from Kill Kill and hit it. "*Now* we playin Western." He added, laughing as he slapped fives with Rasheed.

Them niggas looked like they just hopped out of a GQ magazine. Both of them had on the same green Dolce & Gabanna burnished croc derbies with the Fendi logo socks and the new Saint Laurent denim shorts. It's never a need for a shirt when you as bussdown as them. He leaned his head out of the window to get a better view of the two and shook his head.

"Well, ain't ya'll just the cutest little couple?"

Kill Kill chuckled because he thought the same shit when he pulled up earlier. Macky and Rasheed started clowning with each other because they knew Rarri was going to low-key hate whenever he did pull up.

"Calm down lil nigga" Macky teased as he reached in his car, pulled out a shoe box and a Saint Laurent shopping bag and held them up for him to see. "We knew that you was gon forget us, but we ain't forget you"

For a moment, Rarri was baffled, not understanding what they were talking about. Then he remembered they did all agree to dress alike for St. Patrick's day.

"Damn, my bad P" he apologized as he got out of the car all happy and shit.

"Yeah, whatever" Rasheed replied as they P-shook. He opened the shoebox and was stunned. Not at the shoes but at the price. The receipt showed the cost of eleven bands a pair.

He looked at Macky but macky pointed over to Rasheed who just shrugged his shoulders.

"You said we gon break the world, right? Let's do it like no other."

"On P's" Rarri said in approval at the same time thinking about Maria's similar statement. She didn't leave a number or nothing for him to get in contact with her and he had been dying to see her again.

He still hadn't mentioned their encounter to anyone. In reality, it hardly seemed real. Maria was not only the plug but she also was sexy as fuck. She looked like a better version of Roselyn Sanchez. How is that possible? Only God knows.

As Macky, Rasheed and Rarri clowned around, Kill Kill sat there steaming. He felt left out like a mothafucka. Macky didn't tell him nothing about dressing up for Saint Patrick's Day. He shook it off then kindly excused himself from the group and you don't have to guess who was on speed dial once he got in his car and sped off.

"Get ready, I got another one" he said into the phone then quickly hung up. Wasn't no need for small talk. He knew, just like everyone else, that Tana Jay stayed ready.

All that day Macky, Rasheed and Rarri went around campaigning but not the usual campaign of choppin on hoes. This was a campaign to gather some of the flyest and well known pimps, players and hustlers around the city. With the three of them on it together, it was anything but hard to accomplish. Especially how they pulled up rocking the same fit symbolizing a way of structure.

Deep down, niggas was dying to be apart of something new. While some hesitated, others didn't. Word spread so fast that by nightfall all three of their phones were blowing up nonstop by niggas who had missed them in traffic. Now everybody wasn't invited. The three of them carefully selected the people they agreed on fuckin with and of course, not many took kindly to being rejected. Especially the old niggas because not one of them was called on or asked to participate in this new lane. Quickly, they began to group up against it, before it even started.

A couple of days later, in one of Tony's extravagant hotel ball rooms, Rarri found himself standing in front of a room full of young, hungry pimps who was all known to be with the bullshit. They had been listening quietly for the last hour to the game being dropped on them with widened eyes. Never had they been so touched by another man's words. A lot of them at that moment, found out who they truly were.

As he closed his father's book and looked at the people around him, he knew without a doubt that they felt just as obligated to do better as he did. He took a sip of Remy from a cup them held it to Macky.

"Breathe with me"

He took the cup and repeated the same thing before passing it along in the room. Everyone sipped from the same cup, initiating a new beginning. Vowing that they now had each other's loyalty. After a few hours of polipimpin, weed smokin and drink sippin, they hit the highway and went back to the city, acting a motha-fuckin fool. Every blade they hit was immediately lit and the way they moved as one let everybody know that the rumors were true. The takeover was now in effect.

While Rarri was putting together his crew, lil Dink, Trigg and the flocks were puttin together theirs. Lil Dink gathered all the money getting dope dealing niggas, Trigg all the young killaz he knew and the Flocks all the known flockers and jack boys around the city. Even though they all did different things, Rarri, Lil Dink,

Trigg and The flocks stressed to every member that they all were together on the same team. No bigger me's or little yous. Everybody was each other's equal. It was everyone's job to always make sure that everyone ate. Being broke was considered a sin so getting money was a must. If one person had a problem, they all had a problem.

It was mandatory that every member pitched in a monthly fee. The fees were to go towards vacation trips, legal issues, business start-ups, school tuitions and anything else that would benefit *everyone* in the long run. These young niggas was about to become more organized than an economy of army ants. Big Meech was right when he said there will never be another B.M.F and respecting him to the fullest, Rarri sought out to be better.

He had studied the rise and fall of all the great leaders who were an inspiration in the black communities across America. Big Meech was his favorite because he made sure everybody ate and lived as he did. His organization was worldwide. What Rarri respected the most was that Big Meech went down and never tried to mention or throw nobody else under the bus for a lighter sentence. He also favored Pappy Mason like a mothafucka, he was a fasho joint.

Rarri had a habit of wanting to surpass everyone he looked up to. Only time would tell if that good or bad.

TWENTY-FOUR

"Now tell me that shit don't bang.." Stacey said proudly as she finished playing a few songs for Tragedy, a local and well known producer out of L.A.

"I can't even lie" he admitted while rubbing his palms together. "That shit hot. Like real hot. I could get yo artist out mainstream fasho. You just gotta let me know what type of deal ya'll looking for? Honestly, I think my label would be perfect for this type of shit. I could get them to open up for some big names right now and make sure they get exclusive access to the best song writers, producrers, beats, vocal teachers and all that shit." Tragedy pulled out his pen and check book. "What's ya'll price?" he asked looking at Stacey, DJ Janky and the Bentley Bitches.

Like a lot of people, he already knew about the infamous group trending on Social Media. But this was his first time hearing their music. He just thought they were some dumb ass hoes getting rich off selling pussy. There wasn't a shortage of fine ass bitches in his inbox ready to suck some dick or give up some pussy for fame. Initially, that's what he assumed was going on here and the only reason he agreed to meet with them in the first place but *now,* he was all business.

He knew he wanted to sign them before the first song was over. He knew talent when he saw it and these wasn't no one hit wonder type of bitches. With his connections and great production skills, Tragedy could see them with a promising future. They were the diamonds in the rough he had been looking for, so he knew to sign them now before any other label tried to scoop them up.

He thought the Bentley Bitches were laughing in celebration of his offer but they were simply laughing *at* the offer.

"I don't want you to get the wrong impression..." Stacey replied, placing her hand on top of his checkbook. "You are a great producer and I love all your work. Especially that new song you just did with Rihanna. That shit is fire but we not lookin for no deal or label to sign to, and no offense but the label that signed you don't got enough to sign the *Bentley Bitches,* so your personal account couldn't possibly afford them"

They all giggled but cut it short when she cut her eyes at them. The last thing she wanted to do was to bruise his ego any more than she already had but she wasn't there to sugarcoat their agenda either.

"Look, I'm not trying to come off the wrong way. I'm just speakin facts. Time is money and it wouldn't be professional or wise for me to even think about wasting yours. I'm honored to be in your presence and to have you make an offer is simply mind-blowing because it assures me even more that these girls are special. And, just as I tell them all the time, no matter what doors don't open they're are goin to make it, regarless. I believe in them wholeheartedly. Their talent is undeniable but what separates them from any other group out there is the loyalty they have for each other. You can't put a price on shit like that and the industry has yet to see a group as authentic as them. To be honest, I don't think they deserve to apart of their inevitable success."

He continued to listen, looking curious and interested in what she had to say next, so she kept going.

"Those labels want numbers and loyalty. The Bentley Bitches already been getting money and they're goin to keep getting money, but, it's not goin to be for these white muthafuckas." She added seriously waving her hand around the expensive studio they were all standing in. "Hey, I'm not knockin nobody for doin what they gotta do. Label deals are good for *some* people but once you stop being able to produce the type of numbers they are looking for, do you think they're goin to still be in your corner? You know just as well as I do, Tragedy, that these labels ain't never gave a fuck about us. And they never will, but, now that we notice that shit it's only right to start givin back to where we came from. They seen yo talent in the form of a dollar sign and you as just another young, broke, black boy to capitalize on. What they failed to realize was that signin *you* was the biggest mistake they ever made because *Tragedy* is the pawn they overlooked. They doubted your ability to touch the other side of the board and that is goin to prove tragic mistake for them because now you can become any piece you want to be."

She nodded at Bird who on que handed her a duffle bag. She opened it then started pullin out stack after stack getting them neatly in front of Tragedy as she continued talking.

"You see, we genuinely appreciate you because a lot of the music you produced Made us feel good when sometimes there was nothin to feel good about. Watchin you come up made all us motivated to do the same. This is a token of appreciation from the people who really love what you do and I hope this could form a good relationship between us so we can take things further. If not, we'll still wish you the best and look forward to sittin with you at the top"

She stood and extended her hand. He shook his head as they shook hands. He was too taken back to speak. Nobody had ever came in and did or said no shit like this before.

"I don't get it. What is this money for though and what am I supposed to do with it?"

Stacey laughed.

"Do whatever you want wit it. Ain't no strings attached or hidden agendas behind nothin we do. Just enjoy yoself and keep doin what you love doin and if possible fuck with us how we fuckin wit you " she added before turnin to leave.

"Damn, so ya'll just gon bounce?"

"I mean, I know you busy…"

"Naw.." He said, pulling the chair next to him back out. "Ya'll good. Post up. I got some new beats I want ya'll to check out. Plus, I wanna see what Janky could do with this type of equipment."

"We could do that" Stacey replied with a smile.

She had been planning this day for a long time from where she would sit at all the way down to what she would wear. Proving the phrase, *'practice makes perfect.'* To be true. This is the opportunity that would put her in a position she desired to be in. Managing the Bentley Bitches was the blessing she wouldn't take for granted because being known as the person to bring them out to the world would let that same world see what she was capable of.

'Fuck the world, all I need is Rarri…' she thought to herself.

Getting him to believe in her more than them was important because Stacey wanted to be his main bitch more than anything. As far as she was concerned, these bitches were only *temporary..*

————

Betty wap had been going hard as fuck since taking Bird's place watching over some of Rarri's hoe's on the blade. Even though she was making more money dealing with the tricks Heaven introduced her to, She was still lowkey upset about not being able to work the streets of L.A like alot of the other girls. Frequently, she caught herself contemplating about the best way to sneak a couple dates in but never could build up enough courage to go through with it.

The last thing she wanted to do was get caught doing some dumb shit and have Rarri thinking she wasn't capable of handling business. A hoe at heart, she connected best with other hoes. She understood how cold the game could be. She knew the pain that came with selling pussy and sometimes how hard it could be to make money with all of the competition out there. Despite being unfamiliar with the crew, she was nobody's fool, well, at least not anymore!

As Exotic cried and came up with every excuse in the 'hoe book', Betty wap couldn't help but to laugh to herself. Exotic either thought she was stupid or was actually telling the truth about not being able to catch a date. None of that mattered to Wap though. Her job was to make sure bitches made Rarri's daily fee and if she wasn't allowed to be short, neither were they.

"Alright, look." Betty Wap interrupted. "If shit don't pick up in the next hour, you could just ride around wit me for the night and I'll take care of the fee for you"

"You would really do that for me, Wap?" she asked excitedly from the passenger's side.

"In a heartbeat" Wap replied honestly.

Exotic leaned across and gave Betty wap a hug. "Thank you Wap, I'll pay you back as soon as I get it."

"Girl, you know it ain't nothin, we all in this shit together" she admitted.

"Okay, Ima go see what I can scrape up real quick" Exotic replied with her hand on the door handle ready to leave.

"Ain't you forgettin somethin?" Wap asked with her hand out, stoppin Exotic in her tracks.

"I don't have no money on me, you know I would never tuck on Daddy like that" she answered wholeheartedly.

"I'm already knowin but shirt and skirt though."

Exotic's mouth dropped open.

"You really gon make me shirt and skirt, Wap?" she asked in disbelief.

"I'm not *makin* you do nothin but if I gotta pay yo rent, I'm at least tryna make sure you tried to make somethin happen too."

"I been out here tryin all night though, Wap. You actin like I'm out here bullshittin. Just a minute ago you said we was in this shit together, now you tryna shirt and skirt me like you don't trust me?"

"Look, Ima keep it real with you. I don't trust nobody but Rarri, so you either goin to shirt and skirt and try to get Daddy's money like that or slowmo all night till you hit his mitt." Wap drilled.

"I gotta break more bread than all you bitches but yall don't hear me complain or cryin about it" she spat out looking over at Exotic suspiciously.

"If you ain't ready to shirt and skirt *for Daddy*, how far is yo hoe'n really goin?"

Betty Wap asked simultaneously, thinking back on all the stupid shit she used to do tryna get chose by niggas who's Pimpin was nowhere near Rarri's. She couldn't understand how some of these bitches hesitated to do the simplest shit when there was nothing she could think of that she wouldn't do for him.

'*These bitches should be honored to hit the blade in bra and panties for him. Hell, I would walk this mothafucka butt ass naked all day and night if he asked me to, no questions asked*' she thought to herself.

Exotic thought about Betty Wap's question for a moment, wiped the tears from her eyes then handed her clothes to her with her head down. She felt ashamed of herself. It was already bad enough that she was selling herself for money (which is something she never saw herself doing) but now being close to naked was another story.

She was raised to be a strong, prideful black woman with morals and plans of college degrees and accomplishing goals that would someday make her parents proud. Lately, she found herself loosing her dignity and self-respect more and more each day that passed for a nigga she only met a few times. Not even she could explain how Rarri had a hold on her because before him, she had plenty of men bending over backwards for her with hopes of getting their hands around her heart, to no avail. Then came Rarri out of nowhere, flippin the script and turning her into 'his' trick. Even though her future was nowhere near as promising as it was before, she believed being on his team was worth all the pain that weighed heavily on her heart.

Betty Wap had been through too much herself to feel sorry for Exotic. She wasn't close to shedding one tear for her, especially not over no little shit like this. As far as she was concerned, this was part of the game and life was way harder in Oakland.

"You a bad bitch on a winning team.." she reminded her. "Pick yo head up and get yo bread up. Ain't no way you can't catch a date lookin that good, unless all the tricks done turned gay or somethin" they both laughed at that.

Exotic knew she was bad. Everybody always compared her to VEE, the model featured in the 'Cheeks' magazine. She was the perfect shade of brown with perfect lips, a cute nose, seductive eyes, big titties and a perfect sized ass. She gave Betty Wap another hug, thanked her then got out of the car with the confidence she needed.

Just like Wap had predicted, she didn't make it twenty feet away from the car before catching a date. She smiled to herself, smelled her upper lip then turned up her favorite song, 'Time for it' by Azjah.

TWENTY-FIVE

"MA, it's only been a couple of days, calm down." Rasheed told his mother who had been badgering him all morning about the book.

"Don't tell me to calm down!" she yelled, pointing at him in contempt. "You don't know what I had to go through or do to get you here." Mary added.

"I know ma.."

"NO! You don't know, Rasheed." She let him know sadly as she started thinking years back.

Flashback

Mary had been giving every night her all to please her Pimp, but all God seemed to care about lately was Angel and her little sister. Mary was around before Angel so she wasn't feeling being put on the back burner for a new bitch who, in her opinion, couldn't hoe her way out of a paper bag. Mary wasn't ugly. In fact, she and Angel used to tell people they were sisters because they looked so much alike. She thought she was putting

Angel under her wing. The plan was for them to work together and take Candy's place but Angel crossed her on the low and took it for herself.

What had Mary's blood boiling was the fact that the whole idea was hers. She didn't 'need' to have Angel involved but she genuinely wanted to share her spot with her as a bottom. They had been working the streets with each other since Angel came around and Mary was starting to like her more and more. Even though Angel was only eighteen, she caught on to things quickly. The only thing Mary did wrong was underestimate the young bitch's game.

The whole time Mary thought she had a friend, Angel was simply plotting on her too. She didn't have no plans of sharing 'her' spot with 'no' bitch, until Heaven came into the picture. It took almost a year for them to get close enough to being around Candy on the regular. Candy was on point with everything from making sure God's finances were in order to keeping his hoes in line.

Dealing with her ass on a daily was beyond difficult because Candy always made sure nobody forgot who was the bottom bitch. She wore her position on her sleeve night and day. Angel had grown tired of that bitch's mouth so as soon as she seen her opportunity, she took it. Planting 2,500, some dope and a crack pipe in one of the purses Candy kept in the closet was all God needed to find to beat her ass and demote her so far down that hew would have to squint with two pairs of glasses on to see that bitch. All thanks to the one and only, Angel.

He didn't give her Candy's spot just because she let him know Candy was tucking on him and smoking dope. He made her earn her place like every other bitch in his stable. Honestly, he thought Mary would get it, as did everybody else. To their surprise, Angel couldn't be kept up with by none of them. She tried to say something to him but he just told her to stop hating on Angel and step her shit up. After that, Mary started binging on the bottle and most drugs she could get her hands on when reality set in. She was never going to be his bottom bitch with Angel in the picture.

As time passed, the hatred she had towards her grew stronger and stronger. She didn't know everything but one thing she did know was that he couldn't keep his dick out of her for too long. Especially whenever he was high. So, one night, with no other options, after a long night of sex, instead of throwing the condom away, she went into the bathroom, laid upside down with her legs over the tub and emptied the semen from the condom inside of her, hoping to get pregnant.

She remembered how much he would talk about the son he never had but wanted so much and thought if she could give it to him maybe then, he would have no choice but to get rid of Angel and love her how she wanted to be loved. Mary had it all figured out. The only thing she forgot to do was lock the door, so when he walked in to take a piss and caught her doing the unthinkable, he snapped. God grabbed her up by the hair and smacked her around the hotel room for almost an hour straight. He wanted to have baby but not like this. He knew she wasn't 'the one' so after that night he kept her close to him just in case she did end up pregnant, and she did.

Thinking he had been keeping her close because of the baby, she couldn't wait to flaunt her baby bump to him and everyone else when it came. He smiled and treated her with the upmost respect. The nigga even kissed and rubbed her stomach so when he drove her to the abortion clinic and told her to 'get rid of that mothafucka' she was shocked. She had never told him no and wasn't about to start now.

She went in with her mind set on following his instruction as he waited in the car but as she got closer to the receptionist at the desk, Mary started to feel guilty and couldn't imagine living the rest of her life with the blood of her unborn baby on her hands. She turned, peeked out of the entrance to make sure he wasn't looking and as soon as she got her chance, she took off running in the other direction. That was the last time she had seen God.

Mary was so high the day she gave birth that when it came time to name the baby, she couldn't even remember the name he always said he would give him. She prolonged naming him for as long as she could, debating with herself until she was certain, beyond a doubt, that the name he always said proudly was Rasheed. It wasn't until a few years later, after God's death, that she remembered it wasn't Rasheed, it was Rarri. Despite the error, she raised Rasheed to be in the game since a young age, just like his father.

She compared everything he did to what his father would do. Putting so much pressure on him that it was kind of sad. He never had a chance to become something else in life other than what she wanted him to be and that was a pimp. You couldn't tell Mary that God wasn't proud of what he had become. In some weird, twisted way, she even believed that he loved her more now in death than he did when he was alive.

Mary wanted to believe in things so bad that when she talked to him in her 'mind's eye' she could see and hear him talking back. The God in her mind was telling her how sorry he was for not seeing that she was the one he was supposed to be with. Not Angel or her sister and how it was their fault that he had died. They took him away from his son and despite what he and Angel had goin on, she never 'really' birthed his first child.

She had never told *all* of the details of how everything transpired to her son, but basically, Rasheed was supposed to be Rarri. So, technically, all of the books that was putting Rarri on Mary felt belonged to Rasheed. She had always been keeping a close eye on Heaven and Rarri. Seeing Heaven tweeked out and Rarri running around gangbangin made her feel secure in her and her son's status, but when the two just magically did a 360, and started jumping ahead of mothafuckas and getting their shit right, she knew it was because they had their on the game that God must have left behind for Rasheed.

She had already groomed him to be the best. On top of that, pimpin was in his blood. The books would 'only' put him at a level she was desperately determined to see him on. Mary was willing to do anything to bring him closer to his father. 'Hopefully, not too close'

"This is your time" she assured him sweetly and gently rubbed the side of his face with her thumb. "NOT HIS!" she added angrily.

Deep down, Rasheed wished he and his lil brother could have a real relationship because he really liked Rarri. It was only the things his mother said that made him dislike him sometimes. Every time Rasheed caught himself hating his brother, it only made him hate himself even more because he knew they needed each other. Especially now at the start of everything they were putting together. He felt good about being apart of something that had this much potential.

This new lane was going to be big. So big that Rasheed prayed his mother's plan didn't somehow backfire on them because it wouldn't be too many places in California he could comfortably go if it did. One thing was fasho though, Mary didn't know who she was fuckin wit.

TWENTY-SIX

MACKY WAS STEAMIN. He knew niggas would be looking for him on some gang shit so he was always extra cautious when it came down to where he laid his head at. But, most importantly, where he kept his work. He wasn't out lacking like a lot of niggas so he didn't understand how his spot got flocked. All he knew was that it happened.

"It gotta be the same niggas that hit Dink and em"

"Yea, I was lowkey thinkin the same shit" Rarri replied looking around the tarnished house.

"Damn," Rasheed shook his head. "So ya'll just be out here gettin robbed and shit?"

"Hell naw!"

"That's what it look like" Heaven butted in heatedly.

Neither Macky or Rarri could debate that cause that exactly what it was starting to look like.

"Ya'll need to figure this shit out. So, until then don't call me askin for nothin." She let them know as she got up and headed towards the door. "Ima have somebody come pick up the money for the work tomorrow so be ready."

"Still?" Macky asked in disbelief. "Even after the spot got hit?"

"Yea nigga, *still*" She told him like he was stupid. "Them motha-fuckas robbed *you*, not *me* so run me my shit.talkin bout some, still"

She walked out of there talking dumb shit. She couldn't believe the nerve Macky had to even ask that kind of question. Hell yea she wanted her money despite the situation. It wasn't her fault them niggas was getting booked left and right. Obviously somebody had to have been watching them closely, but regardless, this some shit she wasn't about to come out the pocket for.

One of the things she did pick up from Tony was that when it came to business, there's not many excuses to justify a failure. A fuck up is a fuck and everybody must be held accountable for their actions. Macky's baby mama didn't know what to expect but as soon as Heaven left she relaxed a little and was able to stop eaves dropping from the other room.

Teesha, like many others heard stories about Heaven's cold ways so when Macky told her she was coming over, she begged him to let her leave but he wasn't hearing it. Not wanting anyone to see her that shook up, he told her to just stay in the room until everybody left. Teesha didn't know what to expect but she prayed that if Macky got killed, she wouldn't be the one to join him. Some-body had to be the present parent to raise their three year old daughter.

He was always in the streets so she practically raised their child, alone. He did make sure she was taken care of financially, but money can never make-up for a father's presence. She was tired of Armani asking where her daddy was at. No matter how many times she would bring it up to Macky, he just seemed not to under-stand that shit. It wasn't like he didn't love his daughter, she was his world but Teesha didn't understand that a nigga gotta be dedi-cated to his hustle to feel the type of money he was touching.

If you asked Macky, she was lucky to be able to enjoy al the perks of a lavish lifestyle that he provided her with, without her ever having to put no footwork in. All she had to do was take care of Armani and look pretty while he did everything else. He had been dealing with so many bitches lately on a daily that he hadn't touched her in weeks.

Bitches stayed in her inbox telling her his whereabouts and all the shit he be doing. Yea, it hurt because he should be laid up in the bed with her, not running around giving the whole community dick. She done heard it all but after getting hit in the same spot over and over again, she couldn't help but to feel numb now. It was obvious that Macky was going to do whatever he wanted, so she didn't even bring it up or complain anymore.

She put on a smile for the sake of their daughter, but deep down she was starting to resent everything about him. As soon as Rarri and Rasheed left he went into the room with her, who was now sitting on the bed in deep thought. He sat down next to her.

"You alright?"

She looked at him like he was stupid. He put his arm around her and kissed her on the forehead.

"Look at me"

She looked up and into his eyes.

"You ain't never gotta worry about nothin" he let her know, kissing her on the lips. "I promise you that" he added with such assurance that she believed him without a doubt in her mind.

Seeing how serious he was made her cry because she knew he loved her. Good or bad, he never hid his intentions or feelings when it came to her, no matter what. Macky was the realist nigga she had ever met so just that quickly she was back in love with him all over again.

"I know.." she replied and hugged him tightly. I know"

———

"What the fuck wrong wit you?" Tana Jay asked when Kill Kill threw his phone at the wall in anger.

"This fuckin bitch man!"

"You should be thankin her" Tana Jay replied, shook his head and kept countin the money. The money neither of them would have if it wasn't for Teesha.

You see, Kill Kill and Teesha was creeping with each other on the low for a little over a year now. It all started when Macky went to jail for a murder. Everybody, includin them, assumed he was goin to get washed up. Kill Kill, the real nigga that he 'was', made sure to stop by and check on Teesha and Armani on a daily.

Never once did he think about getting at Teesha. He just wanted to make sure his goddaughter was straight, but one night, unbeknownst to him, Teesha had a plan of her own. She sent him on a bogus food run, lying about how hungry she was and her car being messed up. No questions asked he came running to her beck and call. She knew he was a killer like Macky. Even so, he was still no match compared to her caramel complexion, hazel eyes, pretty face, long hair and body so petite it could put a Victoria Secret model to shame. When he walked in the house, put the food on the table then turned around and saw her standin behind him naked, it was over. She fucked and sucked him so good that he's been in love with her ever since. Unlike Macky, he was always there when Teesha needed comfort and someone to talk to.

Still, this was the first time she had ever told him where he kept all of his shit at so he knew that she was ready to leave his ass fasho now, without a doubt. That was up until he got a text from her saying that she was going to try and work it out with Macky *again*, for 'Armani'. He was getting tired of this shit. Every time she got mad at Macky she would have Kill Kill thinking they were going to run off and be together.

The last time, she stood him up and left him hanging at the spot they were supposed to meet at without ever saying she wasn't coming. He had everything he owned packed and ready to go. He even bought some clothes, toys and a brand new car seat for Armani. But, about five hours into the wait, he knew why she wasn't coming. Macky!

'*He always find some way to slither his slimy ass back into the picture*' Kill Kill thought to himself angrily. That was the '*main*' reason he wanted to kill Macky so badly. He knew if something happened to him, Rarri would be too dedicated towards avenging him. So, that night, after peeking through her room window and seeing her and Macky fuckin, he dropped a tear then drove to Compton and pulled up on Tana Jay with a proposition.

He always questioned himself as to why Kill Kill wanted to body a nigga so close to him and it wasn't until now that he understood. In his personal opinion, Kill Kill was in some sucka shit.

'*Doin all this over a bitch*' Tana Jay shook his head in disgust then started laughing. He didn't give a fuck about Kill Kill's lips being in a knot. He walked out of the room and came back with a big towel tied around his neck draped like a cape and his chest poked out dramatically. Then he started running around the room like he was flying, sound effects and all.

"Dun-dun-du-duuuun!" captain Kill Kill to the rescuuuuue!"

As Tana Jay paraded around the room, Kill Kill stood there contemplating on where to shoot him first. He wanted to shut this nigga up so bad but he still needed him in order to pull everything off successfully. '*I'm killin this nigga soon as we done wit all this shit*' Kill Kill smiled then sat back down at the table to finish counting his money.

"I'm glad you find this shit funny, cuh" he said then had a secret laugh of his own…

———

"What you think?" Rasheed asked Rarri as he swerved through traffic.

"Bout what?"

"Bout Macky" Rasheed replied looking at Rarri like he was crazy.

Rarri just kept looking out the window not ready to entertain no bullshit. Macky having something to do with what's been going on never even crossed his mind. He may have been a lot of things but one thing Macky wasn't, was a snake.

"Look, I know that's yo boy but right now ain't the time to put too much trust in nobody. Not when shit comin up missin fasho."

"I hear you but it just don't make sense for him to have his own spot hit when he gotta pay for the shit regardless"

"That's the thing though.." Rasheed cut him off. "..He didn't *think* he was goin to still have to pay for that shit. I mean, 'P' asked yo aunty like he was surprised or somethin. I like Macky, but me likin him ain't got nothin to do with the situation. I don't know, Just don't underestimate nobody because you never know what somebody else got goin on behind closed doors." Rasheed continued.

Rarri looked at him and nodded in approval. He *was* putting too much trust in people. Sometimes that's coo, but not in the drug game. It was too cutthroat to be trusting muthafuckas in that area.

"So what you think we should do?"

"I wouldn't do nothin but watch him"

"A nigga got ain't time to be watchin cuh all day"

Rasheed laughed, "Don't even trip. I know a nigga who do"

"Ight, fasho try to get him to be on it asap because if it ain't Macky then it gotta be some other niggas" Rarri looked over at Rasheed seriously. "You gon be ready to get yo hands dirty?"

Rasheed chuckled, "They ain't never been clean my nigga" he answered honestly.

Rasheed might not have been a gangbanger like Rarri, but he still had bodies under his belt. Unknown to him, finding a reason to kill was just as much in Rasheed's blood as it was in Rarri's, if not more. It's been awhile since he relapsed into his murderous desires. Rasheed only carried a gun for protection. Other than that, he didn't really have too much care for them. As a kid, he found pleasure in dissecting his pets and hiding them in the backyard from his mom.

The day she found him in the middle of a dissection, she was horrified. Little Rasheed had her favorite poodle, Domino, split down the middle over a piece of Canvas he cut from an old tent. What really had her stomach turning was not how bloody he was but how neatly he had the dog's body parts placed on the side of him. Humming to himself, having the time of his life. When Mary's screams interrupted his little date, Rasheed just looked up at her with no expression. His demeanor calm, irritatingly calm.

Mary thought sending him to see a Psychologist would help but really it only helped him get better at hiding his secrets. Pets were child's play. Eventually, they started to bore him and that's when he graduated to people.

"Yea, we gon see" Rarri answered as he lit a blunt….

TWENTY-SEVEN

TONY WASN'T FEELING Heaven's decision about cutting Rarri and his crews off but she didn't give a fuck. These were 'her' lil niggas, not his. He couldn't even keep up with his own clientele these days so he damn sure didn't have no place in tryna manage hers. It was only a matter of time before she made the move she had been planning on this whole time. Until then, she would just keep on playing her part.

"You don't make these type of decisions without telling me first, do you understand?" Tony barked as he paced the room.

Heaven inhaled then exhaled trying to calm herself. She wanted to tell him that he wasn't running shit so bad but now wasn't the time. Heaven walked up and put her hands around him to stop his pacing then put her sad face on.

"I'm sorry, babe. I don't know what I was thinking. I was just so mad and got caught up in the moment, but that's still no reason for me to not tell you first" she kissed his earlobe slowly, how he liked it.

"It's ok" he assured her. His breathing immediately heavy. He felt his knees going weak and a tingling sensation throughout his body.

"No, it's not" Heaven demanded and bit his ear just hard enough to hurt, then walked over to the bed, pulled her shirt up, bent over doggy style, looked back at him and licked her lips seductively.

"I've been a bad girl come and punish me"

Tony's dick instantly grew heard as a rock. Reaching for his pants he couldn't undress quick enough.

"Keep that belt in your hands. I want you to come and spank me with it" She told him as she massaged her pussy.

Tony was mesmerized. Heaven knew how to keep a nigga all the way tuned in. She popped her cheeks like a stripper. Tony was ready to dive in dick first but when he tried, she stopped him.

"I said spank me first!"

He was so excited he forgot he was holding his shinola leather belt. He swatted her ass with it lightly.

"Harder!" she ordered.

He swatted her a little harder.

"HARDER!!" Tony did as he was told.

"HARDER!!" she demanded angrily.

Tony swung his belt with force turning her cheek red.

"Again"

Swat

"Again"

Swat

"Again! Again! Again!"

Tony dropped his belt, grabbed her by the waist, eased into her slowly and let out a manly moan. His dick was so hard it hurt. Never had he been this aroused in his life. Heaven seemed to always have that effect on him. Her pussy did something different every time he fucked her. Tony slid in and out of her slowly then stopped, trying to hold his nut but Heaven pushed her ass back into him.

He gripped her waist trying his best to stop her.

"Wait"

She didn't wait. She threw her ass back again and tightened her pussy muscles around him. Heaven was wet, so wet you could hear her pussy talking and moistening with every thrust. The squishy sounds sent him into overdrive. Tony couldn't hold it no longer, pulling out, he nutted on her ass. She turned around and put his dick in her mouth, twirling her tongue and sucking simultaneously.

He couldn't take it. His dick was too sensitive. Tony tried to pull out but Heaven locked her hands around his waist to keep him there. Her mouth was dripping spit down to her titties. Heaven pulled her shirt down, put his dick in between her breast, spit on the head then used both hands to press together for support, Pushing both of them up and down, licking the tip of his dick with drool dripping as she looked into his eyes was enough to get him hard all over again.

She held her mouth open as he titty fucked her. Every time he pushed up, she sucked the head and let it pop out loudly. He grabbed the back of her head and fucked her face roughly, takin his anger out on her mouth. Thirty minutes later, Tony was passed out with a big ass smile on his face. Heaven went to the shower to freshen up, after all, she had shit to do.

She knew her sex game was too good to be true. Too bad Tony didn't know she was taught to manipulate the best of em. When you leave this world, and go to Heaven, ain't no comin back.

TWENTY-EIGHT

'*MAN, THIS BITCH BE MOTOR MOUTHIN*' Pretty Me da P thought as Lae Lae went on and on about her life story.

He regretted even asking her but he knew sometimes these hoes just wanted somebody to vent to because nobody really took the time to listen to their stories, if they didn't involve sex or money. But, like the rest, he didn't give a fuck either. He just knew how to pretend a bit better. He hated how much she said '*and then*', when she told stories. She seemed to say that shit almost after every sentence describing '*every*' fuckin detail.

Lae Lae was so happy to be talking that she didn't even notice him dozing off. Or maybe she did because she kept tapping on him from time to time. He was just about to pass out when Lae Lae said something that woke his game up.

"What you say?"

"I said '*and then*' that's when I met Rarri. He the one that turned me out"

Her angry demeanor and facial expression didn't go unnoticed.

"How long was you down for him?"

She smacked her lips, "Not for long. I really wasn't feelin him like that so I got on."

He looked at her like was lying. "So, you just left cause you wasn't feelin his pimpin?"

"Daddy, I'm not goin to lie to you because that's not even how I get down" she replied looking him right in the eyes. "I got knocked by one of his cousins and when I tried to go back, he dissed me in front of everybody. I ran into him in L.A tryna get away from this other nigga who was doin me scandalous and Rarri just did me even worse. He made me say a bunch of shit while he recorded me on his phone. I only did it to get away from Macky but after I said everything he told me to say, he just kicked me in my ass so hard that I had to go to the hospital" Lae Lae couldn't stop her tears from falling. "Daddy, I *hate* him"

Pretty me da P wiped her eyes with his thumb then looked at her seriously.

"Me too"

She looked at him in disbelief. "You know him?"

"Yea, that lil bitch ass nigga set me up and stole from me"

She bit down on her lip thinking deeply for a split second then stood, "Well let's go get yo shit back"

He stood from the couch and paced the room in frustration. "It's more complicated than that"

"Then un-complicate it"

"It's not that simple, I-" He didn't want to expose his hand and blow his cover to a hoe who could potentially fuck everything up for him.

"You what?" she asked.

"Nothin, you wouldn't get it" he answered, sitting back down feeling defeated.

She sat down beside him. "Daddy, look at me"

When he looked at her, he could see the pain in her eyes and he knew she could see the pain in his.

"What we gotta do to get him? Whatever it is, don't even matter." She put her hand on his lap. "Let's just do it"

Pretty me da P knew the Tingly feeling in his heart was love. This was the first time he ever felt connected to a bitch outside of pimpin. Lae Lae was the first person to understand him without him having to even explain much. He leaned in and kissed her on the lips. That night they made love like tomorrow wouldn't come, but it did.

The Next Day…

"And you would be willing to testify to all of this in court?" Detective Mendez asked Lae Lae after hearing her story

She looked at Pretty me da P who was already looking at her then back at the detective.

"Proudly"

Mendez looked at Malone for assurance, he nodded his approval. Both Mendez and Lae Lae bit their lips trying to break the smiles on their faces.

"I told ya'll to have faith in ya boy" Pretty me da P told Malone with a big ass smile.

Mendez looked at him with a look of disgust which didn't go unnoticed by Lae Lae.

She locked hands with him, never takin her eyes off of Mendez to let her know the status of their relationship. Mendez cleared her throat in embarrassment because she knew Lae Lae was reading her intentions like a book.

"Just so we're clear, the deal is that if *we* bring ya'll Rarri, Daddy, I mean, Darshawn won't have to go back to jail, right?"

"Right" Mendez assured with a bit of an attitude.

Lae Lae looked at them suspiciously…

"Can we get that on paper? It's not that I don't trust ya'll or nothin, but I'm just tryna make sure that no matter what happens, he not the one who gets played."

Pretty me da P squeezed her hand tightly with love then gave her a kiss.

"Thanks baby"

"You know I got you" she told him with a smile then looked back at Detective Mendez seriously.

"So?"

She rolled her eyes at Lae-Lae annoying ass, "If you find it necessary, I don't.."

"Yea, I don't think this would work without that"

"No problem, but just so we're clear" Mendez pointed at herself and Malone.." If it turns out your lying about any of this, I'm going to throw your ass in jail right alone with your little pretty boyfriend"

Lae Lae pulled out her phone, scrolled for a moment then handed it to her. When Mendez pressed play and saw the video her heart sank and her blood boiled. When it was over, she looked at Lae Lae with sympathy.

"You have my word Laelani, I'm goin to bust his ass" she promised as she handed her back her phone then held out her hand, "Truce?"

She smiled back at the detective, shook her hand then gave her a hug. Mendez was trying her hardest not to cry. These were the moments she lived for. Helping victims lock up the people who victimized them. What Rarri didn't know was that by posting everything on social media for a couple of likes, he was actually helping the police by building a case against himself for them.

"Can I talk to you in private?" Malone asked Pretty me da P

"Yup" he answered as he followed him into the kitchen. Pretty me da P grabbed two sodas out of the refrigerator and gave one to Malone then cracked his open.

"So wassup?"

"Evans attorney wants you to talk to his investigator about the assault"

Pretty me da P looked at the door in mid-sip making sure Lae-Lae wasn't there to hear. He didn't tell her about what Shawn did to him. Telling on a nigga was one thing, but being raped by one was a whole other story. The last thing he wanted to do was run her off or have her looking at him like he was any less of a man then already felt he was.

Malone could see that he wasn't tryna carryon with the case against Shawn. He also noticed how happy he seemed around Lae-Lae.

"Look, Don't tell Mendez I told you but victims don't *have* to talk to the defense, unless they want to"

"So, I could refuse?"

"Yea, if that's what you want to do"

"What if I didn't want to press charges anymore"

"So, it was consensual?"

"NO!"

"Well, we might have to convince the D.A that it was and that you were just embarrassed so you made the whole thing up"

"You for real?" Pretty me da P asked in embarrassment.

"Yea, I mean the D.A is a real dick and he wants Evans. I don't see him dropping this case for any other reason…He's going to want to throw you back in jail for wasting his time with this but after we prove how much closer we are to catching Rarri and how many people we were able to lock up because of you, I'm pretty sure you'll be off the hook, again."

Pretty me da P exhaled deeply. He just wanted to put the situation with Shawn behind him(Well, I don't know if that's the best way for him to put it to people without them finding humor in his choice of words) Regardless, of all that he was willing to say whatever he had to say to keep the incident a secret now

"Thanks Malone, I appreciate that"

"No problem, Just make sure your girl sticks around long

enough to testify in court." Malone warned. "If this thing backfires, I don't know if I'll be able to get you out of whatever the D.A will have in store for you" He looked around the lavish kitchen. "They've invested a lot of money in this. Don't make em regret it."

Pretty me da P nodded, Malone cracked his soda, took a sip then walked out leaving him to think about everything for a minute. He was going to have to keep Lae Lae glued to his hip. He didn't mind though. That just meant he would be able to get to know her even more now and that's something he, for the first time was actually looking forward to. He wanted to do all types of square shit with her, that he never felt comfortable doing with other bitches.

Last night, he let his guard down, put pimpin to the side and showed Lae Lae who "Darshawn" and she understood him. She made him feel different. She made him feel special and he made her feel the same way. Even though they had really just met, Lae Lae knew it was love at first sight. Her pussy ain't never get this wet for another nigga like it did for him. Not only that, she genuinely liked the person he was on the inside.

She knew he wasn't the type to be vulnerable to bitches so the conversations they had last night spoke in volumes. Never in her life has she felt this for anyone else besides her son(Who they planned to go get once all this was over) Lae Lae was determined to prove her loyalty to Pretty me da P by helping him bring down Rarri so he can remain free. After that, he said they were going to move somewhere where they could settle down and start a family of their own.

Deep down, that's all Lae Lae ever wanted to do. Get married, cook, clean and take care of the kids. She just hoped he wasn't running game about wanting the same things.

'Naw, he ain't. This is real' she assured herself as he walked back in the room behind Malone.

TWENTY-NINE

THE MORNING WAS COLD, foggy and moist. Most people were on their way to work or just getting off and headed home. Luckily for them, Trigg was lurkin for someone else today. Today, he wanted to show the lil niggas he picked to run wit how to really slide on some shit. Dula, Sagger, Shooter and Franko was the hardest lil niggas he knew.

They stayed in some shit and was ready to do whatever they had to do to keep their names ringing. They seen how Trigg came up and wanted to do the same. The four of them fucked with Rarri and lil Dink too but they gravitated more towards Trigg because he was younger, wilder and still the same grimy lil nigga they always knew him to be.

Unlike Rarri and Lil Dink, Trigg didn't really floss his money like that. Other than a fly car he didn't spend on nothing other than guns. Trigg loved guns more than gold chains, rings and all that other shit that make niggas standout. He might have been young but he knew the best way for him to creep up on niggas was to blend in with them.

"Man, ya'll niggas better calm the fuck down wit all that in the back of my shit." Trigg said and adjusted his rearview mirror so he could keep his eyes on the trio in the back of the G-ride.

They all got quiet not wanting to fuck with their chance to finally get to shoot somebody In front of Trigg. Them arguing over who was going to bust first made Trigg proud but he only smiled on the inside. They reminded him of how he used to always argue wit Spank over the same shit.

"Ya'll need to be payin more attention to what's goin on around ya'll instead of arguin…you gotta always be on the same page wit the niggas you slidin wit. You gotta look at it like yall a football team. Everybody can't be the quarterback my nigga. It don't matter who get the ball if we don't score when it's on us"

They all nodded

"Soon as these niggas come out yall jump out and get craccin on YAAHMPTON crip, if anybody still breathin when we pull off, all ya'll getting a D.P"

Nobody said nothing but they said alot. They knew right now wasn't the time to play no games because getting a D.P wasn't something to be proud of. Especially when it's over some shit dealing with putting in work. Trigg took this shit serious and wanted to groom them to be the same way.

Losing Spank fucked his life up all ways around. Trigg learned the hard way what lacking comes wit. Never in a million years did he think he would have to bring harm to his best friend's mom. What fucked him up the most was that he knew it was all his fault because he should have kept his mouth shit like Rarri told him to.

Ain't a day go by that he didn't relive that shit. Trigg wished so badly that he would have just let Spank shine so he would be the one who had gotten shot. No matter how many times he tried to rewind time in his mind the reality of the situation was that, wasn't no going back. All he could do now was keep saggin on shit.

• • •

Trigg was probably one of the coolest niggas to hang around because he was funny as fuck. But, when it came time to lay a nigga down he was heartless.

"There they go right there" Shooter pointed out.

"Damn, they got Tinka wit em" he added then quickly looked from the passenger seat to the back at Franko who everybody knew as in love with Tinka.

When Shooter looked at Trigg and seen his expression he cocked his .45 and pulled his mask down. The rest of them did the same. Franko was sweating bullets and his heart was beating so hard that he was surprised nobody else in the car could hear it. He out of all of them couldn't wait to body one of the Nunley cousins. They were all each others nemeses. It was always on sight with them whenever they ran into each other. From first fights to chasing each other with bats, you name it, nothing was off limits.

The Nunley cousins fasho was the lil niggas poppin in their hood. Mainly because the Nunleys had been there for generations and it was a lot of them. Trigg pulled away from his parking spot at just the right speed making sure not to startle or alert the intended targets. He's done this so many times that now he was a pro.

Franco's blood boiled as he seen Tinka walkin hand and hand with lil Freddy. She knew how much he hated that nigga but she still couldn't stop fuckin with him. Tinka looked at him like a brother or something close to it because of how long they knew each other but he wanted more than that. He was tired of being stuck in the friend zone when he knew her better than anybody.

This wasn't no save-a-hoe mission though. Tinka had told Franko that she had broken up with lil Freddy a week ago but here she was the very next day back with him like nothing ever happened.

'I told you stay away from this nigga' he thought to himself as the car crept closer hoping somehow, some way, if possible she could hear what he was thinking and run (she didn't).

The group of young niggas was so busy talking that they didn't even notice when the car stopped just a few feet ahead of them.

"HOP OUT!"

Shooter was the first one out followed by the rest of them. Just as Trigg had told him, Shooter ran all the way up on his man. Lil Freddy and his cousins were froze. Everything happened so fast that they didn't even have time to react. For a split second they thought it was a joke.

BANG!

Without hesitation shooter put one in the young nigga standing closest to him head followed by another two in the face. Sagger and Dula followed suit sending shots at the others standing around. Bullets ripped through the young niggas with no mercy leaving a bloody mess on the concrete beneath them. Everybody was doing their shit. everybody except Franko.

He was looking down at Tinka who had a hole in her neck and blood comin out of her mouth. She was trying to breathe but the bullet sagger hit her with in the lung made that near impossible. Franko was close enough to hear that she was trying to call her momma. 'Momma' was the only thing she could think of at the time. Tinka wanted her momma 'so' bad. He couldn't move after seeing bullets literally knock her shoes off of her feet leaving her on the ground mangled in her now bloody socks. She tried using one of her legs to get up but it kept falling limp.

'mo-mma, mo-mma, mo'

Boom! Boom! Boom!

Sagger coldly put another three in her chest for fuckin with an enemy.

"Come on!" he yelled as he tried to pull Franko out of his daze to no avail before following the others back to the car.

Franko's legs grew weak and he fell to his knees. Everything went black before he could think of anything else. Trigg put one in the back of his head, grabbed the gun from off of the ground, ran back to the car then pulled off leaving Frankos' brains mixed with lil Freddy's.

———

Lil Dink was hot as fish grease. He couldn't believe what was hearing. He wanted to focus more on his money but that was easier said than done with Trigg running around like he Rambo every damn day.

"It ain't no dull moments wit you, cuh" Lil Dink barked angrily. "You just always gotta do some shit."

"You ain't got nothin rolled up?"

"What?"

"Weed, nigga." Trigg replied like lil Dink was stupid. "You ain't got none rolled up?"

Lil Dink just stood there and stared at him in disbelief. Trigg waved him off, went to the cabinet where Lil Dink kept his already rolled blunts at, grabbed two of them, put both of them in his mouth then lit them at the same time then held one out to Lil Dink.

"Cuh, what the fuck is wrong wit you?"

The look he gave him said it all It was one of them *'how 'you' even goin to ask some dumb shit like that?'* looks. That look always made him feel bad because he knew what was wrong with him. Times like these always made Lil Dink wish he wouldn't have left Trigg at home with his baby momma because he would be chilling with his son right now instead of running around town on some crazy shit.

Even though Trigg was the one who fucked up by tellin Spanks mom what happened, Lil Dink still felt more responsible for creating the new demon inside of him. He grabbed the blunt from Trigg then took a hit as he sat on the couch.

"So why ya'll down, cuh?"

"He froze on some scary shit" Trigg replied bluntly.

"His mom's know ya'll was wit him?"

"Nope, I had them lil niggas meet me in the darc."

"Ight, coo, where they at now?"

Trigg laughed, "I dropped them off at school"

"What's funny?"

"You and all these damn questions. When you become all inquisitive and shit?"

"When yo dumb ass start usin words like 'inquisitive'? Lil Dink shot back.

"When he started fuckin with me" Myesha intervened as she walked into the living room. "You ready, boo?"

"I am now" he rushed to say as his heart skipped a beat at the sight of her.

The feelin he got when in her presence was something he never got used to. She always made him happy. She seemed to be the only person who really understood him. Rarri and Lil Dink were his boys but she gave him a different type of love and even though she didn't agree with his lifestyle, she picked his brain and planted the type of seeds that made him better at what he did.

Myesha knew he was going to keep killing shit, she just wanted to make sure he never got caught doing it. He was a young loc and she honestly couldn't see herself fuckin with nobody else. She knew without a doubt in her mind that his love came from a pure place and that's something Myesha cherished deeply. The two of them together assured true love could prosper in a place where most people felt hopeless.

Wasn't a better couple around. Everybody knew them and their story so it didn't take long for others to aspire to be more like them. She was a business owner who came from nothing. He was a young shooter who was still in the hood shooting shit even though he had enough money to be elsewhere. They had it all. The only thing missing now was their 'Happy ending'

He put his blunt out, got up and greeted Myesha with a kiss.

"Where ya'll bout to go?"

"Damn, mind yo business" she replied between kisses.

"You is my business. Matter of fact, is yall ever goin to sit down and tell me what's goin on wit ya'll? Like when all this-" Lil dink waved them down like they were dirty. "..became a thing?"

Trigg and Myesha looked at each other for a second. "NAW" they both said, laughed and made their way out of the house.

"Whatever!" he yelled at them then pulled out his phone and hit stanky pussy you-know-who with a big ass smile on his face.

THIRTY

R<small>ASHEED PULLED</small> up on a group of P's in the Big Lot's parking lot on Sepulveda Blvd.

"Man we was just about to hit ya'll niggas, P" A tall black skinny pimp with about five gold chains on said in excitement as Rarri and Rasheed got out of the car.

Rasheed knew that excitement all too well. It was that excitement niggas got when they had some drama to tell. That excitement *'some'* niggas seemed to live for more that pimpin itself. The smirk on the dude's face told Rasheed that he as fasho one of em.

"What's the deal?" Rasheed asked as they P-shook with the group.

"Yea 'P', it's like this wit no cut, niggas tryna put pimpin in court"

Rasheed laughed, " Fuck out of here nigga. Ain't a pimp breathin got cause to put me in a circle."

"Naw, not you" he replied then looked at Rarri, "Him"

Rarri just looked at him like he was stupid with an even broader smirk.

"On what charges?" Rasheed asked defensively.

"Mispimpin" another P spoke up immediately looking at Rarri like he should be ashamed of himself.

"Mispimpin?" Rarri asked in disbelief "On what bitch?"

"All of em young blood" an older pimp said as she stepped out of the all white benz everybody was standing next to.

The windows were tinted so black that Rarri and Rasheed didn't even notice him sitting in there but judging by his Balenciaga loafers, Salvatore Ferragamo suit and the Patek Philippe on his wrist they knew he was some real pimpin. His hair was short and wavy. The edge up he rocked was more on point than Steve Harvery's (When he had hair).

The scar that cut from the top of his eyebrow down to the bottom of his right eye, along with the cauliflower on his ears let you know he's had his share of scuffles. Probably even been to the pen a couple of times seeing as how calm he was. He looked ready for any type of confrontation that presented itself. Not knowing what to expect, he still stood there cooler than a block of ice.

"First off I ain't yo Blood, *cuh*. I'm Rarri from Parc village crip" Rarri responded..

"So I've heard. my apologies for the misconstruing. I assumed your inadequacy was only in a certain region but now I see you must be feeble in other places as well" He schooled sounding well-spoken knowing Rarri probably couldn't even understand some of the cheapest words he could think of.

He looked at his watch waiting for Rarri's response but Rarri didn't even know what to say to that shit.

"Well. Rarri from 'Parc Village crip', I'm not into the ole gang-bangin thing. I'm 'some pimpin' and a whole lot of it out of the Hollywood division. I go by Fast Track and I been pimpin before yo daddy was swimmin in 'his' daddy nut sack, ya dig"

The other P's laughed, Rarri stepped forward for an altercation but Rasheed stopped him. Fast track looked at Rarri with a blank expression.

"Naw, chill" Rasheed told him in a low voice but was still heard.

He was looking at Fast track through wide eyes. He had heard stories about him from a lot of the older P's he met over time but this was the first time ever seeing him in the flesh. Fast Track was rumored to be one of the coldest pimps to have ever lived. Spending most of his life in and out of prison, he stopped getting the recognition he deserved in pimpin but his jail rep went just as far.. They say he even had some C.O bitches selling pussy to inmates out in Mississippi for him. In Cali he not only had bitches bringing in dope but he also had some hoes to come bust it open in the visiting room for some of the tricks there too. He was getting money all ways around.

They say he got his name by putting his bitches down when it was slow at the oddest times of the day. At first everybody laughed at him claiming him to be crazy and scared to put his bitches down wit pimpin around. That's up until it started slowing down for everybody else speeding up for him. After doing that on multiple blades around he earned the Moniker 'Fast Track'.

Fast Track smiled at Rasheed. "I've heard a lot of good things about you, young blood, Rasheed, right?"

"Yea" Rasheed replied amazed to have his name known by a legend as they 'P'-shook

"Nice to meet you, main. Yo name been ringin in the game the *'right way'*, keep it up, ya dig" Fast Track said proudly.

"Fasho P... All I know is to mash and bash on these hoes"

Fast track looked at Rarri "Maybe after court you could give yo boy here a couple of pointers"

"Pointers?" Rarri asked heatedly "I don't need no pointers from *'no'* nigga. talkin bout takin me to court. I don't even know you nigga. Better go sit yo old ass down somewhere."

Fast Track had heard way worst so nothing Rarri said hurt him. He chuckled to himself.

"We goin to be back right here at 12 o'clock tomorrow night in the same spot.. Show up or not it ain't going to make me no differ-ence, ya dig.." he said as he opened his car door. "Hell, if I was a chilli pimp I would dodge me too" He added with a laugh while getting in his whip.

Fast track rolled his window down, looked Rarri over, then shook his head as he pulled off. The other P's standing there loaded into the car they came in and left as well.

"You believe that shit? Nigga talkin about court." Rarri replied angrily. "FUCK CUH, COURT!"

"Fuck his court?" Rasheed asked in disbelief. " P' a legend and he got 'yo' name on a spike with probable charges.. Open yo eyes niggas this shit fa real"

"My eyes open, yours seem to be closed as soon as you seen the nigga of yo dreams and shit." Rarri looked at Rasheed in disgust. "You ain't even back a nigga, my nigga. You just stood there on some weak shit."

"What you mean, *weak shit,* 'P', I been tellin you about havin yo bitches runnin around all reckless but you don't like to listen to 'nobody'. You know it all so a nigga can't tell you *nothin,* but you quick to turn around and say we all on the same page.. If that's the case then act like it my nigga, don't just say that shit" Rasheed looked at Rarri and shook his head, knowing he wasn't listening to shit he was saying. "You got to get out of that shit, my nigga. You be too quick to let a nigga get under yo skin, then you bringin that gangbangin shit in the game when you know that ain't coo. Rarri, you better than that, 'P "

Rarri knew he was out of line for that shit but his lips were still in a knot. Rasheed didn't give a fuck about him being mad. Wasn't no way in hell he was going to let him blow his coo and fuck up what they got going. He took this pimpin shit serious and despite his hidden agenda, he still couldn't stand to see another nigga run circles around his lil brother.

"You think I don't see 'why' this nigga poppin up all of a sudden?" Rasheed asked as he got in Rarri's face. "Mothafuckas goin to try and stop what we on as soon as they can. I'm game tight, 'P'. I see through all that divide and conquer shit he was tryna do but I ain't expose my hand like 'you' just did...Let him take you to court. It ain't the end of the world. The best of em done been brought up on charges, It ain't about how you go in 'P', it's all about how you come out"

One thing Rarri couldn't stand was another pimp tryna tell him how to run his bitches but this was the game and even though he was creating a new lane, that didn't mean he had the right to disrespect this one. The only mothafuckas Fast Track could be talking about is the Bentley Bitches and they was on some other shit now. Whatever it was, he decided to hear it out.

"You right, 'P'" Rarri admitted. "I was on some bullshit. A nigga shouldn't even had let that shit get to me. My bad, foo. We good?"

"Always" Rasheed replied and the two P-shook.

"So, what know?"

"I'm pretty sure he done called up a cold circle" Rasheed pulled out his phone and started texting away into a group chat. "So, let's call ours."

"On everything" Rarri laughed in approval, "on everything"

––––––––

12pm the next day..

"What I tell ya'll? When you put some big pimpin in front of these young punks, they gon run for the hills, ya dig" Fast track laughed as he slapped fives wit his pimp patnas.

"You ain't never lyin mane, I been servin these lil niggas left and right, thinkin they some pimpin til some real pimpin pull up. They ain't built like us." A pimp in an all blue suit with the matching gators boasted as he lifted his pimp cup, "A toast to the era of the real pimps"

"To the real PIMPS!" They all cheered then sipped out of their cups.

"What they thought, tryna form somethin without permission from the higher ups?" Another Pimp asked in disgust. "That lil shit ain't even last a week"

"Honk! Honk! Honk!

Just as he finished, car after car started pulling up and honking their horns, interrupting all conversations in the parking lot. Nothing but foreigns flooded in heavily. The twenty or so old niggas found themselves blocked in and surrounded by twice as many young niggas. They all hopped and went to the "court circle" bussed down and fly as fuck. Not saying a word, just looking at the old pimps like they weren't as important.

"So, what's up, 'P'? Rarri asked Fast track as he emerged from the crowd.

Fast track was impressed but he wasn't going to show it. Pimpin for so long taught him how to have a cold poker face.

"Young Blood!" he said loudly like they were the best of friends. Really hoping Rarri would blow his cool again in front of the crowd. "Here I was thinkin you wasn't goin to show. I guess in *some* ways, I've misjudged you."

He put his hand out and the two P-shook.

"Maybe, Maybe not" he replied looking him in the eyes.

"I ain't gon sit here and lie and act like I ain't go about the shit the wrong way" Rarri paced around as he spoke thinking deeply. "I was in my feelings for all the wrong reasons. He laughed. "How I'ma be mad at pimpin for being on his job? You ain't no rink-a-dink out here hatin on young niggas cause you ain't relevant no more. If anything, me not knowin who you was means I'm not on my shit as much as I '*thought*' I was. When I think about it, if I was A legend in the game and I heard about a young 'P' out here runnin around all reckless and shit . I would put his ass in a circle too. Then, put his pimpin on a choppin block if he got in his feelings about it. So I appreciate you givin me the opportunity to better my izm. We all plan to be great but I can't do that with closed ears and a narrow vision. I gotta be able to hear and see things from all angles. All of us do" He waved over to all the P's he came with. Then he looked back at Fast Track with a quick smirk then putting back on his serious face, he kept talking.

"So, 'we' was thinkin after all this is over with, if ya'll don't mind, maybe we could come to some sort of agreement. Honestly, we goin to keep doin our thing regardless but if Og's like ya'll could pull over coats that would avoid a lot of mishaps and keep the cycle of good game in rotation."

Fast track smiled in approval. He didn't expect Rarri to come in as he did and he saw the game being dropped on him at the same time. That made him instantly like Rarri. You see, he was a control freak, like almost every other pimp in the world. Initially a couple of days ago when he heard about what some young nigga named Rarri was doing, he knew his phone would soon be ringing off of the hook for an invitation. But, the only calls he received were from the pimps who felt left out.

Not being able to be apart of something meant they wouldn't be in a position to control it. The only option left was for them to go against it, so everything Rarri did was put on display. Fast Track dug up any and every thing he could on Rarri. Once he found out about the Bentley Bitches, it wasn't hard for him to poke holes in Rarri's program. To him, no bitch breathing should be aloud to run around so freely, especially like Bird out there shooting pimps and shit.

Back in his days, some shit like that would have never had happened but these weren't his days anymore. It was different times now. *'The game need a young P like him'* he thought to himself *but it also needs a bit time king pimp like myself to keep order. I could do big things with him under my wing.*

"You know, young blood, for as long as I've been in this here game. I ain't neva seen pimpin come into a circle like you just did" Fast track admitted then put his hand over his heart. "Young pimpin, you impressed me… so much so, that I don't even believe court should be held over you right now" he turned to his patnas as chatter erupted. "Excuse my pimpin but I would like to dismiss these charges brought up against Rarri…we don't hold court to break pimpin down, we hold it to build pimpin 'up'!

He added with passion and his patnas along with Rarri's cheered in agreement. The only ones who were quiet were the group of young instigating pimps who were in the parking lot yesterday with Fast Track. This was not how they expected things to go down. Now they were in a gray area and judging by how Rarri looked at them, they surely would never be accepted on his side.

"Only a good pimp 'see' his wrongs as things he needs to right and we all just seen that Rarri is one of em" Fast Track preached in full blown pimp mode as he paraded around getting everybody hype. He looked at Rarri and shook his shoulders like he had the chills.

"He a 'cold' young pimp and ima make sure he get even colda, ya understand me, you gotta pimp 'hard', Rarri, cause 'hard' is the only way to pimp. Keep your foot on these bitches necks and don't 'ever' let up, ya understand. The back of a hoe head needs to look like the bottom yo shoe, ya dig. Know a hoe ain't nothin without a pimp's instructions, ya feel me, mane? Neva let her lick the tip before she hit the mitt or give a renegade bitch a drip of spit"

"Preach P" Rarri cheered in excitement which made Fast Track damn near catch the Holy Ghost.

"Oh, Ima preach to em, ha, Tell these hoes ima leach to em, ha. Dirty hoes I'm bleach to em, ha. Foggy bitches I see through em, ha. Ooooh I eat through em, ha" He preached really sounding like a preacher then walked up to Macky who was filming the whole thing and put his face to the camera to make a scene and get the spotlight pimps loved so dearly.

"Preach!" Everybody cheered at the same time.

Fast Track shook his sweaty face dramatically making his

cheeks wobble like a fat boy. "They gon shake it till we make it, ha.. Race it to they favorite, ha. mmm, mmm ,mmm I could taste it, ha. Yeaah they gon hate it, ha." He grabbed the camera to hold it steady in Macky's hand and pointed to the lense. "Let me tell ya, I come from a long line of good heifers and big steppas, ha. This chess, not checkers and can't a pimp check us, ha. We gone take what they ain't gon let us, ha. That bread go good with the lettuce, ha. It's cop and blow so we knocked some moe, when them hoes left us, ha. Look around these pimps don't ride buses, ha. Put a one leg bitch down on crutches, ha...I done pimped on the toughest, ha, I'm talkin bout the real-deep down in the street roughest, ha. My bitch sugar daddy bald now, ha. I got a country hoe that'll wrestle a Hogg down, ha. I done rid that bitch so long she need a smog now, ha. Matter of fact, she still on the Track right now with her draws down, ya understand me"

His old ass was going in like a mothafucka. He ain't felt this good in years. This was exactly what his pimpin needed right now because fasho these young niggas social medias would be the endless boost of publicity he needed to go viral. Fast Track felt back again, young even. Seeing some old pimpin look this happy put a smile on Rasheed's face. Fast Track was so into his mode, he animated almost every word he said. This was a moment Rasheed truly would never forget. This was the shit he lived for, pimpin coming together and moving as one.

He knew how valuable having a legend like Fast Track with them could be because most of the well known older pimps didn't even dare to get on a legend's bad side. Though, they would never admit as much.

"Ain't nobody goin to be able to tell us shit' Rasheed thought to himself as he looked at Macky just in time to catch his face harden.

It's like time moved in slow motion as Macky looked at Rarri and mouthed the words "Break, cuh"

"No" Rasheed mouthed as he shook his head hoping they didn't do anything stupid.

Rarri nodded back to him then looked at Fast Track with that million dollar smile.

"Say 'P', goin introduce me so I could tell em what they should have told you, mane" He said in full pimp mode matching Fast Tracks' impression.

"Say no mo young pimpin" he said as he pulled Rarri next to him. "To all of ya'll out there who don't know, please take time to remember this face because this is what the future of pimpin look like. All you young niggas out there perpetration like ya'll some pimpin shoulda stayed in ya mammy ass and that's words of wisdom comin from a real legend in these streets. If ya'll ain't pimpin to ball, ya'll ain't pimpin at all, ya understand. Rarri, go'n and kick that fly shit and tell em what they should have told me."

Rarri looked into the camera as fly as he could while Fast Track stood there looking like a proud father.

"Yea, ya'll know who it is, Rarri da great, AKA, Mr. Bussdown in the flesh. Get a pen and some paper and I'll teach you how to break a bitch easy, ya understand me? I could knock a hoe anywhere you see a bitch cause I'm BABE street certified, ya dig. I'm standin right here wit a legend who done been down and around before I was even born. You know what say, he done touched every blade in the USA. He got more game then you could play. So, I'm wonderin why the FUCK didn't nobody tell this old washed up fossil in the dirt, dinosaur face ass nigga how I dust off antiques?"

The baffled look on Fast track's face was priceless. He didn't even know what to say. Everything was happenin so fast all he could do was stand there and look stupid as the crowd of young niggas went crazy.

"Yo heart was in the right place so I ain't even gon dog you like I want to" Rarri said as he looked at Fast track. "But since you got a problem wit this new shit, here go some old game for yo old ass"

He pulled a banana peel out of his back pocket and threw at fast tracks feet. "You just got peeled nigga" He added as three of Fast track's hoes walked up with their heads down. The crowd erupted yet again. Fast rack and his patnas was standing there in complete shock, Rarri's too. The only person who knew what he was doing was Macky. "*If* you really some big pimpin go'n knock yo bitches back. They only standin right there" He instructed but Fast Track didn't move. Not because he didn't want to, but because he physically couldn't. This shit paralyzed him.

In all of his years in the game he had never been done like this and the fact that Rarri made it seem as if he was going easy on him made him, for the first time in his life, question his own pimpin. He fell right into some bullshit. The last thing he thought when putting his bitches down today was Rarri knockin them. You see, all the talking Fast track was doing about Rarri only made his bitches that much more curious. So, when he pulled up popin that fly shit they ain't hesitate to choose up.

Had he not been overly confident and had not underestimated another man's game, no matter how young he was. He probably would still have his hoes and his career. But, now it was over. Don't get it twisted, he could always pimp but this moment was going to be one he would be remembered by most. The fact that all of this was being filmed was even worst because it gave people the option to see it over and over again.

Wasn't no escapin this shit. Deep down, he knew he would forever be a prisoner of this moment.

"Somebody get this old nigga a towel, he sweatin and shit" Rarri clowned then out of nowhere Fast track fell to the flood as his entire body locked up and shut down on him. The young niggas laughed.

"He havin a heart attack somebody call 9-1-1" One of the other older 'P's" cried out.

"Ya'll bitches get back in the whip, we bout to slide out" Rarri laughed as he turned to leave and they did as told not giving a flying fuck about Fast track who was literally on the floor, dying.

Macky scandalous ass was still filming every moment of the

tragedy with tears in his eyes from laughing so hard. This was the first time any of them had witnessed some shit like this, So, everybody was hyped up to the fullest and couldn't wait for Macky to upload that shit so they could repost it. Rasheed grabbed Rarri by the arm.

"What the fuck was that?"

"That shit was funny, right?" Rarri chuckled.

"Funny?" Rasheed asked in disbelief. "You didn't have to do that. I thought we was comin here to squash shit"

"*We* did and I squashed that nigga career like a bug as soon as I stepped on it"

"Watch that 'B' word" Macky joked as he walked up finger fuckin his phone. Rarri snatched his arm away.

"Let me tell you somethin, Sheed. I will never let a nigga get away with callin me weak and damn sure won't let no old nigga say I'm no chili Pimp. I ain't worried about them coming from us, they need to be worried bout us coming for them" He said seriously as he walked all the way up in Rasheed's face.

"You said we all kings, right?" So is you ready to show these niggas or what?"

Looking in Rarri's eyes, Rasheed could see nothing but sureness and as he looked at all the young niggas standing around, he saw the same thing. The two of them 'P' shook and embraced in a hug, easing the tension.

"Why ya'll at least ain't tell me what was going on?" he joked.

"Cause all you was gon try to do is talk a nigga out of it" Rarri laughed.

"I wanted to but cuh made me bang it on the set not to, before he even told me what was goin on" Macky admitted as he finally uploaded the video. "It's done, ya'll!"

Everybody talked and laughed in excitement as they went to comment and reshare the footage.

"Damn P, yo name about to be ringin like a mothafucka" Rasheed said in excitement as he too went to repost the video. "You done served a nigga into a heart attack, P, on camera. This type of shit ain't never happen"

Rarri looked over at Fast Track as he was still on the floor looking stupid as fuck. "He just another one like the other ones, P" he replied then got in his car with his new bitches. "Ya'll bitches ready to get this money or what?"

"Hell yea!" they all cheered happily rambling about what just happened.

Rarri had already broke on them hoes as soon as he seen them. Not only did they hit him with a knot of gwap, they also gave him the drop on the spot, so off top, Rarri hit his boys making sure Fast Track got knocked and Flocked. He pulled off bangin 'Rather give you my bitch' by Sugarfree...

THIRTY-ONE

"HELL NAW!" G-man said seriously as he stood from the lavish Oakwood table. "I thought you said it was an emergency and that Rarri needed me"

"It is and *he* do need you" Heaven replied.

He shook his head, "Naw, this sound like somethin you need"

Heaven jumped up angrily. "You damn right I need it! Just like I needed my father"

"That trick ass nigga stabbed me so I shot em. What the fuck was I supposed to do?"

"You could have shot him in the leg, arm or anywhere else but you shot him in the back of the head as he was walking away." She recalled.

"Where the fuck do they do that at?" he asked looking her right into her eyes.

She hated those eyes but loved them at the same time. Really she just hated them on G-man but she loved them on Rarri because they always made her feel close to god. If it wasn't for those eyes, G-man would have literally been close enough to touch him.

Heaven blew out in frustration as she palmed and rubbed her forehead to calm down.

She hated debating with mothafuckas. This wasn't no negotiation and if this was anybody else she was talking to, the conversation would have been terminated and the new topic would have been on where to bury the body but He didn't know that side of her, yet.

"Look, I'm not tryin to argue with you. I guess you did what you had to do. Fuck it, It's over now and talkin about it ain't goin to bring nobody back and I wouldn't wanna talk about it wit *you* anyway" she explained calmly. "..But, what I wanna talk about is what Rarri need and yea, you damn right, *his* needs are my needs too because I'm the bitch who's gon make sure shit gets done." She stared him down as she kept going. "Now, I know you don't like my momma. To keep it real, I don't like her neither, but that boy…" she pointed to Rarri who was outside with a couple of his boys smoking and laughing causing G-man to look out at him too. "That boy is important and he's the gift that yo son and my sister gave us before they left."

She couldn't hold back her tears but Heaven still stood there strong.

"He's all I got and no matter how we feel, that boy out there loves my momma a million times more than any of us could *ever* hate her"

She wiped her eyes and straightened herself. "She was doin so bad the last time we went to go see her that it almost broke em… and you've seen how strong he is. That boy don't break nothin but a pimp's profits."

"When a hoe outta pocket" they said at the same time, quoting one of god's lines and shared a laugh.

Both of them for a moment found themselves lost in good memories.

"I gotta see him at his best, pops." Heaven went on as she looked back out of the window. "I really do"

G-man walked to the other side of the table and gave Heaven a hug so warm and loving that she immediately broke down in his arms. It was a hug only a proud father can give to his child and she had never felt that until now. Seeing as how she never called him Pops before, he knew in his mind and felt in his heart that her last statement was spoken through Heaven from god himself. He was certain of it. He could feel him in there.

"You couldn't of copped better" he said never wanting to let go.

'What the fuck?' Heaven asked her self after a moment then pushed him away, hating that she allowed herself to look weak in front of a man. "Don't ever hug me again!" she said, pointing at him shamefully.

When he put his hands up, shrugged his shoulders and took a step back with that same million dollar smile, she instantly smiled because it reminded her of god on her eighteenth birthday. She couldn't stay mad at G-man.

"So, is you gon do it or what?"

"Yea, I guess I could have at it, one more time." He answered.

"Damn, ok. Ok. That's wassup" Heaven responded looking at him in approval. "I thought yo old ass was gon have to check in wit your wife first or something." She added, laughing

He gave her that, 'yea the fuck right' face.

"Don't let the gray hairs fool you. I still run this shit like a sewage line" he boasted.

"So, you ready to go?" Heaven asked as she picked up her purse and keys.

"This a one man rodeo, sweetheart. You can go on and sit this one out"

"You still know how to get there?"

"How could I forget.." He said as he turned to leave.

Now, G-man would never admit this, but once in the car he did call his wife to let her know what was going on, not to ask though... never that😳😂.

THIRTY-TWO

TWO WEEKS HAD PASSED and Rarri and his boys were pimpin up a storm in the streets. Bitches couldn't even get kicked out of their folks car without getting pressed before he pulled off. Niggas was bouncing out on hoes, bussdown in new pieces, draped in designer and pushing the latest foreigns, not giving a fuck about the police. It was a bullshit nigga's nightmare and a bad bitches' dream.

They had the option of fuckin with the flyest of the flyest. It seemed as if overnight life sped up to a whole new pace. Pimps and hoe's flocked in groups. It was nothing to see twenty bitches standing on one street hoecializing then drive down to the next block and see the same thing. The blades were poppin but the back streets were where it was really at. That's because not everybody wanted to be seen. Especially not the lowkey hoes whose brothers and family members be lurkin, ready to trip on a pimp for having her out there.

From the inside looking out, squares come in different forms, shapes, colors and sizes. So those with the capability of inverting the normal laws of geometry can see it clearly. Those who can't are who we call squares Aka the stupid mothafuckas who don't know that no matter what, the bitch was going to get out there and sell that shit regardless. Blame the bitch, not the pimp.

The only thing pimpin goin to '*make*' a bitch do is wanna pay him *willingly*. To all those who need the formula of simplifying like exponents explained, let me tell you, as sure as Pi equals 3.14, you could bet your last dollar they will stay the same. Translation: Shut the fuck up and listen and you will hear these bitches tell you step by step on how they *want* to be played.

This applies to all bitches not just prostitutes. Not many people know this but pimpin on a prostitute is really the lowest form of it. Now a days, it's nothing to see pimps from all nationalities but originally pimpin was only a black man's game. You see, after slavery, wasn't too many ways for blacks to make decent money. So, seeing as how whitey still loved black pussy, the black man figured a way to manage it better. The days of fuckin for half a steak and a piece of cornbread was over. Niggas wanted that money and they got it.

Looking at the young niggas in the game right now, it's easy to see that we still getting it. The square will always criticize the pimp because he hates having to pay for everything the pimp gets for free. Deep down, he wishes he had what it takes to be a pimp, but he doesn't. That's why he's envious over the lifestyle he doesn't understand. He may swear up & down that he's never had such an idea but double back and ask yourself this, How many straight men in the world are there who hasn't fantasized about being surrounded by beautiful women?

Maybe some, but not many. Ain't no shame in my game, I'm a realist. I've never had bitches like Hugh Heffner but I sure as hell wish the fuck I did. That white nigga was pimpin on another level. He understood it's not about what you sell, it's about how you could package the product and make it appealing to America.

He got away with doing all the shit we blacks are still going to jail for because he did it on a level we weren't known to tap into.

Don't hate the player or the game though, Just take notes and step it up.

"P, ya'll ain't goin to believe this shit!" Rasheed said as he walked back up to the group getting everyone's attention. "They talkin bout Fast track died last night."

"Yea?" They all seemed to say at the same time.

"Yea." He replied in deep thought as he and everyone else took time to process the information looking off into nowhere.

"So, where ya'll tryna go eat?" Macky asked.

"I was thinkin bout Roscoe's" said Rarri.

"Man, a nigga tired of Roscoe's. Lets go to Red Lobster" Rasheed interjected.

"Red Lobster been played out. Let's hit the crab shack." No love butted in.

"A nigga damn sure ain't goin to that mothafucka" Macky laughed. "They ain't getting none of my money, on babies.

"Alright, I'm paying then" No love countered.

"*Ima real blood*" Macky mocked, sounding like Pinochio. "Ole Pinocchio ass nigga. You tryna *pay* a nigga to eat the homies, cuh" Everybody started bustin out laughing.

"We might as well hit up Trap Kitchen." Rarri suggested. "Spank food better than all that shit."

"On everything" No love agreed right before they all pushed out.

———

""I had my boy look into that situation" Rasheed said as he licked the buffalo sauce off of his fingers then grabbed another wing. "Macky straight. He ain't been doin nothin out of the ordinary. You got somebody else you want me to look into?"

Rarri thought about it for a minute then stuffed his face with some more fries. "Naw...Honestly, I don't give a fuck about that shit right now. Ain't nobody dumb enough to do no shit like that in my circle. The niggas who did it goin to try some shit again but this time we gon to be ready for em. The only work out right now is with Dink, in the hood and ain't nobody able to take nothin out of there. I like it like this though. It gives me more time to focus on my game and not be worried about the bullshit all damn day."

Rasheed nodded "I dig the fuck out of that 'P' mashin ain't never been as fun as it is right now"

"You feel me?" Rarri was thinking the same thing. "A nigga could push all the weight in the world but don't nothin feel this good... we out here deep as a mothafucka bustin bitches like it ain't nothin, fly as fuck. Maan, when we pull up, then hoes go crazy, P. These bitches be lookin at us like we famous or somethin my nigga. This only the beginnin, sheed. Watch, we goin to look back years from now like, damn, we really did all that." Rarri answered with passion thinking about everything he's ever been through. "On god, sometimes I don't even be thinkin this shit real. I used to Pinch myself hard as fuck tryna wake up. Lowkey hopin I didn't though. Then it just hit me one day like, this ain't no dream, a nigga really here." He looked up "Sheed, niggas really right here P" Rarri shook his head almost in disbelief. "We *really* right here"

'*Damn*' Rasheed thought to himself feelin like straight dog shit. He wanted his father's books just as bad as his mother did but the way she was forcing him to get them was killing him in the inside. He just wanted to talk to him as a brother and be there for him like he should be, not plotting against him. This shit was foul but he promised his mother to do things her way.

Still he wondered if there was some way he could get the books without Rarri knowing he had them, that way he could please his mother and Pop P's with his brother. The only thing about that was, he didn't even know where to start looking for it at. The only time Rarri read from it in front of him was at the Ballroom and that was weeks ago.

'*It could be anywhere*' he pondered. 'But then again, it might be right in front of me'

"On everything 'P', we done really found a way to live a pipe dream" he admitted.

"Let's celebrate, you think yo aunty will let us throw a lil part at her shit?. I lowkey wanted to jump in that pool earlier but I ain't know if she would be trippin"

"Nigga that's *my* shit. You should have just jumped in foo" Rarri replied then turned to everybody else who was eating on the hood of Macky's car.

"AYE! Ya'll tryna go back to the spot and turn up?"

"Hell yea" they all said.

He turned back to Rasheed, "There it is there. Hit the squad and tell em we bout to throw a lil get together"

THIRTY-THREE

"I'M glad we did this shit, P" Rarri slurred as he hit his blunt then his cup as he held the smoke in. "We need to do shit like this all the time" he added after exhaling while looking around at everybody enjoying themselves.

They had bottles, weed, bitches and a nigga cooking on the grill going crazy.

"Cuh" Macky slurred back. "I wish my car was close by cause I would pop the trunk on yo dumb ass"

Rarri laughed and passed him the blunt. "You just a violent ass lil nigga for no reason, what the fuck you goin to pop the trunk on a nigga now for?"

"Cause, you be sayin dumb shit. My nigga, we *do*, do shit like this all the time" He replied and started laughing like it was the funniest thing in the world.

"For real though" Rarri realized after he thought about it.

They probably didn't do it at that specific spot but they did turn up and did fly shit everywhere they went, so this really wasn't nothing new.

"Aye, 'P', a nigga gotta take a piss" Rasheed said as he got out of the pool.

"What, you want a nigga to hold it for you?"

"Fuck outta here nigga" he laughed. "I didn't want to just push up in there on some weird shit."

"'P', you askin to use the bathroom *is* some weird shit, foo" Rarri joked.

"On everything" He admitted then staggered towards the house, pretending to be drunk. As soon as his feet touched the marbled floor and the door was closed behind him, the act was over. Now it was time to handle business.

Heaven had left earlier to go meet with Tony so he felt more comfortable roaming around knowing he was alone. He moved quickly, not takin one second for granted. His heart was beating excitedly and his breathing became harder with each step as he made his way to his brother's room. This was the moment he had been waiting on his entire life, so he didn't hesitate to put his hand on the knob, turn it and walk in.

He listened with his ear towards the hallway to make sure nobody was coming in as he simultaneously scanned the neatly decorated room. He's been here before but never alone. The fragrance of new clothes flooded his nostrils, so he knew Rarri must have just went shoppin, (Again), The pang of jealousy didn't last long. He would soon be greater.

Rarri, an MCM fanatic had almost everything in there matching his favorite brand. His blankets, pillows, curtains and everything was made by them. He even had 7 leather poodles standing next to each other in front of his dresser. He looked up and his smile and eyes widened at the same time when he saw the book, sitting on the top of the dresser next to some of Rarri's chains. Paranoid, he looked around making sure it wasn't a trap. Apart of him was waiting on somebody to jump out of the cut and grab him, asking what was he doing in there.

Another part just wanted to run out of the room and go back

outside but the part that carried the thought of his mother's hatred towards him for not succeeding with the plan out weighed everything else. Also thinking about all the game he would have and everything Rarri had, that his father actually left for him, gave Rasheed the courage he needed to go ahead and take what he felt was rightfully his anyway. He hurried and grabbed the book and quickly left out of the room. He went through the front of the house and left the door cracked as he put the book in the trunk of his car under a pile of clothes and inside the space where he kept a spare tire then went back inside.

He didn't expect things to be this easy but it was. Having the book in his possession gave him a sense of relief. He felt as if the weight of the world had been lifted off of his shoulders.

'*Ma bout to be happy*' he thought as he made his way back through the kitchen.

"Aye, you know what I was thinkin?" Macky asked as he closed the refrigerator door, scaring the shit out of him. "When you first started comin around, somethin was tellin me '*don't trust cuh..*' It's like this lil voice in my head that be tellin me not to fuck wit niggas and on babies that shit ain't *never* lead me wrong, cuh." He added seriously as he walked up on Rasheed.

Rasheed clenched his fist not knowing how he was going to get out of this one. At least a dozen or so cars had him blocked in so driving out of there after an altercation like this was impossible. He dreaded the thought of leaving without the book but reasoned leaving with his life was way better. He would just have to make a run for it.

"Until now.." Macky kept going as he handed him one of the gallons of cranberry juice. "I'm glad you stood yo ground that day at the spot, you said some real shit, cuh.. I guess I just ain't like how tough Rarri was fuckin wit you or somethin. That lil nigga gon ride for you like no other. I ain't met too many niggas like cuh. I really love that lil nigga like a brother. I will knock a nigga whole family down for cuh bitches and all You feel me?"

"Yeah, I feel you P, I mean I don't know about the bitches and shit but..."

"You don't know about the bitches?" Macky asked sarcastically in disbelief. "Let me tell you somethin, sheed, fuckin wit 'us', you goin to have to start lookin at knockin a person down as the same way you look knockin a hoe, you just gotta tell yo mind *one thing*"

"What's that?" Rasheed asked. Macky laughed to himself wickedly and said "They all knockable..." Then headed back outside "Come on, let's go get fucked up, 'P"

Rasheed forced on a smile and followed Macky back outside for the first time thinking about what he was getting himself into.

"Arrghh!!" Rasheed screamed in anger as he flipped his mother's dinner table over. Breathing heavily like a madman.

"Calm down, Rasheed!" Mary ordered, glad Frank wasn't home to see this.

"Calm down?" He asked in disbelief. "Ma, you said once I get the book all of this would be over. If they catch me doin some sneaky shit, they go'n fuckin kill me!"

"I understand that, but this isn't the book" Mary replied as she picked it up off of the floor and opened it for the first time.

Mary knew it wasn't the book she used to see god writing in because that one had *"The book of God"* on the front of it, but as she looked closely to the words on the pages on the inside, her eyes grew wide in excitement. She knew his handwriting like the back of her hand. Mary closed it, to look at the cover, the writing was different so it threw her off but she was certain who it was written by.

She looked at her son joyfully. "Rasheed, this isn't the book that I was talking about but I never forgot his handwriting" Mary opened the book again and scrolled with her pointer finger. "You see how the letter 'Y' resembles half the shape of a heart?"

"Yea" he replied, as he examined the letter she was talking about.

"That's how *your* father writes *his* Y's, Rasheed"

"So you tellin me he wrote *this* book too?"

"Yes, that's exactly what I'm telling you" she happily replied.

Rasheed was so excited when he grabbed the book that he didn't pay attention to or think to stop and read the title. He just assumed the one he saw was the same one he's seen Rarri reading from at the ball because it was the same make.

"So, what was the name of the book you saw, ma?"

"The book of God" she said proudly, then looked at him in question. "Why"

"Because if the one I seen him with had 'Breathe" on the front of it and the one you saw my dad with said something different, then why does this one have '*The Crown*'?

"That must mean"

"He wrote more books" They said together.

"Ok, we'll worry about that later" she assured as she handed the book to Rasheed. "Right now, you need to read."

"You not goin to read it with me?" He asked.

She placed her hand on the side of his face, gently rubbing her thumb on his cheeks as she did when he was a child. "No, this has always been for *you*, Rasheed, '*always*'"

He nodded as his mother turned to leave. He instantly started feeling bad for thinking his mother was a selfish woman. This whole time he thought she wanted the book for something else but she *really* only wanted it for him. He promised himself never to think such things of his mother again. As soon as she closed the door behind her, he sat down on the couch and rubbed the surface of the book.

"*The Crown*" he read once more with patience then quickly opened it up feeling as if butterflies were fluttering around in his stomach. He had been waiting on this moment his entire life. Just to be able to touch something that his father had created made him feel special. He started to read.

'He who is not down for the crown, could never become a king in the game. Some say the streets have no king. Whether they do or not, is not of our concern, for BABE STREET will have plenty of kings and zero peasants. He who is not down for his crown is not affiliated with us, neither is she who is not down for her crown of queen. Our queens must be able to move in real life as those on a chess board. No pawns, no knights, no bishops, no rooks. For who can beat the king playin chess with all Queens? The answer is nobody. So, every king's dream hoe should be a queen hoe. One must remember that every hoe is not a queen and every queen is not a hoe.

Not all but most bitches know who and what they want to be in life. They shall call you the motivator because your job is to motivate her to become whatever it is that she wants to be. Aim high so whatever it is that she wants to become is within reasonable standards of your program. Never settle for those who are lesser than but have an eye for those who are capable of being something more than what they are at the present time. Not everyone is aware of their strengths, so always be prepared and genuinely willing to bring out the best in people.

A good king is considered a great king and great kings do great things. So always bless those around you with game to be as great as you are and pray for them to be even better. There is no heart better than a pure one, so your intentions towards your family should be just as such. Whosoever so crosses a king shall be dealt with accordingly and whoever so crosses a queen should rightfully receive the same punishment for our loyalty, love and respect is fair, but never cheap. A life or a reputation is at the discretion of the Royal who is ever wronged by another.

Loyalty before royalty, no one who Is justifiably disloyal was never one of us to begin with. Your heart should never warm or soften for 'the foul'. It should be frozen, cold and hardened by the deceit. Do with them as you wish and receive not a single letter from a word of rebuttal from another royal. "Off with his head" they shall chant "Off with his head"

He closed the book quickly and wiped the sweat from his face.

He felt as if his father was speaking directly to him. Like as if somehow or some way, god knew this book would end up being the one in his hands. Thinking of all he's done to get this far, Rasheed felt as if he was 'The Foul' his father spoke of but quickly shook it off as a coincidence. It's impossible for someone to make such a prediction. right?

Rasheed cleared his throat, opened the book and began reading where he had left off.

'Off with his head' they shall chant, off with his head' The crowns we wear can only be severed off. So get rid of 'The foul' before it turns into 'The Fuzz' I've given you pieces and I've given you clues, if you've made it this far, you will make it further. In dark times I will show you the light but good game always stays tight. From who you were, to who you are and who you will become, the switch will change your life. Son, can you crack this code?'

He smiled then turned the page, then another and another and another. He scanned through them all. Nothing! Not a single word. Every page was completely blank.

"Son, can you crack this code?" he read out loud then scanned through the book once more. He hurried out of the room in search of his mother. When he found her, she was in the kitchen enjoying a glass of wine reminiscing on all the good times she had with his father and thinking of how great he would become with the game he would soon have.

She wanted him to shit on Rarri, so then she could openly laugh at Heaven for her sister's failures. 'When she finds out that Rasheed is God's first born and how they were outsmarted for-

"We have to find the other book, ma." Rasheed said cutting into her devious thoughts.

"We will" she assured him with confidence. Wine glass close to her lips. "But finish reading that one until then.." she added before taking another sip.

"That's what I'm trying to tell you, ma." He flipped through the pages slow enough for her to see. "He never finished it"

Not believing in what she was seeing, she quickly sat the wine glass down, snatched the book out of his hands and began scanning the pages closely. Just as he had said, the rest of the book was empty. She couldn't believe this shit, feeling cheated yet again. She examined it one more time in desperation, dropped it on the table in defeat, then swatted it to the floor in anger as she screamed at it painfully.

He hurried to pick it up, dusted it off all while checking the surface and interior making sure it wasn't damaged. After being satisfied, he turned back to the last page written.

"I've given you pieces and I've given you clues, if you've made it this far, you will make it further" he read out loud.

"We didn't fail ma. This book is just one piece to the puzzle. I bet money if we get the other ones, we'll be able to make sense out of this one. The other ones must have the pieces and clues he left Rarri and that's how he's been getting on"

"No, Rasheed, These are the pieces and clues he left for you, not him!"

He closed the book, "Well, why doesn't it feel like it, ma?" he asked seriously. "Why am I the one sneaking around for my shit?"

"Because it was stolen from you, we can't go and ask for them back. Since when do thieves return the things that they have taken, Rasheed?" she asked.

When he didn't reply, she knew she had him. "Our advantage is them not knowing who you are, because if they find out before we have the books, we may never get them. I only want this for you. All I've ever wanted was for you to have what was yours. I'm not your father, there is only so much I can teach you. Yea, you've learned a lot from me and people I've introduced you to and people you have met but what have you learned from *him*, Rasheed?" she asked, then again more passionately as she reached out and touched the book in his hands, looking into his eyes. "What have you learned from *him*?"

He answered by shaking his head.

"You are my son and I love you. I don't want to push you to do something you don't want to do. So, if you want to go and *ask* them for *your* things, I guess I'll support it. but even though I'm your mother, I'm just like the rest of these bitches. I'll only ever *respect* what you *take*" Mary told him seriously.

He nodded in approval, Set the book on the table and left without saying a word. He was going to do whatever it took to get the books and once he did, then cracked God's code. Mothafuckas was goin to see him break the world. They would know without a doubt in mind that Rasheed was *'Down for the Crown'*

THIRTY-FOUR

BETTY WAP WAS GOIN on and on and on about how she and Pinks were on their shit. Rarri had missed her talking and for a minute, he felt like the old Betty wap was back. He liked who she was now but secretly he wished something would bring the old Wap out of her.

He felt bad for making such a wish because he knew she loved her new self. He couldn't help but feel selfish and he hated himself for it because being aware of his selfishness wasn't enough to make him stop being selfish. Rarri knew he was wrong but he didn't care. Yea, she was bringing in gwap but so was every other bitch in his stable. The money she was making might have been new to her but it damn sure wasn't new to him.

He never cared about that type of shit when it came to her. When he sent her to fuck with Heaven after 'the show', he wasn't expecting these types of results. He thought his aunty would give her a lil bit of game, make her feel welcome and some shit like that. Not literally, physically and mentally make her a new person.

"What's wrong? You looking like somebody kicked yo dog?" she joked.

"Nothin" he lied as he forced a smile on. She didn't say nothing but he knew she noticed by how she looked at him.

"Well, if you ever want to talk about it or need a shoulder to cry on, I got you" she joked as she patted her shoulder like a big dog.

He couldn't help but laugh. "Yo ass stay flippin some shit around and clownin a nigga."

"And yo fine ass stay flippin shit around to make a bitch break" she countered biting her lip seductively as they locked eyes.

"I do, huh?" he said with that sexy fire in his eyes as he slowly leaned towards her from the driver side of his Benz.

"Mmhmmm" she replied slowly as she leaned in to meet him halfway. Her heart was damn near poppin out of her chest in excitement.

She always fantasized about what their first kiss would be like. The more she thought about it, the more frightened she became. The closer they got, the more her stomach fluttered as if a million butterflies had awakened on a beautiful summer morning. Time couldn't move slower, Betty wap stopped. For her, it was that moment on a roller coaster before the big drop. That moment when you look down finally noticing how high you are then grip the sides thinkin, *Why'd I get on this ride?*

As soon as his lips touched hers, she leaned out of the car and started throwing up.

"Damn bitch, what I make you sick or somethin?" he askes, slightly bruised.

She reached back up with her left hand "Nooo, give me something to wipe with"

He shook his head, opened the middle console, pulled out a small pack of Kleenex and handed it to her. She pulled a few from the pack, wiped her mouth, then turned around with her lips puckered out to him.

"Okay, I'm ready."

They both started burstin out laughing knowing damn well that wasn't about to happen. He gave her a small bottle of mouthwash to rinse with. Rarri always kept some type of personal hygiene close by to make sure he stayed fresh. You could be fly and buss-down but if you run up on a bitch stanky breath and musty don't none of that shit matter(Vice versa).

"Let me find out yo ass out here pregnant or somethin, Wap"

She stopped swishing around the mouthwash in her mouth, looked at him like was crazy, continued swishing for a bit then spat it out in the gutter and closed the car door.

"We ain't never did nothin yet so how ima be pregnant?"

"I don't know, you out here just throwin up out of the blue and shit"

She rolled her eye. "It wasn't just out of the blue. I just.. never mind you wouldn't get it."

"Cause you ain't tellin me shit" he laughed.

"Because it's embarrassin" she blushed.

"Embarrassin?" He asked in disbelief.

"What about that time when we first met and I came out the bathroom and you was butt ass naked on the bed with the blunt hangin out of yo mouth, lookin like this" He grabbed the blunt out of the ashtray and imitated her position almost to the T.

She playfully snatched the blunt from his mouth, "I was not looking like that"

"Yea, ok, that's the moment I will never forget Wap. That was damn near like the start of my journey. I remember that day like it was yesterday. Seein you knockin on my door with that bullshit ass weed talkin bout it was bomb, lacin me up on the Pitt and all that" he recalled happily then his face hardened. "That shit you told me yo bitch ass pops did too."

She blew out in frustration, "Yea, look daddy, that's kinda somethin I been wantin to talk to you about, cause he—"

"Hold on real quick" he said cuttin her off to answer his phone "YAAH, what's the deal? Say no more, I'm on my way" He hung up then turned to her. "I gotta sagg out but we gon chop it up later, ight."

"K" she replied and got out of the car as soon as the door closed he sped off.

"Fuck!" she swore then walked back to her car, got in and sat there quietly.

Too much shit was on her mind these days. Right now, she just wanted to go home, take a hot shower and give her teeth a real brushing, but she still had to wait on Exotic and the rest of the bitches to get done first. She was getting tired of this babysitting shit, if bitches couldn't get out there and get it on their own, they should even be on the team in her eyes. Watching these bitches was making her miss out on the money she could have been making. It wouldn't have been a problem if she was able to work the streets too but just sitting around looking at other hoes getting dollars was getting boring as fuck.

It wasn't like she was getting any younger and all hoes have expiration dates, so time was of the essence. She pulled out her phone and called Heaven.

"Hello"

"Hey, can we talk?"

THIRTY-FIVE

WHEN RARRI PULLED into the Sunny coves he could see the police lights flashing a short distance ahead. Not wanting his car seen by them, he parked in someone's driveway and power walked to the crime scene where people were gathered on the sidewalk. Some crying, some yelling, some shaking their heads in disbelief while consoling others as best as they could.

He rushed right up to the yellow tape in anger, not saying a word, not dropping a tear. He just looked at the two lil niggas's lifeless bodies that been mangled, twisted and riddled with bullets. The smallest ones bloody hand was caught in the rim of the bike. The older ones foot was slightly still on the pedal. It was obvious that the older one was riding the younger one on the handlebars when everything happened.

The cold part about it was that they weren't even affiliated nor anyone in their family. The only time their pops let them come outside was to ride that bike and that wasn't often. Seeing their father out there crying his heart out had Rarri hot. He didn't give a fuck about them not being gangbangers. They grew up over there so that was good enough for him to slide for them.

"YAAH! YAAH!"

Looking down the street, he saw Lil Dink and Trigg standing far away from everyone else. He knew what that meant. He looked at the bodies once more then walked away. As soon as he walked up, they jumped in the front seats of the g-ride not saying a word. When Rarri got in the back, he saw the same AK-47 with the hundred round drum he used the day Spank died. A mixture of emotions flooded his body. He was happy to have it back in his hands but sad from the memories he had the last time he shot it.

He checked the drum, making sure it was full then closed it back before grabbing the blunt from Lil Dink. The three of them smoked in silence as they drove but being together doing what they did best felt good to them all. This was their fun. He missed times like these. He knew no matter how much he loved doing other shit, his heart would always be tied to the set. He would never turn his back on where he came from, NEVER! Especially in situations like these. Letting niggas come through and do shit like this was unacceptable. No matter how much money he got or bitches he knocked, Rarri would always sag for his section.

———

"Oh, yea these niggas bold as fuck" Lil Dink said as he drove pass a dozen or so niggas hanging out in front of a house without a worry in the world. They were obviously celebrating something. They knew this was a known Nunley house, as did almost everybody else in Compton. Trigg's aunty used to get her hair done there whenever she didn't want to fuck with Myesha. He hated that shit but his aunty and their aunty's knew each other before Trigg and his generation of niggas was even born.

"Ya'll niggas ready?" Lil Dink asked in disgust.

They didn't say a word but that said everything. Lil Dink made a U-turn and pulled up right in front of the house. Rarri and Trigg was out of the car before it even stopped, taken everybody by surprise.

"BOOM!

Rarri shot the closest nigga by him in the back of the head sending the front of his face to no-mans-land. Then moved on to the next as Trigg sprayed the crowd with his signature 9mm.

"Kill Cuz!" Lil Dink yelled angrily from the car like a coach on the sideline watching his team dominate the other.

That hyped Trigg and Rarri up to the max, making them go even crazier, chasing niggas down as they ran for their lives. Some got away the ones too slow weren't so lucky.

"PAT! PAT! PAT!"

Trigg shot a nigga trying to run in the house, dropping him in the doorway then focused on another target. Rarri noticed the nigga in the doorway trying to crawl in the house. He ran up and kicked him in the ass.

"Turn yo bitch ass over!"

"Come on, man" he replied, turning his head to see who he was talking to.

"BOOM!"

Rarri knocked the side of his face off then stepped inside of the house.

"FUCK!" Lil Dink swore to himself then looked around in a panic.

The plan was to Spray shit up and get out of there as quick as possible before the police came but things took a drastic turn. The last thing Lil Dink wanted to do right now was get caught up for some shit like this. His nerves were at an all time high. The first thing Rarri saw was two bitches curled up screamin on the floor next to a couch.

"BOOM! BOOM!...BOOM! BOOM!"

He shut them up with two each. Trigg came running past him through the house and down the hall kicking in doors shooting everything in sight, not wanting to be out (because this was a competition) Rarri followed suit and went right along with him tearin shit up. He quickly switched clips. Rarri kicked open another door and froze. When he saw a lady in there crying in fear and craddling a baby .

As soon as she looked up he instantly thought of a picture his grandmother had hanging on her wall of him and his mother. The woman in front of him looked just like her and the baby resembled him.

"BOOM!"

Before he could muster another thought, Trigg put one in her head.

"Boom! Boom!

He turned to Rarri in a rush. "Come on, we out"

Trigg looked at Rarri, then at the lady and back at him with a sour expression. The disappointment on his face was evident. Rarri's lips knotted as he sniffled his nose, aimed his choppa at her slumped face with precision then pulled the trigger.

"BOOM!"

The bullet literally knocked her forehead off and the baby fell slightly out of her hands crying it's heart out. As reality set in, they both ran out of the house and jumped in the car where an impatient Lil Dink was waiting. He was so nervous that as soon as the door opened his foot, pressed on the gas damn near leaving them. Rarri and Trigg literally had to jump in the car.

As soon as they made it back to the hood safely, they instantly began clowning on him. Glad to finally have something like this over his head. They called him 'gas pedal' all night. Coming up wit 'GP' for short. Just a little inside joke between the three. They hung out for a moment reenacting everything that happened for Lil Dink (AKA Gas Pedal's) amusement.

He was mad it was on him to drive, especially with the new moniker. He couldn't wait till his turn was up. Rarri and Trigg was actin like they were all of a sudden the big homies now. Walking around wit their chest all poked out and talking to lil Dink like he was a lil nigga. Even going as far as calling him 'lil cuz'. They was getting on his nerves, but he loved it.

"Look, lil cuz" Trigg said as he put his hand on Lil Dink's shoulder. "You gotta really step yo shit up, YAAH. We hit mothafuckas outside and ran up in there and chipped shit. Fasho we like real serial killers now. And we yo niggas, so '*know*' you ain't one of those yet"

"Shut yo dumb ass up" Lil Dink replied laughing as Trigg swatted his arm off of him. He nodded his head in approval with a proud smirk.

"Yall did that though cuh, on YAAHAMPTON."

Rarri pushed up in his face with the extras. "We don't need you to tell us we did that. Cuh we '*know*' we did that, nigga. Matter of fact, shut yo nice ass up!"

Lil Dink jumped up from the couch and playfully punched Rarri in his side.

"Get off the homie, cuh" Trigg said as he jumped in, throwing punches at Lil Dink. Then they both started packing him out, laughing.

Lil Dink pushed them off, sat back down, grabbed the blunt off of the table, lit it and inhaled deeply.

"Damn, I miss my nigga Spank, cuh"

"On god" Trigg agreed.

"Aye remember when that nigga from tacos got up and ran after Spank shot him in the face, then cuh tried to chase cuh but couldn't catch him?" Rarri reminisced and they all laughed.

"On YAAHMPTON, cuh was '*steamin'*', when we got back to the hood" Lil Dink cracked into tears.

"Naw, what about that time when cuh got burned by Shondra?" Trigga asked then they all started crying, laughing, thinking back to how mad Spank would be every time he had to take a piss.

"Then cuh got craccin on Rarri for showin everybody the green shit in his draws"

They couldn't even breathe laughing at that shit. Spank

whooped Rarri's ass that day. You see, Spank probably ain't have aim and couldn't kill a nigga if his life depended on it but he had a cold squabble.

"A nigga gotta go check on cuh moms in the mornin. I ain't been there in a minute" Rarri said after catching his breath and grabbing the blunt out of Lil Dink's hand.

Trigg and Lil Dink shared looks. They had been debating on the right time to bring it up but couldn't see how. He had been in the blind for long enough and they knew they were wrong for not saying something sooner. Lil Dink blew out in frustration with his head down.

"Aye YAAH, we gotta tell you somethin cuh but you gotta bang that, that you ain't gon trip, foo"

Rarri hit the blunt two small times. "On V's, what's the deal?"

"We had to knock Ms. Benitt down" he replied sadly.

He chuckled, "Get the fucc outta here nigga, what's really up?"

Lil Dink looked at Rarri seriously. Rarri looked at Lil Dink, then Trigg, then back at lil Dink in question.

"We had to cuh, she was about to go to the police and turn us in" Trigg admitted as Rarri stood in a daze, dropping the blunt.

"YAAH, it's all my fault foo cause I couldn't 'NOT' tell her like you told me to do. I just couldn't. I thought her knowin would give her a peace of mind because she wouldn't stop askin. It's like she already knew and just needed me to say it to know it wasn't us who did it to him. We would be in jail doin life right now if we didn't do what we did-"

"Naw" Rarri said, still in a daze, then looked at him with a blank expression. "She would still be alive if you ain't open up yo mouth. us goin to jail would have been on you for talkin. I would have sat in a cell forever before I did what ya'll did"

He swatted Lil Dink's hand off of his shoulder as soon as it landed then turned to walk out of the house. He didn't want nothing to do with them no more. He really felt betrayed by the two niggas he trusted the most. Rarri specifically told Trigg not to say shit and he turned around and did the complete opposite.

The crazy part about it is that something told him to kill Trigg when he was still in the backseat crying when they pulled into the garage of the vacant house in the Sunny coves, but he couldn't do it. Trigg didn't even see that Rarri had his choppa aimed at him because his head was still in the seat.

When he asked what they were going to tell Spank's mom, Rarri lowered his gun as well as his head as he spoke. That day changed his life in so many ways. He had no choice but to start getting money so he could pay for Spank's funeral. Never in a million years did he think Heaven would be the one to get him where he's at right now. The thought of her stopped him at the door as he opened it.

"Did my aunty know about this?" He asked looking at the two. When they dropped their heads he shook his in disgust. "Of course she did" Rarri told himself then slammed the door behind him.

Lil Dink pulled out his phone and called Heaven...

THIRTY-SIX

"DAMN NIGGA, twenty missed calls? Ima just assume ya'll gutted the niggas who been robbin ya'll" Heaven joked then ashed her cigarette in the tray just as Rarri walked through the door. She smiled but his look was stone.

"Naw, I been tryna call and let know that Rarri found out about Ms. Benitt-" Lil Dink explained

Heaven looked like a deer, caught in the headlights. Lil Dink was still talking but she couldn't hear nothing he was saying. Rarri eyed her coldly.

"Hey Daddy!" Betty Wap said excitedly as she ran to him for a hug like she hadn't seen him in years.

"Why you smell like the 4th of July?" Betty Wap asked as she leaned back to look at him then noticed the spots of blood on his inner shirt. "You bleedin daddy" She panicked tryin to feel around him but Rarri blocked her with his hand, never takin his eyes off of Heaven.

"What you doin here?"

"I wasn't turnin in early or nothin like that. I just stopped by after you left because I been thinkin about workin while everybody else down, but I wanted to come ask first, to make sure it was coo"

"Ask who?"

"Yo Aunty"

"You ain't gotta ask her 'shit'" Rarri stated coldly. Heaven put her head down in shame.

She knew she had fucked up by not telling him what had happened. Heaven was going to tell him when he got out of the halls, but the day he got released was when his grandma started tripping, so she took him to the bay.

The last thing she wanted to do was stress him out with too much shit on his plate. Heaven needed him to focus on his father's guidance more than anything and this situation would have had his mind all over the place. Was she wrong? Yes. But some wrongs are necessary. Still, she could have had told him sooner instead of leaving him in the dark for this long.

I know this may sound fucked up but honestly, Heaven had been doing so much crazy stuff since then that she really forgot all about that shit. Telling him that would only make things worst. The killing was one thing but the hiding it was the fuel to the fire. Heaven put the pressure on Lil Dink who then put the pressure on Trigg. The three of them were as equally guilty. If he couldn't trust them then who could he trust.?"

Heaven and Rarri were as close as can be. Betty Wap didn't know what to say or do so she just stood there feeling out of place. Rarri shook his head in disgust as he looked down at his aunt then turned to leave.

"Come on Wap, we outta here"

"What about my stuff?"

"Leave it" he replied bluntly over his shoulder. " you don't need none of that juju shit on you"

"You ain't even gon let me explain myself?" Heaven asked in desperation finally looking up as they walked off.

He stopped in his tracks, "No matter how much I love and trust a bitch, if I gotta *watch* her" he turned to look her in the eyes so she could see the pain, hate and anger in his "I don't even *want* her" he added with a foul taste in his mouth.

Heaven literally balled up and fell to the ground, cryin her heart out, feelin as if he physically punched her in the stomach. She actually rather that he had. His words cut her deep but he didn't feel sorry for her or them. From here on out, he was only fuckin with his 'P' partners.

'Fuck everybody else' he thought as he pulled out his phone.

"Sheed, what's the deal?" was the last thing Heaven heard before the door slammed.

She felt as if her world had shattered into a million pieces. Heaven didn't know if she would ever get his trust back but if need be, she would spend the rest of her life trying.

THIRTY-SEVEN

"Kɴᴏᴄᴋ, Kɴᴏᴄᴋ, Kɴᴏᴄᴋ, Kɴᴏᴄᴋ!!" Peso looked back at his car shaking his head exhaling deeply, obviously irritated.

"Bang on that mothafucka Bruh bruh" Kid Doe suggested from the passenger seat as he texted back and forth with some potential work.

Peso smiled wickedly and nodded his head in agreement.

"BAM! BAM! BAM! BAM! BAM! BAM—" The door swung open.

"Damn, I said hold on!" The nigga barked from the doorway.

'WTF?" Peso immediately thought to himself noticing that the person in front of him looked hunched with his head stuck in his shoulders.

He quickly looked Peso up and down, looking just as shocked.

"Oh you *fasho* you got the wrong house" he said stepping outside then pointed a few houses down.

"Termite and Hector stay right there. Wait! Did them niggas send you down here over that punk ass five dollars?, here my nigga, damn" he added in frustration as he dug in his pocket before Peso could even respond. "Tell em they ain't gotta be sendin decoy

Mexicans down here for me to pay em either. It ain't even that serious nigga, on P's"

"Man is Voice box here?"

"Oh, oh my bad, you the nigga with the Molly's?" he asked putting his money back in his pocket then extended his hand out into a 'P-shake' "What they call you?"

"Peso" he replied as they shook causing the other nigga to chuckle at the name.

"That's crazy. Anyway they call me No Neck, leave a bitch wit no check for the record though"

"Voice box in the back...follow me" he added with extras and smoothly flickered his nose before turning and walkin back in the house with Peso behind him.

Kind Doe was in the car crying laughing at both of em. He was laughing at Peso cause he know how much being called a Mexican boiled his blood. He was surprised Peso held his composure. But that ain't have shit on the nigga No Neck and his intro. This shit was comedy at it's best. Not because it sounded stupid but because he said it fly as fuck. King Doe could tell that No Neck was one of them type of niggas despite his handicap and no matter what anybody said. He knew without a doubt in mind he was the flyest of all mankind. You couldn't convince him otherwise. Point. Blank. Period!

"Aye, hold up!" Kind Doe called after them as he quickly pressed the button to roll the windows up, grabbed the key out of the cup holder, pressed the ignition button to turn the Power completely off and got out of the car, racing to catch them in the house.

He handed Peso his car key and introduced himself smiling from ear to ear, with his hand extended. "They call me King Doe 'P'"

Peso shook his head but he was smiling too. He knew by the look on King Doe's face that he wanted to hear No Neck say that bullshit again. Especially when he leaned in a little towards No Neck waiting on it, hand on ear.

"They call me No Neck, leave a bitch wit no check for the record though"

King Doe leaned back, face stanky, nodding in approval. "That's what the fuck I'm talkin bout, 'P', mothafuckas out here motivated bruh, bruh."

"On P's" No Neck replied as he closed the door, then he and Kind Doe was walking towards the back of the house talking, laughing and clowning like they knew each other for years.

Peso just shook his head as he followed them through the dirty ass house, looking disgusted. Two things Peso didn't do was like or Trust dirty living mothafuckas. He never understood why people didn't like to keep they shit clean. It was easy. just clean the fuck up.

King Doe didn't seem to mind or notice much shit like that but that was K.D for you. He always embraced niggas who was some pimpin without a second thought. To keep it real, if it wasn't for him, Rarri wouldn't have made it a full day in the Pitt without somebody tryna rob him. Soon as G-man would have pulled off niggas would have been plotting on whether to run in his room or wait till he come out.

The fact that K.D didn't let Rarri get at Betty Wap said a lot to everybody else around. It said Rarri was some pimpin. K.D was some pimpin. K.D wasn't feared in the Pitt, he was loved. Either one could save yo life or get you killed. Love simply got him ahead. King Doe was genuinely happy for Rarri prevailing in the Pitt without the slightest pang of jealousy. Apart of him felt like he was prevailing too because he seen it in Rarri before anybody else did. He might not have pimped his way out of the Pitt like he swore he would, but being him, staying true to who he was, what he stood for and what he believed in, is what gave him opportunity.

That's what connected him with other pimps most of all. He believed in Unity within the lifestyle and that real pimps should always stick together. Not only that, but instead of being so quick to bash a nigga for mispimpin. Show em how to pimp correctly. After that it's fair game, Fuck em. King Doe stopped No Neck before they walked into the back room.

"Sometimes, less is best 'P'. It's always better to be *'me'* but if I was *'you'*, I would put more swag in it by saying *'rec'* instead of *'record'*.. You feel me burh, bruh.?"

"They call me No Neck leave a bitch wit no check for the *'rec'*. No Neck said to himself "on P's less is best" He added smiling as they 'P shook then No Neck opened the door to the backroom.

"Five Deuce on the come out mothafuckaaaa!"

Soon as they stepped in they noticed Voicebox screaming through the top of his lungs or his neck, really I can't even describe this shit but the nigga was yelling, holding that lil thang to his neck looking like he bout to tell you why you shouldn't smoke cigarettes.

'I was wonderin why they called him Voice Box' Peso thought to himself. *'He gon fuck around and blow that mothafucka up yellin like that'* Peso was shocked though cause the backroom was like walking into a whole new house. It was really like a completely different environment. New furniture, sectional couch, two big screen TVs, wood panel floors, surround sound speakers in the top corners of the room, couple of pictures of Bob Marley, 2 Pac and a few big booty bitches. It was real spacious, clean and lowkey had a comfortable feel to it. Peso was slightly impressed.

Voice Box set his Voice Box on the table, Slid one of the twenty dollar bills that was in the middle of the floor next to his right foot with the rest of his money, grabbed the dice, waited for the nigga he was shootin with to put down, then rolled as soon as the money hit the floor, not wanting to cool his shot down. He probably should have schooled em cause he came out wit snake eyes.

"s-s-s-show me the t-t-titties, bitch" The other dude stammered as he picked his money back up along with the dice, happy they were on him now.

Voicebox looked at No Neck heatedly as he slid his twenty back in the Pot. If looks could kill, No Neck would have dropped dead.

"Ain't nobody tryna hear that shit V.B, you was goin to crap out regardless" No Neck said knowing Voice Box was going to blame him simply walking in the room as the reason for him falliy off dice.

Voice Box is one of them type of niggas if you do 'anything' while he on dice and he crap out. He's going to blame whatever you was doing as the reason he fell off. No matter what his point is or how long he was on dice. Oh, and don't let him be low on his doe, getting hit.. You bet not even be in the same room when that's happening if you ain't in the dice game cause he going to swear to God by you just looking at him shooting the dice, is fuckin him up.

Mothafuckas used to take it personal until it was just obvious that Voice Box is simply going to do that every time he lose. Sure signs of a gambling addiction. The nigga on dice rolled a four then he grabbed the dice, got low to the ground and popped them up real lightly bouncing instead of Rollin and back door's a lil Joe. Voice Box shook his head in frustration and slid another Twenty from his pile. No Neck stepped in the middle of the game putting them on temporary pause.

"Hold up, 'P', this the Molly man, handle ya'll business first, they probably got shit to do V.B"

Voice Box grabbed his voicebox, "Oh my bad, I forgot ya'll was comin through."

He extended his hand to a 'P' shake "I'm Voicebox for the record"

"Naw, it's for the '*rec*' now, not record, P" No Neck corrected.

"What?" Voice Box asked confused by the sudden change.

"Nevermind" No Neck looked at King Doe. "He don't get it yet, P"

"Less is best" The two said at the same time and shook hands.

"I'm Peso" Peso told V.B as they shook as well. He couldn't help but notice No Neck did that same chuckle he did a minute ago when he said his name on the porch.

"Let me show you around, 'P'" No Neck put an arm around K.D's neck as they walked. "This the homie Two-Time. He always stutterin sayin shit twice with his ugly ass"

"F-f-fuck you nigga at l-l-least I could see my neck"

"Mothafucka you need to go 'see' why you can't stop g-g-glitchin" No Neck and King Doe started laughing hard.

K.D introduced himself then proceeded to finish the tour. Peso kept a eye on King Doe. He really didn't like how he was always friendly wit niggas. Especially out of town niggas.

"Rarri said you got some shit that's gon go crazy mane. Is they really that fire?"

Peso took his backpack off and set it on the table while he opened it.

"I don't know what ya'll been fuckin wit out here but this the best shit you goin to find fasho..This a Q.P... You gotta cap em' yoself though bruh" He instructed, handing him the four ounces of Molly and a bag of empty pill capsules.

"D-D-Damn!" That's all Molly?" Two-time asked as he walked up to the table. "P-P-Put me one in a pill. Im-m-ma pop that bitch right now"

Peso pulled out a lil scooper he used to fill the pills wit and stuffed like eight good ones. By this time, K.D and No Neck was at the table too. K.D was puffin a blunt that he rolled on the way there. He took two more big pulls then extended his arm to pass it. No Neck attempted to reach for it because he was closest to him but King Doe dodged his greedy little fingers dramatically and passed it to his boy.

Peso hit him back wit that same chuckle *fuck you thought nigga* he thought as he hit it. That made Peso's day.

I don't like this Bad Bunny lookin ass nigga No Neck thought as he openly waved off Peso's expression. With his hand and a smirk of his own.

No Neck didn't like people who acted black and Peso didn't like people who acted like they was some pimpin even more but he wasn't here to discuss his personal opinions. He was here to handle business. Business he ain't even want to be doing in the first place but he knew Rarri wasn't bullshittin when he said if Peso brung the Molly's down his way it would put him on another level. On top of that, he was in high pursuit of a new group of prostitutes above anything else. Peso wanted hoes.

No money felt better than hoe money to him. But that still was never enough. Peso wanted Moe Money. Maybe even yo money. Who knows but one way or another, he was going to get that bag. Rarri paid for the Molly's and told Peso to just drop a Q.P off to each one of his people's in Long Beach, Compton, Watts and now his last stop in LA. Rarri just wanted them to pass them out for free.

What Peso didn't know was that V.B might have been a lil game goofy but damn near everybody in LA knew who he was, like literally, EVERYBODY! Even though he was pushing 30 he still happen to keep up with the up and comin. The best part was that V.B wasn't into bangin so he would be in places all over L.A that most people couldn't think about going without getting shot in their imagination.

In a crazy way that made him not only standout but it also made people remember him. He so ugly you can't even describe who he look like but fasho you knew you was ugly if somebody said you look like V.B. Everybody knew he was the one to go to fro the best ecstasy pills in L.A. Really it was his Mexican homie Termite a few houses down. Voicebox would play middle man and make his money that way. Which was coo for Termite because besides V.B he couldn't stand dealing wit niggas. He was from Florence 13. He was somewhat of a young shot-caller. Nobody would dare fuck with him over there because his family ties to his hood and especially because of their positions in Prison. Which, for political purposes ran even deeper.

Termite and VoiceBox has been friends since elementary. In fact he was the only black person to ever be allowed to step foot in his house. He done been there for dinner, holidays, weekends. They even threw him a few birthday parties over there. V.B got his first piece of pussy from one of the hoodrats from Florence because Termite told her to do it.

V.B done jumped in fights for Termite. He didn't give a fuck if you was black, Mexican, pink or purple. If he seen it, he was getting in for Termite and vice versa. Despite their racial differences, the friendship between the two had never been questionable.

Peso passed the blunt to V.B knowing No Neck wanted to hit it but regretted doing so immediately when he seen Voicebox hit it from the hole in his neck.

"Damn, V.B., how you know we ain't wanna hit it before you start doin all that weird shit?" No Neck complained.

He exhaled back through the same hole and laughed. "My bad"

"I-I-I ain't even get to hit it" Two time was mad too. "H-H-He think that shit c-cute"

Nobody took it as he tried to pass it around the circle.

"Fuck it" He added through his Voicebox and kept smoking. Two time grabbed a pill off the table and popped it angrily but he didn't say nothing else. A good 15 seconds passed with no talking like everybody was in deep thought.

King Doe just started burstin up laughing. His lil body ass was already high.

"Wassup P?" No Neck asked with a smile.

K.D looked at Two-Time then Voice Box, then No Neck and looked them over one more time.

"I ain't even tryna clown right...But...I was just thinkin.. All ya'll missin is a nigga in a wheelchair 'P'"

Peso and King Doe started dying laughing.

"On my Pimpin I was thinkin the *same, shit, bruh*" Peso said lightly hitting the table three times with his palm simultaneously with his last three words.

The three laughed lowley with somewhat of a nervous look

between each other as K.D and Peso shed tears holding on to each other, so they ain't fall on the ground. It took about a full minute in a half for them to calm down and catch their breaths and recover, only to start laughing again.

"This why I don't go nowhere wit you, bruh" K.D pointed at Peso.

"Whachu mean this why I don't go nowhere wit 'you'! You be on that bullshit Bruh on P's" Peso shot pointing back at K.D.

The two of them trying not to look at the goofy looking trio just to avoid further laughter.

"You supposed to be more professional bruh, bruh real shit" K.D said straightening himself out takin the smile off his face.

"How I'm supposed to be more professional wit you on that bullshit?"

"Alright, we both goin to be professional"

"Yup, fasho on 'P's'" Peso replied wit a more serious demeanor and straighten himself out also.

"You ready?"

"Is 'you' ready?"

"I been ready, I'm waitin on you" King Doe said with confidence.

"You ain't gotta wait on me P, I'm already ready." Peso replied the same way.

Both of them talking to each other like they were the only two in the room. King Doe even going as far as cracking his neck and some of the muscles in his back. Then he looked at the Trio seriously.

"My bad P" He said as sincerely as possible.

"Naw, you good my nig-"

"Naw P listen" King Doe said cutting No Neck off seriously. "It's some real pimpin goin on in this room" he looked each one of them in the eyes.

"We 'must' always and I repeat 'always'...maintain being

respectful, civilized and professional at all times amongst other P's bruh bruh"

Voice Box, Two-Time and No Neck nodded in agreement at the real shit he was kickin, feeling every word with more passion than the speaker.

"Anything less is inexcusable and I mean that with all of heart...from the deepest depth of the lowest crevice of M- What was that?" King Doe looked towards one of the closed doors where the noise came from. "I just heard something, P, what was it?"

Peso reached in his bag ready to whip out and fuck some shit up wit his 30 round. No Neck stood up in agitation mixed wit a little bit of disappointment, regret and only lord knows what else.

"Look, that's the homie, Willie"

"Oh, okay fasho, I thought some other shit was goin on" King Doe admitted as he and Peso eased up. "But, like I was saying-.."

"Naw listen, P..he" No Neck stopped short of what he was going to say causing King Doe and Peso to get back on edge.

"He what, 'P'?"

The door starting shaking...

"He what, 'P'?" King Doe asked louder but No Neck was speechless as the door started shaking harder and the knob was turning back and forth.

""What is he, 'P', gotdamn!" He shouted as Peso had his hand back on the trigger but the gun still in the bag. He tightened his lips, something he always did unintentionally before he shot somebody.

"H-H-HE, He-H-He-He-He-.." Two time started but was major glitchin,

Voicebox forgot he put his Voicebox in the blunt box so was just checking his pockets furiously for it to no avail. The door flung open and he rolled out "Top of the mornin 'P's"

Peso and King Doe broke out of the room and ran all the way to the front porch, falling over each other, neither one of them able to breathe. It was a free for all. Every man for himself as they literally almost had to crawl and stumble all the way to the car. Peso was laughing so hard that King Doe had to physically grab the key out of his pocket for him, open the passenger door and let him climb in first because if he stepped in the street fasho he was getting ran over.

"Go bruh bruh, get the fuck out of here!"

Peso pushed the start button with his foot on the brake but left it in park. "I can't see nothin, KD, we goin to crash. Wait a minute, give me a minute, FUCK!" he laughed as he fought King Doe's hands away from the gear shift.

"Alright.." he replied tiredly giving the struggle and rolled his window down as he rested uncomfortably in the seat, fanning his shirt out by the collar while catching his breath with closed eyes.

Peso had his head stuck in the steering wheel with both hands clamped on tight, looking like he just got done running a marathon. A few moments of recovery had passed a few 'long' moments.

"Alright, I'm ready, bruh" Peso said, lifting his head from the steering wheel and rested the side of his face on his right arm, eyes still closed. Peso inhaled then exhaled deeply one more time for good measure and opened his eyes.

'BAM, BAM!'

"What the fuck!" King Doe jumped.

Peso had hit the steering wheel hard as hell and was laughing so hard that no sound came out. King Doe looked to the right of him towards the house and started screaming laughing, Stomping his foot over and over immediately losing his breath again. The four of them was just standin there lookin. Willie didn't know what was goin on so he was the only one without his lips in a knot.

Peso didn't give a fuck no more. He was either going to die from crashing or laughing. Maybe even both. He put the car in gear and smashed off, gassing it before he found out.

"What was so funny?"

No Neck smacked his lips, waved Willie off and walked back in the house. Voice box shook his head, looking down at him in disappointment and followed him back in. Willie looked up at Two-Time confused as hell.

"What happened?" he wanted to know.

"Y-Y-Y-You be makin us look bad" He replied before following his boys.

THIRTY-EIGHT

"So, WHAT YOU THINK?" Rarri asked in open arms as he stood center of the magnificent twin stairway, looking down at Rasheed and Macky.

"Man, that's mothafucka big as fuck, cuh" Macky replied in amazement. "What we supposed to do with all this?"

"live in it nigga" Rarri answered as he came down the stairs.

Rasheed nodded in approval. "This *is* livin" he admitted.

The mansion Rarri had just purchased looked like some shit that could be featured on 'Beautiful home and estates.' Pulling up into the long ass circular driveway, you could see the four car garage and huge double glass doors that lead inside to where they were standing now. It had Fourteen bedrooms, which included four master suites, eight bathrooms, two dressing areas for the bitches to get ready when they were there and four gas fireplaces. That was just to start. The new crib also had an indoor and outdoor pool with a pool house with two more bedrooms and bathrooms in there. The outdoor pool area had a Jacuzzi and an area where they could barbeque along with an outdoor living area with a DJ booth built in for when they threw parties.

The swim-up bar in the deep end and the waterfall would have been enough, but not for Rarri. In addition to the fire pit, it also had an outdoor oven so they could make pizzas and other shit they would want to fuck around and eat while smoking, drinking and swimming out there. Back on the inside there was a movie theatre with a popcorn machine with butter dispensers and a hot dog warmer. The oversized theatre seats were plush and could be reclined all the way back. They also had pop up tables to sit the drinks, popcorn and food while watching the movies in there.

The floors in the house were marble throughout and it had two separate kitchens, a butler's pantry and another bar area. There were two of each living spaces. One that they would use and the other for showpieces. You could literally forget someone was in the twelve thousand square foot home. Which is why the security system was top of the line and he planned to stash guns all over in case anyone tried to creep on them from anywhere in the mansion.

"This the new 'chop shop p" he stated proudly as they 'P' shook.

"The new what?" Rasheed asked. "Ya'll niggas stealing cars now" he joked looking at Macky like he was crazy.

"On babies I ain't even know cuh was into that type of shit, but if it got a nigga livin like this, he might as well go on and count me in" Macky mumbled lowly as he palm brushed his hair.

Rarri laughed, "Naw, I got this shit from my cuzzins out there in the bay. The house they pimped out of if legendary"

"Why they call it the chop chop?" Macky asked.

"Because, that's where bitches get chopped, rebuilt and brung back brand new." Money Mike said as he walked into the room with Money-Mitch, J-money and Dolla. PayDay staying back. Not that he wanted to. It was just that the others didn't see no point in him coming along without no toes.

He got knocked by J-money and Dolla before the hospital cleared him to leave and hadn't had a bitch since. That together with being stuck in a shit bag, PayDay was bitter as fuck. He wasn't even funny no more or takin care of himself properly. He done let his bag burst many too many times to count and literally just say in that 'shit'. If it wasn't for the fact that he didn't have anywhere else to go, they would have been kicked his ass out. He had a dark cloud hangin over him, rainin and pourin everywhere he went. It felt good for the rest of them to get from under it with him.

Rarri introduced everyone then they made their way back to the living room, where KD and Peso were waiting in excitement, laughing with each other as they read from a piece of paper each of them had in their hands. Macky and Rasheed had met KD and Peso a few days ago and instantly took a liking to them both, but they had their favorites. Rasheed took more of a liking to King Doe because of the Pimpin. On the other hand, Macky favored Peso because he could see he was with all he bullshit and stayed clutchin on something just in case shit got ugly.

"What's this ya'll lookin at 'P'?" Rasheed asked as he sat down then picked up a paper of his own.

"These the rules of the new Chop Shop, P" Peso spoke up proudly.

Macky and Rasheed smiled as they read in silence but laughed out loud at the rules they loved.

"So, ya'll tellin me I got action at anybody bitch in here at any given time with the 'challenge' game?" Macky asked like a happy lil kid.

"All you gotta do is drop a bitch name, P" Dolla assured.

"What if a nigga say no though?"

"Say no?" J-money, Dolla and the twins asked at the same time with sour expressions.

"Listen, if a nigga say *no* to a *challenge* he's outta here." Money-Mitch joked seriously as he pointed his thumb to the back of him. "Ain't no exceptions. That's basically cuffin on these hoes and we don't do non of that" he added making a mental not to challenge Macky for even asking some dumb shit like that. Then, he proceeded to explain. "Ain't no wrong way to challenge a nigga cause his pimpin should be ready for anything and if it ain't he don't belong at the Chop Shop."

"Witnessing my first challenge was crazy" Rarri chimed in with a big smile. "I ain't even know what the fuck was goin on. At first these niggas was talkin about lions and guerillas. The next thing I know, Money-Mike and Dolla was at each other bitches in the garage"

"Who won?" Rasheed questioned excitedly, looking at them both.

"Look at me, 'P'" Money-Mike said as cocky as can be and posed in a fly squat. His chains jingled dramatically at the slightest move. He palm brushed his hair once and thumbed the bugger in his ears, looking at Rasheed as if he was in the mirror. "Who you think won? I got an identical twin and *he* don't even look as good as me" Dolla made a sarcastic face and shook his head as everyone else laughed.

"Look, we all live in the same house and the bitch face stay to the ground, so she ain't seen Dolla since, ya feel me, name?" Money-Mike asked with his hand extended and the two P'shook.

Everybody broke out in good laughter, even Dolla. This was the shit they loved to do and the life they loved to live. Wasn't no feelings involved over losing no bitch because these hoes come and go, so it's always better to get knocked by a nigga around you rather than a nigga you don't know. These hoes belong to the game first, *'then'* the pimp, if he's in it correctly. But, a lot of niggas out here got it fucked up thinking these bitches are theirs to keep, forever.

Yea, they will tell you that but that's hoe-say and hoe-say is no-say unless you 'Jose' and 'Jose' gets no way of hoe-pay, you feel me? Rasheed had never been around none of his family members on his father's side and it felt good to know that he came from a bloodline of some pimpin. He only wished things were different. A part of him wanted to just say, fuck those damn books and let them know who he was.

His pimpin was already established before the books, so it's not like he was drowning without them. One thing he did know though was that there is no such thing as havin 'too much' game.

'He don't know that I already got a book. Maybe I could get the other ones on the low too now that we're all under the same roof' Rasheed plotted to himself. If everything went as smooth as he hoped it would, he would be able to grab the game without fuckin up what they had going. Being around Rarri was something he loved because they had so many similarities. On top of that, the game really needed what they were offering. Wasn't a group of young niggas in America coming together like them.

Rasheed felt guilty for being the only shady one in the group… but, was he really?

―――――

Two months had passed since the Chop shop had opened up and it was pop'n beyond any of their expectations. It was a mad house yet still sophisticated at the same time. The competitiveness of the house was crazy. Money-Mitch knocked Rarri for Diamond and Rarri knocked Ne-Ne from him that same night.

KD was in a panic because he was knocked hoeless on a couple of occasions but niggas respected his pimpin because he constantly bounced back before being eliminated from the shop. Peso and Macky was challenging each other almost every other day. Well really it was Macky challenging Peso in hopes of getting his bitch back. Rasheed had been knocked twice by Money-Mike and once by J-money and for some reason he was the one having the hardest times when it came to challenges and he wasn't feeling that shit at all.

What really had his head fucked up was getting knocked for Brandy by K.D. He honestly didn't get that shit because he knew he was Ten times flyer and had way more money than him. Rasheed couldn't see why she would wait all these years just to downgrade and end up hoe'n for a nigga like K.D. Yea he was some pimpin but it's levels to this shit and Rasheed felt that King Doe wasn't nowhere near his level and financially he wasn't. Where KD lacked in money, he made up for in game and had a personality that took bitches by surprises.

Remember when I told ya'll that you could knock a bitch by doing nothing but that's still doing something because sometimes doing nothing does something to her? Well that's exactly what happened with Brandy, when Rasheed took King Doe's last bitch. Seeing how much humor K.D found in being hoeless tickled her stomach and made her love his little heart. Brandy was a real hoe through and through. So she knew she was out of pocket for simply thinking about King Doe so much.

But no matter how hard she tried, she just couldn't help it. Him clowning himself made her smile when he wasn't even around. Especially when he started singing 'Oh Sandy' like John Travolta in the movie Grease, to the bitch he got knocked for, every single time he seen her. That was beyond comedy at it's best. When King Doe did that nobody in the room could hold back from laughing into tears not even Rasheed, or any other bitch within ears reach so King Doe's antics really had all them hoes out of pocket.

It was so funny to the point where none of them could be mad at their toes for cracking a smile or burstin out laughing because it seemed impossible not to. Brandy seen how much KD's personality could light up a room and the night before he was due to eliminated she found herself holding a handful of money walking into his. King Doe sat up in the bed when he heard the door close behind her. He looked at Brandy in question then noticed the money in her hand along with the smile on her face.

"Bitch stop playing wit me" he joked and laid back down.

"I'm not playin" Brandy laughed as she walked to the bed.

"Sheed bring yo ass out here bruh bruh, I ain't fallin for this shit 'P'... I know you hidin"

"Ain't nobody hidin" Brandy assured as she slid into his bed which instantly made him slide out and eye her with humorous suspicion.

He looked under the bed, in the closet, the bathroom and out his bedroom door down the dark hallway.

"I see you" He lied and listened for any type of movement, still thinking Rasheed was lurking somewhere in the shadows.

K.D closed the door and looked at Brandy. "So, I got some new Toe's ?"

She smiled seductively, held up the money and let the bills fall to the bed. K.D twiddle all of his fingers together with a devilish grin like an evil super villian as he pondered. The next morning all the 'P's of the house sat at the table eating breakfast as they did every morning.

"No lie ima really hate to see you go P Dolla told K.D and everybody chimed in, in agreement as they ate.

They didn't want him to leave, but nobody was above the guidelines of the house. Everybody knew K.D was some pimpin so it was only a matter of time before he bounced back.

"It's coo 'P' You know the game God goin to always bless K.D" King Doe spoke proudly.

"You better get to prayin then" Rasheed joked.

"To keep it real, I'm the type of nigga that prays for the people around me, instead of prayin for myself, but back to the pimpin. You taught me a valuable lesson and I really appreciate that 'P'. The game is priceless but this gift is all I can give at the moment"

K.D reached down beside him bringing up a gift wrapped box with a ribbon on it, then passed it across the table to Rasheed. He looked at everyone, shrugged his shoulders then started unwrapping it with a smile.

"What the fuck" the mouthed, as he opened it and seen what was inside. Then flipped the contents onto his empty plate. Which were some baby back ribs.

"I want my baby back, baby back, baby back, baby back riiiibssss" King Doe teased.

"Knock, knock, King Doe at yo door wit some toes that ain't Yo's!" He jumped up with ambition and everybody went crazy when Brandy came and stood behind him with her head down.

"Yea that's right 'P', she came wit a fee and chose me. I might be short but I'm in it for the long haul, we face to face but this ain't nothin but a phone call, everytime you doze off, ima chop yo toes off. All you niggas better remember what I told ya'll. My list of victims. Go'n need a rollcall. I'm bout to be the nigga on TV known for playin Toe's Ball. Im talkin bout pro's from the old law, cocaine nose raw, stone cold Steve Austin when the show off, Ima be the reason these hoe's never chose ya'll, on P's I got every nigga in this room wonderin how Sheed fuck the hoe off. Let me expose it then mane. He actin like he pimpin really lovin on the low, A baby if you playin me I don't wanna know, ass nigga." King Doe chopped and started laughin as did everyone else.

"Well played" Rasheed said as he stood with a smile clappin in approval then the two P-shook.

"I kept it light" K.D admitted then sat back down.

"Dismissed" He added waving his hand nonchalantly then Brandy walked out of the room.

Rasheed played it off coo but inside he felt that shit. It's like everything they had been through together blew up right along with her. The craziest part about it is, he 'was' wondering what he did wrong to lose the bitch.

Was it cause I went too hard on the hoe? Got too many bitches for the bitch? Damn when is the last time I took that hoe out? Yea that was a while ago I shoulda put-

"I want my baby back, baby back, baby back, baby back, baby back riiibsss" K.D teased again seeing how deep in thought Rasheed was.

Everybody started crying laughing. Rarri and the Twins damn near spit their food out, Peso, Dolla and J-money all ran out of the room and Rasheed just shook his head laughing. He knew he would have to redeem himself because K.D was going to clown every chance he got. They were technically even but K.D knockin Brandy kinda trumped Rasheed's knockin because she was his best hoe.

K.D knew with a bitch like her down for him it was only a matter of time before his paper elevated. Brandy was his breakthrough bitch and a new King Doe was definitely in the making. None of them in the house really played the blade no more. They all had stepped it up and started sending bitches out of town, in escort services, Sugar Daddy events and all type of shit like that. They ain't have to try hard at all because word about the Chop shop spread quickly but only the baddest of bitches were ever invited.

All the other well known young pimps came by the Chop shop almost everybody, to hang out and chop game. It was decked out with vending machines, old school arcade games, and all types of fly shit. The pimps of the house were so cocky that they even had paintings of themselves hanging up throughout it. They rode around on motion boards lazily, dressed to impress knowing damn well they probably weren't going anywhere because they lived where anybody who was somebody wanted to be.

Even celebrities started coming by trying to be around some new era pimpin. It was funny because they would come around then next thing you know, their trick asses would be putting out music videos talking about how they were all of a sudden some pimpin now. Rarri and them didn't give a fuck though because they were actually living the lives others rapped about. On top of that, when them niggas weren't getting knocked for bitches, they were trickin on the bitches getting sent at em. They called rappers Eazy money and T.O.A.T's(Tricks of All Time).

It's crazy how game goofy niggas can look coo on T.V but behind the scenes in real life it's a different story. Every time a bitch gave up a drop on their spots Rarri sent the Flocks. Not to all of them though, because not every rapper is fake. The real ones always got respected and it showed.

Rarri and his crew would literally roll out the red carpet for the real ones and make them feel at home, with a grand entrance. They loved it and found the challenges to be more exciting than anything they had ever seen. The games they played were unheard of. Niggas died over takin niggas bitches. Some even killed themselves over losing a bitch. But not at the Chop shop. They ran through bitches like it wasn't shit. Losing your hoe was like losing your phone. Eventually you'll get another one.

"So, what's on the agenda for the day?" Peso asked as he came back in the room and sat back down trying his hardest to avoid eye contact with Rasheed.

"Ain't that nigga Lucci supposed to be comin through?" J-money reminded.

"Oh yea 'P' and that nigga Philthy and Sauce walka" Money-Mike threw in "Ima try and knock both of them niggas" he added as he slapped fives wit Macky, Money-Mitch made a sarcastic chuckle and had a yea right expression on his face as he sipped his orange juice from his cup.

Money-Mike noticed as did everybody else in the room.

"What was that?"

Money-Mike didn't answer right away, in fact he just drunk the juice from his cup slowly until the very last drop then looked inside the cup like he couldn't believe it was gone. He even tilted his head back with his mouth open and tapped the bottom of his cup dramatically trying to get the last drop that wasn't even there, knowing he had everyone's attention. Then he looked around in surprise. "Oh you was talkin to me?"

"It 'sound' like you got somethin on you mind" Money-Mike replied with a more stern look at his brother.

"You remember Tawanda and Raynisha in Elementary or what about Chante and Dorothy in Junior high?" Money-Mitch asked with a smile full of diamonds. Seeing his brothers lips instantly knot up made him laugh because he knew how to get under his skin. "Naw the funniest time was at Castle Mont high with the other twins Kandice and Krystle, remember them?"

Money-Mike didn't say nothing he just looked at him.

"You don't remember that, Mike?" Money-Mike playfully asked in disbelief. "When I had Kandice and you had Krystle then everybody was like *'damn Mitch really him'* When I had Kandice and Krystle on my arm just like I did with Tawanda and Raynisha and Chante and Dorothy?...I been knockin you, yo whole life 'P'. It goes Money-Mitch *'then after that'* comes Money-Mike, not the other way around. We even came out the pussy in that order. Why you think they call you Twin Duece back home? It's cause I'm number one nigga. I mean don't that go without sayin?" He asked looking at everyone else in the room who were visibly trying to hide their smiles.

"I'm thing one and *'he'* thing two, right?" Everyone snickered but didn't speak. Money-Mitch turned Rarri by the shoulders.

"Right?"

"Yea 'P' damn" Rarri laughed as did everyone else.

"You see, everybody know it" He told his brother with his arms open in victory. "Keep it real Mike, you know it too"

"I know you a dirty Macker" Money-Mike replied bluntly replacing the snickering with exaggerated gasp's the room went mute for a split second then everyone chattered to one another obviously finding his statement appalling.

Being labeled a dirty macker is not something to be proud of. It's acutally frowned upon in the life of pimpin, but still mothafuckas do it all the time on some sucker shit. K.D stood up to get everyone's attention. "'P' that's a serious accusation to be makin on somebody who some pimpin, *'especially'* here at the shop" King Doe explained to the accuser then turned to the accused. "So you sayin that Money-Mitch *'THEE'* MONEY-MITCH is really a dirty macker? Naw not break a bitch Mitch I don't even believe that"

K.D waved the thought off and sat back down like nothing had ever happened.

"I ain't believe Raynisha!" Money-Mike spoke loudly inter-rupting the chatter with his 'P'-fingers in the air lettering everyone know how serious he was. "Or Dorothy because we was raised not to trust '*no*' bitch. But, when Krystle said the same shit that those two said, I had no choice but to believe the shit. yea, he got the bitches, I'll give him that. But, I also wanna give him the opportu-nity to tell ya'll '*how*' he got em because they told me, I just never told him that I knew"

Money-Mike sat back coolly in his chair as his brothers face flushed red in embarrassment and shock. He couldn't believe his brother held water for this long. They told each other everything and I mean '*everything!*', this though was obviously something they both kept secret. Time moved in slow motion as he looked at his brother's smirk from across the table and felt the assuring look in his eyes as he nodded his head knowingly.

Money-Mitch was baffled, he didn't even know what to say. His lips were moving but no words were coming out. He was stuck and everybody saw the look of shame all over him.

"Say it ain't so, 'P', say it ain't so!" K.D cried but his along with everyone else's fell on def ears. They were all begging him to say something, but he couldn't. At least not in time.

"We was fuckin kids, man" He blurted out after a long moment then they all cried in defeat. While Money-Mike laughed.

"Aww Naw, not Mitch"

"Damn P"

"Fuck"

"I can't believe it"

"Psssh" was all Money-Mike could hear as he desperately tried to explain himself but wasn't nobody trying to hear it.

You would have thought somebody had died how they were looking and actin. This shit all started when Money-Mitch told Raynisha that Money-Mike had another girlfriend that went to Highland elementary. He did the same thing with Dorothy in Junior high then turned around and did the same shit wit Krystle in

High School. They all only really did that to make Money-Mike mad but even as a kid he never gave a fuck.

That's why he never said nothing about it and sometimes that's the best thing to do because people tend to expose themselves at the worst of times. You see Money-Mike would have never said anything like this but seeing as how his brother tried to clown in the open by bringing it up, he just played the game with him. By now everybody including Money-Mitch had a smile on their faces. He knew his crucifixion would be in good nature but fasho this was something they would 'always' use against him, especially in times of need.

Money-Mitch knew he would now have to hold his tongue a little more and allow some shit to slide to avoid further clowning on this matter in the future.

"You ain't shit" he laughed.

"You started it.." his brother replied with that same diamond crusted smile.

Rarri, Rasheed, Macky, Peso, J-money and Dolla all had a group huddle going on in the corner looking like a real football team making a secret play.

"Aye, twin, check it out real quick" Rasheed said with his head up from the huddle.

Money-Mike squeezed in with Rasheed and Dolla's arm around him as they congregated. Rarri peeked his head from the circle to look at Money-Mitch, then went back in.

"Yea, on everything" He said loud enough for Mitch to hear.

Money Mitch shook his head every time one of them would peek up at him, then ducked back in laughing. After coming up with the perfect plan everyone could agree on they all put their P-fingers in the middle, counted to three then said, "On P's" together, then everyone sat back down.

"Alright, this the deal 'P',you been demoted" Dolla said as he flickered his nose coolly.

"Demoted? To what?" Money-Mitch asked with a sour

expression.

"Well we was goin to make you sleep in the back wit the hoes but that's givin yo lil ass too much action to keep Dirty mackin, so we decided instead of yo name bein BREAK-A-BITCH-MITCH, yo new name is-.." Dolla paused for the group drum roll then used his hands for special effects and said, "TELL-A -BITCH- MITCH" Everybody started cryin laughin, even Money-Mitch.

"We was kids, P. That shit shouldn't even count"

"But it does" Macky assured. "I know niggas' that told at 13 and they still is considered a Snitch"

"Fa real" everybody agreed.

Mitch stood in agitation, this shit was funny but it was also getting on his nerves. "So what, now ya'll goin to just hold this shit over my head forever?" He looked at this brother "What about forgiveness 'P', what about 'forgiveness'"

"I forgive you" Money-Mike admitted as he stood level with his twin "But I will never forget." He added seriously shaking his head then walked away smiling, followed by the rest of them doing the same.

"You know what, fuck ya'll" Mitch shouted, waving his finger around in contempt. "And, what ya'll talkin bout and if ya'll call me Tell-a bitch-Mitch in front of *'anybody'* Ima Dirty Mack all you niggas and let ya'll bitches know *'all'* the little secrets. since the cat out the bag now!" he added sounding hard as a mothafucka.

———

"Who let the cats out? Meow, Meow, Meow, Meow!" They all sung together pointing to Money-Mitch who was now steamin, because his boys were still clownin with a house full of people.

What really pissed him off though was all the other drunk mothafuckas who kept joinin the sing-a-long and all of the antics not even knowing what it was really about. Money-Mitch had his lips in a knot looking at King Doe coldly because he was the one that kept on starting everybody up with this shit. He was out of his mind thinking they weren't going to keep this shit going when people were around. Shid, really that's the best time to do it. It's always more funnier and if the shoe was on the other foot, Mitch would have been doing the same shit.

Usually, he didn't let little shit like this get to him but for some reason, this shit was sticking hard. It might have been because the Flocks were there. Mitch always seemed to act different when they were around, like he had something to prove or something. They were extra'd out to the fullest *and* getting money. Mitch wanted to be more like them. He and his brother even been with them to their hood a few times and had a ball.

Seeing how much love and respect they got made him low-key idolize them niggas. None more than Baby flock, because he was the shooter, fighter and everything else. Money-Mike idolized himself too much to wanna be like the next nigga. Yea, the Flocks was coo to hang around and fuck with but he didn't want to be like them. Least of all like Baby Flock because he was always trying to pressure somebody up. Just like right now, he knew him singing along had Money-Mitch boiling inside, but that's exactly what he wanted.

"P, why it look like bout to cry-"

Mitch socked K.D in the jaw before he could get out another word. Instinctively K.D socked him back and they were in a full fledged fight, Falling to the floor and some more shit. Peso tried to jump in but Baby Flock grabbed him up.

"On Piru ain't none of that goin on"

Rarri, Rasheed, Dolla, J-Money, and Money-Mike snapped out of their drunken state and broke up the fight. They damn near dragged the two upstairs away from everyone else.

"What the fuck is wrong with you niggas?" Rarri barked at them both. "Both ya'll out there lookin dumb as fuck, puttin on a show in front of mothafuckas like ya'll ain't got no class."

"On P's that shit wasn't coo" Mike pitched in as did the rest of them.

K.D and Mitch adjusted their clothes in embarrassment knowing they were both out of line. King Doe for continuously keeping the joke going and Mitch for letting it get to him.

"FUCK!" They both swore in tandem and pulled out a knot of money and started counting as Dolla held out his hat.

K.D looked at Mitch "I only got four on me"

Mitch glanced back at him like he wanted to say some smart shit but just kept his thoughts to himself, counted out another band, gave it to King Doe then they both put 5 bandz in dollaz hat, P-shook gave each other a hug and walked out of their room laughing at the shit like it was nothing followed by everyone else.

"Come on, let's get back to the party" Rasheed said with both hands on Macky's shoulders as he guided him out of the room but just before walking out, something caught the corner of his eye and he grinned to himself, then yelled, "God blessin all the PIMP niggas!"

They spent the rest of that night getting fucked up popping Mollys, smoking weed and drinking. Having a good all time. Rarri ended up takin three bad bitches to the room and calling it a night. The rest of them kept the party going then the funniest shit happened. The twins challenged Philthy Rich and sauce walka and ended up getting knocked instead of doing the knocking so they were a lil down about that but hey, at least they tried.

Then Philthy Rich and Sauce walka really clowned when they broke on them bitches, threw the money back and pulled off on them hoes because they ain't have enough. Neither Philthy or Sauce wanted them bitches no how. They just wanted to clown and make a spectacle for the gram and let the world see that it's levels to this shit. Wasn't no hard feelings, it was just part of the game. Philthy and Sauce been in the game longer because they were older and had more money because of the music shit. All the young niggas idolized them both so they always dropped game and help sharpen the tools of the up & comin because that was something important to real niggas. The Chop shop was a place like no other, it was a place where pimps could be pimps and hoes could be hoes.

As the sun rose, Rasheed pulled into his mother's driveway, parked, grabbed the book from the Passenger seat and walked into the house. Mary's heart skipped a beat when she saw what was in his hands but she kept her cool this time, not wanting to Jinx the situation.

"Is that what I think it is" she asked calmly.

Rasheed nodded proudly then sat down on the couch next to his mother.

"*The Book of God*" he read out loud, looked at Mary, then back down at the thick book, exhaled to calm himself, secretly praying this wasn't another one of his father's unfinished projects. Quickly, he used his thumb to scan the pages back to front just to be sure. Seeing the filled pages caused both of them to cheer a smile and a quiet shriek. Mary grabbed on to him tightly in anticipation as he made it back to the front page....to read.

'*I had everything I wanted in growin up. My pops was a pimp from L.A and my momma was a ho from Oakland so I was destined to be great, understand me? From middle school to High School I stayed with a ring on every finger and a fat chain around my neck.*'

As Rasheed continued to read, he and his mother hung on to every word. He spent the next few days getting to know the man her never knew.

THIRTY-NINE

HEAVEN HADN'T SEEN Rarri in months and it was killing her. Betty Wap had been keeping her updated on his whereabouts and what's been going on, but still that wasn't enough. She wanted to talk to him herself, not have Betty Wap leave messages all damn day. Besides, she obviously wasn't a good mediator because Rarri never sent a response back. Well at least not one Betty Wap felt comfortable relaying.

"You know what, fuck him?" Heaven yelled at Betty Wap as she went to the bar to make herself a drink. "Let him ignore me then. Let's see how long his lil punk ass could do that for" she added recklessly before downing a shot then double downed on another one.

Wap cringed in disgust. "You don't think you should slow down a little bit?" she suggested as Heaven went in for the refill. She looked at Betty Wap, batter her eyes and chuckled sarcastically while shaking her head.

"What was all that?" Wap asked defensively.

Heaven downed the shot, slammed the glass down then leaned over the counter teasingly. "I'd let a pitbull hit bareback before I take advice from my one-eyed flunky" she replied coldly before laughing like she just told the funniest joke in the world.

Her word's hit Wap hard because she looked up to her more than any other woman she had ever met. She thought Heaven loved her but hearing how she really felt brought her back down to reality.

'she don't give a fuck about me' Wap thought as she looked back at Heaven with a mix of emotions. Mostly hurt, the anger in her dared for a challenge but she couldn't build up enough courage to do so. She tucked the envelope she wanted to show Heaven back in her pocket then stood to leave.

"At least I got somebody that wants me" she said, sadly tucking her bottom lip into her mouth in deep thought then looked at Heaven with a bit of pride. "And that's worth more than *'anything'* you got"

"You think you somethin now?" Heaven yelled to Betty Wap's back as she walked away. "I made you, BITCH! ME! And since we bein honest, Rarri just felt sorry for yo raggedy ass, my nephew don't want you"

"Well, I guess that makes two of us then huh?" Betty Wap one-upped over her shoulder before walking out.

Heaven threw her shot glass at the door and screamed out in anger, Knowin that Waps' statement was truer than hers. Rarri loved Wap. He just had a lot on his plate at the moment. They had been spending more time together and doing things like going to the movies, out to eat, walking the beach and shit like that. They even hit a few clubs together, but, Rarri hadn't made any other sexual advances towards her since the kiss in the car.

She didn't want to put pressure on him by whining about it. The situation was just starting to make her feel insecure and question herself again. More so after what Heaven had just said. Betty Wap knew she was just drunk but still, she made it her mission to prove her wrong. She wiped the tear from her face, got in her car and headed for the Chop shop. Tonight she was going to make love to Rarri and tell him everything that's been weighing her down.

It might not be as romantic as the *'first time'* fantasy she had on her mind but at least it was going to happen. She had been doing everything a good hoe could possibly do. She never came in short or did anything out of pocket. In fact, she *'always'* hit Rarri's mitt with more than he expected. She put in more hours than any of his other hoes, now that the Bentley Bitches were gone.

Anxiety started to build up as she pulled into the driveway. All of the cars in the front didn't make it any better. Betty Wap hoped to catch him alone but that was near impossible because the Chop shop was never empty.

"You got this" She assured herself in the mirror making sure her eye was in-place, make-up and hair was straight then got out of the car and walked up and into the house with confidence, seductively bouncing everything she had.

The house was packed and the crowd of people put a strain on her catwalk but she squeezed by and found Rarri in the kitchen spitting game to some white bitch she had never seen before. Betty Wap frowned to herself at the sight of her daddy choppin at a bitch. Usually, that would make her smile and put a damp in her panties but tonight was supposed to be her night. She wasn't about to let no silly white bitch stop that though. Wap faked a smile as she walked up.

"Hey daddy, can I steal you for a minute?" she asked, surprising him a bit.

He looked back at the white girl with that million dollar smile instantly making her blush.

"Stay yo pretty ass right here, Ima be back before you can say, *"I choose"*

"I choose" she teased immediately biting down on her bottom lip and looking into his eyes like she was ready to eat him alive.

"I know" he replied as they eye fucked slowly. Betty Wap cleared her throat loudly interrupting their moment.

"Ima be right back" he walked over to Wap slightly irritated. "What's the deal?"

"I was thinking maybe we can spend the night together and talk about some stuff?" she asked slyly as she pulled him closer by the bottom of his shirt looking up at him with sex in her eyes.

Rarri moved her hand and distanced himself a bit. "I know you see me choppin at some new toes. You don't get paid to think, Wap. What we gotta talk about?"

She looked down at her feet. "I mean, it's not nothing I feel comfortable talkin about in front of nobody else"

She looked at the white girl who was literally watching her mouth not wanting to miss a word even though she couldn't hear them clearly. When he looked back at her also, she turned elsewhere not wanting to *seem* nosey but he noticed. Wap was looking back up at him in question when he turned to her again. She wanted him to tell her off, get her number, call her later or something. anything! Hell, he could have made her stand in the corner for all she cared. But, like a lot of *'niggas'* who get caught up in the moment, his vision was clouded by *'Snow'*. He was tryna catch a bunny and she was in the way right now.

"Look, obviously it ain't nothin that important, right?"

She didn't know what to say to that. Maybe it wasn't important but that's why she wanted to talk to him about it and find out. She didn't like keeping things from Rarri but every time she tried talking to him, something either came up or someone was around. This was a personal issue and she wanted to keep it that way. If she couldn't talk to Rarri or Heaven about it, she was on her own to be honest and that's not something she *wasn't* used to.

"Right.." she agreed sadly then smiled awkwardly.

"That's what I'm talkin bout" He replied slapping her on the ass. "We gon holla later" he added turning his attention back to the white girl, then placed a hand on the small of her back guiding her out of the kitchen so they could talk privately.

From where to send her and how to send her, he already had it all figured out. He knew exactly what to do with this bitch. She was going to go with Pinks and the rest of his high priced white hoes. He was going to have so much snow dough his finger tips would be frostbitten after checkin his trap. He could see it clear as day, but-sometimes we *'want'* something so bad we overlook the people we *'need'* the most.

"Riiight" Betty Wap agreed like she finally got it once he left the room. She was disappointed in him but she pushed that feeling in the same place in her mind where she used to put things and told herself what she wanted to hear. "Riight" she repeated again then burst out laughing. And just like that, mentally at least, the old Betty Wap was back.

"Ain't nobody seen that nigga, Sheed?" Rarri asked as the group sat lazily in the living room scrolling through their phones.

"I ain't seen that nigga since the day I knocked 'P'" K.D pointed out proudly and everyone else agreed in unison.

"He out there in pursuit. Probably choppin bitches up as we speak" Rarri boasted, then added in disgust, "Look at ya'll, layin around all lazy like. The twins lookin like they bout to take a picture together doin double duck lips for the gram. Make sure ya'll hashtag *"Kissyfacepimp"* on ya'll next post…Then look at this nigga.." he pointed at Peso. "Puedes traerme un poco de agua?"

"I don't speak Spanish, 'P'" Peso admitted.

"Then what is you good for?"

"Pimpin!"

"I can't tell" Rarri spat back, shaking his head and moving along to King Doe. "You a made man now you got some toes again, huh? You got too much game for that K.D. One bitch is too close to havin none. It seem like every time you knock a *'new bitch'* you forget that shit" He then turned to J-Money.

"'P', you gotta start makin better impressions. It's like you don't stand out at all. We be steppin out lookin like the Migos and you always on the side lookin dull like Take-off...somebody asked me who you was the other day. How they don't know you, 'P'?"

Next, he looked at Dolla and Macky and their shiny ass shoes. "Simmer down cuh ya'll be tryin too hard." He added then plopped down on the couch to relax.

"You ain't forgettin nobody?" Money-Mitch asked.

"Naw, Sheed ain't here to defend himself so I ain't even goin to speak on him"

"No, not Rasheed, I'm talkin bout you, 'P'. He reminded him.

"Me?" Rarri sat up in surprise, then laid back after a moment of thought. "Nope, ain't nothin to forget when you're on yo shit, 'P'"

"On yo shit?" 'P', do you know what we lookin at right now?" Money-Mitch said holding out his phone.

Rarri grabbed it and saw Betty Wap smiling from ear to ear standing next to some suited and booted old school pimp nigga. He knew all bitches were knockable, but damn, seeing Betty Wap with somebody else was a hard pill to swallow and something he never expected. And by some old school pimp too? It couldn't possibly get no worst than that.

"Who is this nigga?' He demanded to know.

"That's her pops, 'P'" K.D's words hit him hard.

He seen that the picture was posted 2 days ago and nothing been up there since. Which was unlike Betty Wap who had become a creature of habit, posting something everyday. Even if it was just a meme or what she was about to eat. So, Rarri knew something was wrong. He pulled out his phone and called her but it went straight to voicemail. He did that a few more times getting the same results. Then he sent a text. "Where you at?"

No reply came. He felt stupid for not paying attention to what was going on. This is what she had been tryna tell me the whole time. He thought to himself. 'If he did that to her as a kid, he couldn't even imagine how hard on her he would be as an adult. He picked up his cousin's phone to look at the picture again. Betty Wap's father had a cold menacing look and crafty eyes. He could feel the monster behind his smile. Betty Wap stood there as happy as can be, oblivious to what was going on. The saddest part was really how excited she looked to be with the man who went to prison for shooting her. Just thinking about that shit had his blood boiling all over again.

"I gotta go find her" he said then jetted for the door, not even knowing where to start looking. All Rarri knew about her father was what she told him when they first met.

As soon as he opened the door, he saw Rasheed walking up. He said 'what's up' but Rarri brushed by him, not even hearing that shit, Then jumped in his car and sped off.

FORTY

Hours had passed and Wap was nowhere to be found. He had looked everywhere she was known to be to no avail. She was officially off the grid. It was only one other place he thought she could and even though Rarri dreaded the idea, he had to find out.

'Knock, Knock, Knock, Knock.."

"Who is it?"

"Me!"

"Where yo key at?" Heaven asked with a hint of attitude after a long pause.

He blew out in frustration, put his forehead on the door, his right hand on the knob and stood there in sadness, regret and a whole lot of defeat.

"I..." He stopped himself from telling a lie. Apart of him wanted to hurt her but the other half of him hated doing that. Even so, the truth was no better, but it was the truth. "I threw it away"

She shook her head, slightly bruised. "So what you want?"

"Wap missin...I been lookin everywhere. She ain't answerin her phone or nothin..."

Heaven opened the door after hearing that.

"When's the last time you talked to her?"

"Like, a few days ago" He answered letting himself in.

"A few days ago?" She asked in disbelief. "What, ya'll got in an argument or somethin?"

"Naw, I was lowkey on some bullshit the other night when I met this new bitch.. Wap as tryin to holla at me about somethin but I brushed her off"

"Damn, now that I think about it, I kinda did the same shit" Heaven confessed sounding disappointed in herself too. "I got faded and she came over here tryna talk about somethin wit me too but I was still mad at you for bein mad at me and ended up goin off on her for no reason." She let her head drop, "That's probably what she was tryna to tell you."

"Naw, it's way worse than that. She ended up meetin with her pops" He replied as he pulled out his phone.

"How is that worse? I wish we had a chance to meet our fathers."

"Not if ours were like hers" he countered then passed her his phone. "Her eye like that because of that bitch ass nigga. He went to jail for shootin her when she was six. Talkin bout she was comin between cuh money because she kept getting sick. What type of nigga shoot his own daughter??"

Heaven's heart nearly popped out of her chest when she saw the man Betty Wap was standing next to. Rarri was still talking but she couldn't hear a thing. Frozen in fear and panic, Heaven quickly felt herself becoming light-headed. She slightly stumbled to the sofa and took a seat, staring ahead in a daze. Rarri picked his phone up from the carpet then looked at his aunt with questions in his eyes.

"You straight?"

She didn't respond but the look of terror on her face was evident. Rarri had never seen her this distraught in his life and it angered him deeply. She was literally shaking like a wet dog outside in the wintertime. He looked at his phone then back at his aunt.

"Who is this nigga?"

She looked at the phone, then back up at him.

"Sir Master.."

"Sir Master? Ain't that the same nigga you said had somethin to do with my pops getting killed?"

She nodded sadly.

"..But, how is this even possible?" he asked in confusion.

"I don't know" she replied, shaking her head, just as baffled as he was. "I mean, now that you said what he went to jail for, it does all make sense. After everything happened, Sir Master left, probably thinkin I was goin to say somethin to the police when they came askin questions but I ain't say shit. The rumor was he went up North and got locked up for a shootin that happened out there. I heard a kid was involved but I ain't know nothin about it bein his daughter."

"I know you said he was fuckin with that nigga, Juice, but how exactly was he involved?" he asked as he sat next to her.

"Pass me those" she pointed to the cigarettes and the lighter on the table. He grabbed them both and gave them to her. She pulled one from the pack, lit it and hit hard to calm her nerves. "Yo dad had a plug on this drug called 'The Devil's Breath'. It's some shit that will make a mothafucka give you any and everything you ask them for. You could literally tell a person to give you everything in their account and they would do it with no questions asked"

"So, why we ain't got none of that shit?" He wanted to know.

"I guess I just never had too much care for it. Especially after everything that had happened."

She pulled on her cigarette and continued.

"..anyway, yo dad came up with a plan to rob Sir Master for all of his shit. He wanted everything 'but' his bitches and against our better judgement, me and your momma sought it through. After he got hit

with 'The Devil's Breath'. Yo dad told him to put all the money and
jewelery in the house in a bag and give it to me then to let me leave and
he did. Back then, Sir master was the most cruel and heartless pimp
around. He would degrade hoes in ways you couldn't even imagine.
Especially the white bitches. One time, one of them tried to leave him
for another nigga and he burned her pussy with a hot curling iron so
nobody would want her. He even tarred and feathered a bitch before.
Every story I ever heard about him always outdid the other and when
his hoes would come up missing or found dead, everybody knew he
had killed them. Sir Master had the whole city terrified. Even the
pimps because he would get on them too." She grabbed a drink she
had on the table and took it straight to the head because the cigarettes
weren't enough on their own as she talked about him.

"Keep goin" Rarri pushed her.

"..yeah, So, Nobody ever stood up to him, that's why I think yo
dad did what he did. The next day, he woke up to nothin and when
his bottom bitch told him what had happened, he knocked all of
her teeth out thinkin she was lyin. The best thing about that Devil
shit is that mothafuckas don't even know they are on it cause they
don't feel high and can't remember nothin when they come down.
We got away smooth"

She put the cigarette out in the ashtray as she exhaled the
smoke, shaking her head in regret.

"But, he didn't want to stop there. Sir Master was just the start
of something that ended up being bigger and eventually, being yo
father's downfall. You see, after that, he had us doin something to
every gorilla pimp he could think of. We was bookin shit left and
right. When word got back around to Sir Master, he knew what was
being said had to have been true and that's when all the conspirin
began."

"Against my pops?"

"Right. Now, Juice always wanted to be my nigga. We was
supposed to go to the prom together and all that but nothin
compared to being touched by god. So when I left him hangin he

was hurt. So hurt that he linked up with the people who hated your father the most. One of them being...."

"Sir Master" Rarri finished for her as she nodded that he was right before going on.

"I don't know the exact role Juice played but I kept hearin about *'why'* he was involved. He thought if God was out of the picture that me and him would get together. All I know is that one night, yo dad dropped us off at momma's house because she wanted to see you and a couple of minutes after we made it in the house, I heard more gunshots goin off than I ever heard in my life. As soon as they stopped me and Angel ran outside and seen yo dad's car crashed at the end of the street. When we ran to the car it looked like a million bullets had ripped through it and your dad was----"

Heaven wiped her eyes and Rarri put his hand on her shoulder to console her. She then exhaled to strengthen herself and continued.

"He was unrecognizable. Angel was yellin at me to help her get him out of the car but.... I wouldn't touch him. It was just, it was just too much for me to deal with. I froze and she couldn't forgive me for that. Two days later, she killed herself by swallowing a whole bottle of pills. I felt so alone that I contemplated doin the same thing but I couldn't leave you here by yoself.... He made me promise to make you great.."

"Damn.." Rarri whispered to himself, letting it all sink in. He knew that his dad was murdered and his mom killed herself but hearing some of the details was new. He found it crazy how the laws of the universe could bring people together. "I can't believe Betty Wap is his daughter.

"I can't believe I let that bitch stay in my house" She replied honestly.

"What you mean?" he asked, snatching his hand from her shoulder.

"What I mean is, I don't want her back over here."

He stood up in anger. "Are you serious?"

She gave him a look that said everything. She grabbed another cigarette from the pack, lit it and pulled on it hard, thinking deeply to herself.

"You actin like it's her fault he did what he did. She don't know nothin about none of this shit. Cuh obviously got her brainwashed or somethin. Look what he did to her and she still tryna fuck with him" He protested. It was falling on deaf ears. She gave him that same look again and shook her head.

She didn't give a fuck about none of that shit. She had her own problems to worry about and Betty Wap's father was the main one of them. "So you still want to fuck with her after everything her father did to yours?"

"You still fucked with my dad after his killed yours, what's the difference?" He shot back looking at her impatiently for an answer.

Her once frightened eyes now cold and replaced with the malice she usually carried. The anger inside of her dwarfed all of her fears. Heaven knew what she had to do so all of his reasoning's continued to go unheard.

"The difference is that I loved your dad and never had a *chance* to love mine. I seen yours grow into somethin beautiful and within seconds look like he got thrown into a fuckin blender. The difference is that my sister killed herself over that nigga. The differences don't even matter, Rarri. I'll do a lot of things for you but reconciling with the daughter of the man who took everything away from me, that's not one of them." She spat out looking at him seriously.

"I'm sorry but you are on your own with this one." She got up and left out of the room. She missed Rarri but he had the option of coming back. His parents didn't.

After everything she endured wasn't no way in hell Heaven could see herself sitting in the same room as Betty Wap without trying to kill her. The mere fact of her DNA made her guilty in Heaven's eyes and just like her father, she was as good as dead.

Rarri slammed the door in frustration on his way out, feeling like he was back at square one. Deep down, he knew coming here was a mistake because It really only made things worse. He knew Heaven like the back of his hand, so he didn't need thermal goggles on to see something was up her sleeve. He drove around for hours with no destination. Hopelessly hoping to see Betty Wap somewhere. Now her phone was going straight to voicemail and she still hadn't made any new post or answered his text.

It was late and he was getting tired but he didn't want to go home and deal with everybody laughing and cracking jokes and shit because he would snap on one of them niggas. None of them would understand him needing to find her. The only thing they would see is the cape on his back and the Capital (SAVE-A-HOE) 'S' on his chest. Thinking about it, Rarri didn't feel like he had anybody to talk to without him feeling weak, so he checked himself into a hotel room for the night to be alone. He was tired as hell but he still couldn't sleep.

His mind was going a million miles a minute. He couldn't do nothing but lay there until the sun came up. He went to get the complimentary breakfast that the Embassy suites provided every morning. The woman who made the plates eye fucked him desperately. He knew damn near every bitch in the room was enamored (How could they not be?), but, he wasn't in the mood to entertain nothing. Not even potential toes.

'*I gotta find this bitch*' he thought to himself as he took a bite of the eggs then let the fork drop on the plate making a sharp noise.

"Is everything okay?" The woman who had served him the food asked while walking by to collect empty plates.

She was beautiful but that was meaningless at the moment. Rarri wanted to talk to her but didn't even know what to say to the bitch, so he just got up and left. When he got home, he crept straight up to his room and locked himself in there, not wanting to be seen by anyone in . A week had passed and the only time he came out was to get a bottle of drink or to raid the fridge. He did shower everyday and brush his teeth, so he didn't let himself go completely.

K.D and the rest of them tried to cheer him up whenever they could but he was in a world of his own. He even stopped answering his phone for the Bentley Bitches and that was rare because they kept him updated on everything they did almost everyday. He missed them too but the thought of Wap somewhere crying her heart out or possibly dead somewhere was too over-whelming. He didn't want to talk to nobody else until talking to her because he felt responsible for everything.

Sitting at the edge of his bed, slumped, with his head down, he twirled the bottle of Remy to hear if it still had liquor in it. It was empty but he still put it up to his lips attempting to get the last drop. The bottle dropped to the floor as he stood. He tied his Versace robe as best he could as he stumbled to his matching house shoes, somehow managing to slip them on. He looked in the mirror in front of him and belched loudly as he tried his best to adjust his disheveled dreads, looking like he hadn't had a edge up in ages. Not recognizing the man in the mirror, he looked at himself in contempt.

Grabbing three of his chains off of the dresser, he put them on then looked at himself again, this time with a drunken smile.

"There you go" he said proudly.

As soon as he opened up his room door, he could hear music playing in the distance.

"Ayee" he cheered to himself doing a chef dance as he came down the stairs almost falling on a couple of occasions. It was people everywhere so he knew they had thrown another party but he just wanted to get his drank and go back up to his room.

His vision was blurry but he somehow made it to the bar area. He squinted hard, literally putting his face up close to every bottle looking for his liquor of choice. Not finding it in sight, he opened the cabinets behind the bar, stood and started throwing everything inside to the floor, breaking glass and spilling alcohol everywhere.

"WHERE THE FUCK ALL THE REMY GO!!" he shouted angrily. Almost everybody in the room started laughing at him. "Oh, ya'll mothafuckas think this shit funny?"

He started grabbing bottles and blindly throwing them around trying to hit whoever he could. Bitches screamed and ducked as they fled out of the room for help. Rarri was about to throw another bottle that was in his hand but somehow in midthrow, he noticed it was some Remy.

"AYEEE" he cheered doing his little chef dance again before twisting the cap off and takin a big ass sip. Satisfied now that he had found what he came for, he was ready to head back upstairs.

As soon as he walked into the other room, everybody burst out laughing and pointing.

"What's up wit you, 'P'?" Rasheed asked as he and the rest of the group came to his aid.

"What uuup" Rarri responded, took another big ass sip then held out the bottle. "Ya'll niggas want some of this shit?"

"'P', get it together" K.D pleaded sympathetically. Macky agreed not feeling seeing his boy like this.

Rarri laughed to himself as he tried his hardest to stand up straight. He looked at them with a sarcastic smile them waved them off. "You niggas buggin, 'P'"

" 'P', you walkin around in a robe, butt ass naked wit yo shit hangin out" Money-Mitch pointed out.

Rarri squinted down in disbelief for a long moment then looked with suspicion and said, "Where my drawers go?" before falling out.

You would have thought that would have been a wake-up call or turning point for him, but it wasn't. The next day he was at it again, drinking his life away. Solving his problems through a bottle. He wasn't even checking his trap no more so his hoes were running to pimps who were actually *trying* to pimp.

Everybody at the Chop shop tried to play it down for him but they could only keep up with the façade for so long and around there, that was being *too* nice. Sometimes pimpin gotta learn the hard way or he won't learn at all. They played a lawless game but the house itself did have guidelines. Rarri had so many toes ready to leave that it was ridiculous, but who better to have them then his own squad? If any of them said they weren't excited to take his bitches they would be lying. It was the main talk of the house. Among the bitches for sure.

Everybody but him seemed to care. He would literally walk right pass them hoes like he never even knew them. He was hanging on by a limb at the Chop Shop. He only had Pinks left but she was ready to fuck with Rasheed now because out of all of them, he was the one poppin the most recently. It's like out of nowhere his game had elevated to a new level and everybody noticed it. Rasheed was handlings every situation like a boss and stepped up without hesitation. He was a natural born leader. This shit was an episode of big brother and he was now head of the house.

Rasheed could be cold but sometimes, depending on the topic, it's just better to be calculated. When he found out Pinks was ready to choose up, he called a meeting and everybody agreed upon what must be done. Silently hoping this would snap him back to reality. The seven of them went to his room to let him know if he didn't get at Pinks right now before she chose, he would be eliminated from the Chop shop.

This was the push he needed so they just knew Rarri was going to come out, go downstairs and chop on the bitch but to their surprise, he came out with his bags packed.

"Ya'll goin to help me take this shit to the car? He asked miserably and rugged looking while still in his robe and house shoes.

They was all in a state of shock, not believing he was really throwing in the towel over Betty Wap leaving. Macky was heated.

"Cuh, you really bout to go out like this over one bitch? HELL NAW!" he grabbed the latch to his MCM backpack "Take this shit off!"

Rarri pushed him away, leaving Macky ready to fight him over this shit but K.D grabbed him.

"You can't make him pimp, 'P'" he said seeing the emptiness in Rarri. King Doe didn't understand what was going on, but he accepted it. "I got you, bruh bruh" he added then grabbed two of his bags. The rest of them reluctantly did the same and walked him outside to his car, trying to talk some sense into him the whole way.

It didn't seem real until Rarri pulled off. Peso shook his head in disbelief waiting to see if he came back laughing like this was really another one of his jokes. Only it wasn't. He turned out of the driveway and kept goin...

FORTY-ONE

The Next Morning…

TAP, Tap, Tap…

Rarri jumped up out of his sleep in shock hearing the noise on his car window. He looked lost when he seen who was standing there.

"You comin in or you just goin to sleep in the car all day?" G-Man asked, then opened up the back door, grabbed some of his bags and headed towards the house.

Rarri adjusted his robe, slid back into his slippers and got out of the car looking like a Vampire trying to hide his face from the sun as he bee lined behind his grandpa.

"What you doin over here?"

"Something I should have been done a long time ago" G-man said with a smile lookin at his grandson proudly as they reached the door. "Come on, yo breakfast gon get cold"

The first thing Rarri noticed was how clean everything was which was a surprise because the last time he came here it was filthy and his grandma was pissy drunk, Spitting at people and all types of shit. This time when he seen her, she was sober and looking happier than he had ever seen her. She nearly ran up to him giving him a big hug.

"Hey baby, I missed you so much" she said, giving him a few hard kisses on the cheek.

"I missed you too, granny" he admitted holding onto her tightly.

He missed her so much that he wished he could hold her like that forever. This was the last thing he expected to see coming here. He just wanted to drink, Pop Xanax and be miserable in peace and wasn't no better place than his grandmas house *'he thought'* but this was better. His grandma leaned back to get a better look at him. He looked away. She hugged him again, tightly.

"Everything goin to be okay" she assured and gave him another kiss. "now come eat yo food before it get cold. Cristy know she goin to hear it when I see her. Got my baby out here lookin like he ain't ate in weeks."

Rarri followed her into the kitchen where his grandpa was already seated and eating. He sat in front of his plate and dug in. It had been a while since he had her cooking and everything she made was always good. She cleaned quietly with a smile as they ate just enjoying the moment. The way she kept their glasses full, refilling them with orange juice almost after every sip, he knew his grandpa had gotten her straight.

Thankful, Rarri nodded at G-man when their eyes met. G-man nodded back with a sly smile, took another bite of his sausage, then grabbed a napkin to wipe his mouth and fingers.

"So how you likin 'The Crown'?

"What Crown?" he asked.

"The book, I left it in yo room" he replied pushing his plate away.

He thought about it for a minute then looked back at G-man "Naw, I never got that one, but I haven't really been goin over there like that lately."

"So what you been doin?" G-man and anybody else with eyes could see this wasn't the normal Rarri, plus the twins had told him what was going on already.

Rarri put his fork down, wiped his mouth with his hand and pushed his plate away. He opened up his mouth but didn't know what to say so he just shook his head.

"What is?" G-man shook his head, mocking Rarri.

"NOTHIN!" I ain't been doin nothin..DAMN!" he replied with an attitude.

"So you just goin to let everything you learned and all of yo hoes go to waste over one bitch?" G-man asked

Rarri looked at his grandma, he wasn't used to speaking about shit like this in front of her. She didn't seem the slightest bit bothered.

"What you looking at her for? You know what, it don't matter, 'P'" G-man got up, walked over to him and held his hand out. "I need that back though"

"You serious?"

G-man gave him a look that said everything. Rarri's lips knotted. He was hot aint need nothing or nobody so he snatched the diamond crusted link with 24k Ferrari medallion off, threw it to the floor and stormed to his room, slamming the door behind him. He felt like the whole world was against him. Everywhere he went, somebody had something to say. It was like nobody understood what he was going through. They just expected him to say fuck Betty Wap and move on but he couldn't, not without at least knowing she was alright. Something was wrong and he could feel it.

He couldn't imagine Betty Wap leaving him willingly, especially without saying something. Hell naw! Not knowing where she was at was killing him inside. He couldn't hide his pain even if he wanted to, so he didn't. He laid on his bed and stared at the ceiling having de ja vu. He had been holding this in for too long. Tears fell from his eyes as he thought about everything that's ben happening in his life . The shit with his mom and even the murder of spank, even though he didn't have nothing to do with it, he still felt responsible because if he didn't put him in a position to get killed, the both of them would still be alive.

'All of this shit is my fault' He thought to himself. On the outside, everything used to look good, but on the inside, he was always feeling fucked up. All of the killings was starting to think about where before, he never give them a second thought. Even though the lady Rarri shot inside the Nunley's house that resembled his mother was already dead, shooting her again only made things worse. The blood pouring from her head and the baby crying haunted him almost every night since it happened. In his dreams, he was the baby and his mother the lady.

He used to love the nightmares but now he hated them. Everything that was going on was things he brought upon himself. That's why he needed to find her. If she was dead, that would be the straw to break the camel's back. She would end up another one of his nightmares and that's something he didn't want to happen. Tired of thinking, he closed his eyes and tried to rest his brain a bit. He was just about to doze off when a thought caused him to open his eyes.

"The Pit" just a fast as he said it, he was out of the door.

Knock, Knock, Knock, Knock, Knock, Knock!

Rarri had been knocking on Betty Wap's door repeatedly and was about to start kicking on that mothafucka like Supreme.

"You just missed her" Tasha said as she stepped halfway outside, looking sexy as she always did. "You could come in and wait if you want. unless you still mad at me"

He looked at her for a moment. "Naw, I ain't mad at you" Rarri forced a smile as he walked in.

She closed the door, grabbed the blunt from her ashtray and sat indian style on her bed as she lit up. He sat on the bed across from her.

"You look....comfortable..." Tasha joked.

He looked down at his robe and house shoes, slightly embarrassed. "Yea" was all he managed to say.

Tasha held the blunt out but he declined so she just kept on smoking solo.

"So, you kicked Wap to the curb huh. I knew that wasn't gon last long. I mean, she look 'way' better now but can't no nigga fix what's up here in a bitch" she said, tapping her head and started coughing from the smoke in her lungs.

"Man" He agreed, thinking about how crazy Tasha was.

She laughed thinking he was talking about Wap too.

"Now, she back here at the Pit, where she started, doin the same shit" she joked like she was doing something different.

"How she been though?" he was eager to know.

"She been ight, I guess. It kind of surprised me though"

"Why is that?"

Tasha hit her blunt one more time then put it out.

"She just seemed 'too' happy to be back. I guess I would be too if I was her and I got my eye fixed and body hooked up. What made you pick her at the show, anyway? I mean I know why you ain't pick me but I never understood out of all those bitches there, Why her?"

Rarri smiled to himself as he thought about Betty Wap then looked at Tasha.

"She was special"

"Yea, special ed" she replied sarcastically and got up from the bed. "You want somethin to drink?"

"Naw, I'm bout to bounce. If you see Wap, tell her I said to call me" he said as he walked to the door.

"Rarri, can I ask you somethin?" she asked as he opened the door.

"What's the deal?" He looked at her over his shoulder.

"Before you leave again, are you goin to think about takin me with you?" she closed her eyes tightly, waiting on his response.

"Probably not" he admitted and walked out.

She was heated. Angry and feelin played *'again'*, she ran to the door and started going off as he walked away.

"Fuck you then, nigga! I don't need you or yo weak ass pimpin. My hoin *'been'* goin, mothafucka!" she yelled then slammed the door.

He didn't give a fuck about nothing she was talking about. Tasha's true colors always came out when she got mad. Her crazy ass was obviously on the same shit as before. He jumped in his Benz and pulled out of the hotel. God must have been listening to his prayers cause about five blocks down, there was Betty Wap standing on the corner with some other woman.

"Yes!" he cheered happily, gassed it to her and hopped out excitedly. "Wap"

"Rarri!" she replied just as excited.

He hugged her tightly, glad she was still alive.

"I'm sorry Wap. I should have listened to you. I was bein stupid. I ain't going to never do that again, I promise."

"Marquesha!" the lady behind them yelled.

Betty Wap moved out of his arms sadly and put her head down. He looked at her in shock then at the lady in anger. She looked like a smoker. Even though her mouth was closed due to the killer mean mug, one tooth peaked out dramatically.

"You know this nigga?' she sounded like she smoked a hundred cigarettes a day.

"Yes momma" Betty Wap replied.

"Momma?" Rarri asked himself in disbelief as he seen the resemblance.

"Who is he?" she demanded to know. Betty Wap got quiet which seemed to anger her mother even more. "I asked you a question, Marquesha, don't make me ask you again"

"I'm Rarri" he spoke up.

She huffed, looking at him like she wanted to kill him. "Well, she got folks now" Her mother grabbed her by the arm and pulled her away from him roughly. "Bring yo ass on. Daddy gon hear bout this shit. You could bet on that"

"I told you we was gon be a family again, Rarri! I told you, you'll see!" Wap yelled happily to him as her mom pulled her to the other side of the street.

"What are you doing, Wap? You don't want to be here, not with her...not with 'him'" He pleaded with tears in his eyes as he stepped off of the curb, falling out of his slip on.

"Nigga, look at you. You out here in a robe and some slippers, cryin over a bitch like a trick or somethin" her mother joked with her see through smile. Then she looked at Wap. "Ain't that funny, Queesh?"

"Yea" Betty Wap laughed and her mother looked at Rarri in victory.

He was hurt, he felt like fire stood between them. He reached out for her.

"Come on, Wap. All you gotta do is get in...just like before."

Her mother huffed again, looked at him shamefully, then turned to her daughter.

"Do yo dance on this nigga, Queesh"

Without hesitation, Wap started bouncing her shoulders and shaking her head with her tongue out like her favorite song was playin looking goofy as hell.

"AYE! AYE! AYE! AYE!" her mom cheered dramatically which made Wap turn up even harder.

His heart sank. Wap was back looking like a damn foo. He wanted to save her bad but by the looks of it she was too far gone. He shook his head as she continued to parade around, put his slipper back on and walked back to his car.

"Yea, that's right mothafucka. Go on back home cause I got this" her mother taunted loudly.

When he got in his car he looked at Wap one last time. She was still over there dancing but now her mother was back to cheering her on. He pulled off and didn't look back. She was alive and breathing, so he was at least grateful for that. No matter how much he didn't want to, he knew at that moment that he had to let Betty Wap go.

Was this enough to wake him up? HELL No! A week had passed by and Rarri found himself stuck under the same dark cloud as his cousin, Payday. The both of them doused in each other's misery. They didn't even talk. When one of them wanted something they just pointed to whatever it was and grunted, creating a pathetic way of communication.

He was so lost in the sauce that he didn't even care when Payday's shitbag would burst. Who was he to judge him? This was a place where they could be themselves and not care what people thought in the outside world. Rarri would stay here forever if he could. All they did was smoke, drink and watch back to back episodes of Black-ish all day. If you were lucky, really lucky, you might catch a laugh every now and then.

Payday pointed at the bottle of Remy in Rarri's hand and grunted, Rarri chugged some, passed it then pointed to the blunt in his. He took a pull then passed it on to Rarri. He took two hits and exhaled lazily. It felt good to be ducked off and off of the grid. Rarri 'thought' nobody knew where was at. Unknown to him, Payday, being as bitter as he was, wanted to make his cousin's jealous for leaving him behind to go fuck with Rarri in LA. He found it funny how Rarri was now in the Bay fuckin with him. So much so that he would send long text messages ranting about much 'fun' they were having and all the shit they were doing. He even sent a picture of Rarri when he was passed out on the floor with the caption 'white boy wasted'. They knew it was bad seeing as how Rarri had the same robe on from the day he left.

The Chop shop used to be lit, colorful and full of life. Now it was dark, dull and dead. Payday had every curtain closed. The only light illuminated came from the T.V and his phone. Rarri was getting tired of moping around but was discouraged and didn't know what step to take next.

'*I need my pops right now*' he thought to himself. He plotted on going to spend some time in his father's room but didn't want his grandma to see him right now. Not like this anyway. He stood up, snatched his bottle from Payday, took another sip, passed it back, grabbed his car keys off of the table and headed out.

The night was cold but the liquor kept him warm. He poured some out on the ground for his father, took a sip and sat down on the damp grass. He came here to talk but ended up just sitting in silence, not knowing what to say. Hours had passed and Rarri hadn't even taken another sip. Instead, he just kept pouring it out for his father, not knowing what else to do with it. He blew out in frustration then stood.

"What do you want me to do?" he asked as he emptied the bottle and as soon as the words left his mouth, it started pouring down raining. He nodded and said, "I got you" then walked off with the answers he had come for.

When he got back to the Chop shop, Payday was still in the same spot. He walked passed him, went into the kitchen and opened a drawer where he had seen Payday's .357 a few days earlier. He checked it, noticing only one bullet chambered, then walked back to the living room in question. Payday saw the gun in his hand and the look on his face and knew what he wanted. He pointed to the entertainment center. Rarri rushed to the closed cabinet, opened it and saw a box of bullets, grabbed them and left again.

FORTY-TWO

RARRI HAD BEEN STAKED OUT, watching the hotel parking lot for three days now and still there was no sign of Sir Master. Not wanting to miss too many moments, he had empty water bottles to piss in,(Well, some empty). He was just about to call it a day when an old school Cadillac pulled into the lot. He ducked down low in his seat but kept his eyes on the driver and sure enough, after parking, Sir Master got out of the car in an all white suit.

His blood boiled at the sight of him. He wanted to get him right then and there but it was too many people around. Sir Master reached into his car, pulled out a teddy bear, closed the door then went and mingled with a circle of pimps for a minute before walking off with a big smile on his face. Not even ten minutes later, he was storming back to his Cadillac in anger, Teddy bear still in hand. This time he didn't say shit to nobody. He just got in his car and pulled off, nearly crashing into another car as he came out.

Rarri followed him for about thirty minutes until he pulled into some rundown duplex apartment building. Not wanting to be seen, he lurked from a distance but was still close enough to see his mark use his keys to open the door and walk in. He cut his engine off and got comfortable like a spider in the back of the web until something got caught in it. Sir Master came back out, got in his car and pulled out of his driveway. This time, he didn't follow him. He had a better idea. Dressed in all black, Rarri was ready to hunt.

———

Sir Master put the key in his door knob, twisted it and walked in with a brown bag in his hand. He didn't waste no time going to his couch to sit down. He pulled Hennessey out of the bag along with a small plastic cup, poured himself a drink and took a sip with his eyes closed, loving the burning sensation.

"I'm more of a Remy man, myself" Rarri interrupted startling the hell out of Sir Master who instantly reached for the gun he kept in the crack of the couch. "You lookin for this?" he asked, stepping out of the dark corner with Sir Master's 9mm in hand. "You slippin on yo pimpin 'P'"

"I ain't in the game no mo" he replied seriously.

"Yea, ight, I hear you" Rarri pulled one of the plastic chairs that Sir Master had in there and placed it across from, then sat down.

"Look, I don't got no money. I don't know what it is you want but what I do know is that this not the road you want to go down, son"

'BOOM!'

Rarri shot him in the stomach with his own gun.

"Arrghh" Sir Master groaned in pain as he held his wound, white shirt turning crimson.

"You gonna kill a nigga then talk to his son like he yours? Rarri asked looking at him like he was crazy.

"I don't know what you talkin bout" He yelled, then groaned again in pain.

"No?" Rarri leaned in closer and pulled the dark blue rag down from his face to his neck. "What about now?"

He was the spitting image of his father and Sir Master recognized it immediately and put his head down. Satisfied, Rarri sat back clutching the gun in his lap and shook his head in disgust.

"I would have thought you would have been way more on yo shit from all the stories I done heard. But, you just a washed up old nigga"

Sir Master grunted as he looked at his wound, then covered it back up when he noticed how bad it was.

"I told you I'm not in the game no mo"

"Nigga, stop lying. I just seen you come from yo daughter spot earlier. Probably checkin trap" Rarri replied through clenched teeth. "You went to jail for shootin her cause she kept getting sick. Now you back out tryna fuck up her life all over again? Nah, I ain't lettin that happen."

"I had twenty years to think about my mistakes. Especially the one with my daughter." He managed to moan out through the pain. "I NEED A DOCTOR!"

"Nigga, you better put some OOVO on it" He replied pointing to the bottle on the table, thinking about the Blackish episode that Chris Brown played in. "Let me get that for you" He grabbed the bottle from the table, opened it, then started pouring drink all over his face. "There you go"

He sat back down looking at Sir Master as he shook his wet head. He knew that look all too well.

"You ain't no better than me."

"What?" Rarri asked in disbelief. "I would never be the type of nigga out here pimpin myown daughter"

"That's not what I'm talkin bout. You a killa, just like I was"

"Man, miss me wit all that rehabilitation shit. Ain't nobody buyin what you sellin, nigga" Rarri drilled.

Sir Master looked at him seriously. He wanted Rarri to see that he wasn't playing.

"Ain't nothin to sell, man. I'm not the same person I used to be. I swear"

Rarri just waved him off. "I don't know what you bein desperate for. You not walking out of here."

Sir Master nodded in agreement, never breaking eye contact. "I know"

"Well if you know so much, why keep lyin?"

"You said you heard stories about me, right?'

"Yaahp" he replied.

"Ahhhh" Sir groaned, half out of breath. "Has...a liar...ever been one of them...?" he managed to get out.

Knowing that he would be lying if he said yea, Rarri studied his face for any signs of bullshit, not seeing any.

"If you ain't sendin Wap, then why you pop up all suited and booted in the Pit?"

Sir Master tried to chuckle sarcastically and instantly regretted it when the pain shot threw his body. He groaned then nodded his head to the Teddy bear sitting in the empty chair.

"Today her birthday...I wanted to give her that and take her out to eat but her momma....she still the same and can't accept the fact that I ain't....she....ahhhh, she...brainwashed Marqueesha into thinkin that I want her out there workin corners....I should have never left her alone...with her. I ain't choice. I had to check in with my Parole officer...." He stopped to try and catch a breath before talkin some more. " When I came back, they were gone."

Rarri thought about it deeply and it was Wap's birthday. He had just forgotten due to everything else that was going on.

"That still don't explain why you shot her when she was a kid"

"Honestly...I was so gone off PCP that I still can't...tell you what happened." He explained, his words coming slower and slower. It didn't stop him from explainin though. "All I remember is wakin up...in jail wit a charge...It was all downhill for me after yo dad did me how he did." He managed to get out just before he spit up some blood.

"Then you did what you did" Rarri spat back in contempt, connectin the dots.

"I did" Sit admitted seriously.

"You and Juice" he coached.

Sir Master tried again to laugh and ended up hurting himself even more.

"Juice was soft…he wasn't nothin but an inside…source."

"Inside source?"

"You.. ain't know?" he asked Rarri, stopping to spit out more blood.

"Know what?" he countered.

He coughed more and spit up more blood instead of answering which just pissed Rarri off more.

"KNOW WHAT?!"

Sir Master smiled, teeth stained red from the internal bleeding.

"The only ..person…that wanted yo dad gone mo…than me and Juice….was Angel's momma…Yo granny set…your father up to get killed…ain't family a bitch…" he said then let out his last breath and died with his eyes wide open.

Rarri didn't want to believe him but how could he not? It all lined up perfectly. His grandma tried having his grandpa killed twice so being the one to set his dad up didn't sound far-fetched at all. Every word she had ever spoken after he would mentionq his father played in his head vividly. She hated him because G-man embarrassed her in front of everyone and deep down she knew he would never take her back. She could never be his. NEVER!

Rarri shot him in the face two times, grabbed the Teddy bear from the chair and left, not knowing exactly how to handle the news. All these years he had been loving and living with the person he hated most. The same person who had raised him was responsible for him being parentless. He never could explain the connection he had with Wap but before he knew it, he found himself knocking on her door holding the Teddy bear her father had gotten her.

She opened the door with a look of shock on her face.

"Happy Birthday" He said and before she could react, he

started kissing her with everything he had in him. He stepped inside, closing the door behind them, never takin his lips away from hers.

Wap kissed him back with just as much heat, her hands wrapped around his back, feeling him the way she always wanted to as they made their way to the bedroom. He pulled his shirt off and she eagerly helped, then she pulled hers off and helped him too. Both of them started fumbling with their pants, racing to get naked. He wanted Betty Wap, bad. He laid her on the bed, kissing her gently while looking into her eyes. He then slid inside of her wet pussy, making her moan out in ecstasy. Wap was tighter than he had expected. Her pussy felt like the home his dick had been waiting for it's entire life.

"I love you.." The words came out his mouth without a second thought.

Wap dropped a tear and said, "I love you too" in between kisses.

He thrust slowly in and out of her, both of them moving to the same beat. It was as if their bodies were one. She had never had this feeling before. It was better than anything she had ever anticipated experiencing. When they had both finished, they laid next to each other sweating, tired and smiling from ear to ear. He looked over at her with a question.

"Why'd we wait so long to do this?"

She blushed, closing her lips in excitement, "I don't know"

He locked his fingers with hers. Rarri had missed Wap. They had been through a lot and it's like life was finally giving them a fair chance. He began to think deeply about where to go from here. His way of living had no fairytale ending and he knew it. He and Wap wasn't going to run off, square up and live happily ever after. He was a pimp and she was a hoe. Not only that, but he also couldn't take her around Heaven anymore. He didn't care though, as long as they had each other, nothing else really mattered. Rarri just needed her on the same page.

Another thought came to his mind as Betty Wap started smelling her lip.

"Do you love me?" He asked.

She looked him in the eyes, all lovey dovey and shit and answered, "Duh, I do"

The way she responded let him know she was still lost. He had to get her out of here to wing her back to how she was. He got out of the bed and started quickly getting dressed.

"Look Wap, pack yo shit up. Ima go get the rest of my clothes from my cousin's house, make a couple quick stops, then we gone."

She sat up quickly in a panic and confusion.

"But, but, what about momma? She-she gon be worried. She gon be lookin for me..and my daddy"

"Listen, fuck yo momma Wap. She don't give a fuck about you. not like I do. Not yo dad di-" He stopped himself then went and gave her a kiss on the lips. "Just trust me."

She looked into his eyes seeing nothing but love.

"K" she nodded.

He smiled at that, "Alright, I'll be right back"

He left quickly, he was moving so fast he didn't stop to check his surroundings. Maybe if he did, he would have seen her mother lurking in the shadows. She was just on her way back from the dope spot when she saw him walk in. By the time he came out, she was high as a kite with a crack induced rage.

Later that night…..

As promised, he handled everything he needed to do and came right back. He was about to knock on the door but seen it was slightly cracked open, so he just walked in, not thinking much of it. He was in the middle of poppin some fly shit but when he noticed how messy the room had become in such a short time, his antennas were up. One thing Betty Wap always kept was a clean room.

"WAP!" He called out but no reply.

It looked as if a tornado had come through there. *'Maybe she had a panic attack and trashed the room'* he thought to himself, hopin for the best. Then, it was like the world stood still when he saw her feet on the far side of the bed. He rushed over to her and when he seen her laying face forward on the floor, his heart sank.

"Wap!!"

He turned her over onto her back and couldn't believe what he was seeing. She had been beaten severely. She was almost unrecognizable. Her lips looked like hot links that had been left in the microwave for too long. It looked like her nose was broken and a lot of her hair had been pulled out so her scalp was showing, but the worse was her eye, it was missing. Her body looked lifeless. Rarri sat beside her and cradled her in his arms. Telling her how sorry he was and how much he loved her.

'Cough! Cough! Arrghhh!

"Wapq..?" He cried out then grabbed the room phone and dialed 911.

She couldn't speak. All she could do was moan in pain and he kept holding her. When the first responders came and put her on the gurney, Rarri noticed the white piece of paper in her hand and grabbed it as they pushed her to the ambulance. Everyone in the hotel stood outside in shock, some crying, others talking bout what they thought had happened. He unraveled the paper and instantly teared up. It was a list of the future kids they were going to have when they decided to settle down and get out of the game.

He chuckled to himself as the tears poured down his face, finding humor in all of the adjustments she had made over time because the end result was all of their kids looking just like him.

"Sir, are you coming?" The First responder asked, ready to close the door.

He looked up just in time to see Betty Wap's mother standing in the crowd with a sinister look on her face. His jaw tightened and his eyes hardened because her expression said it all.

"SIR! Are you coming?" They asked once more.

He wanted to kill but Betty Wap need him by her side.

"Yea" he replied, then ran and jumped in.

Two Weeks Later....

Heaven cleared her throat from the middle of the doorway. Rarri jumped from the bed proudly and protective over Betty Wap but still slightly embarrassed because he had been caught playing Patty cake.

"At ease soldier" Heaven said sarcastically in her manly voice as she walked in, looking just as stunning as always. Her casual, two piece black and white Balenciaga fit matched perfectly with her heels. She always looked as if her clothes had been painted on, flaunting her curves dramatically like a model ready for a photo shoot.

"These are for you" She said handing Betty Wap a dozen gift wrapped roses.

"Thanks..." she replied with an eye roll.

"So, what, you just gonna stay mad at me?" Heaven asked picking up on the sarcasm.

"Uh, yeah. You called me a *'One eyed flunky'*, remember?" she answered pointing to her missin eye and Heaven"s heart sank.

She had paid good money for that eye and seeing Betty back without it pissed her all the way off.

"We need to talk" She said to Rarri, then walked off without waiting for an answer. "NOW!" she ordered with authority when she looked back and saw him still standing there.

He followed her just outside the room.

"Wassup?"

"You have to go back home-"

"Home? What home? I don't have a home. Qnot no more. My home is with her and you made it clear she ain't welcome at yo house, so as far as I'm concerned, neither am I" He drilled.

"Look, I'm sorry, okay? I'm sorry for not tellin you about

Spank's momma. I didn't mean to keep you in the blind for so long. The last thing I ever wanted is for you to feel like you can't trust me. I was out of pocket for that but I promise you that will *'never'* happen again, *'on my sister'''* She pleaded as she took his hand and kissed the back of it "..and on yo dad" she kissed it once more and he believed her instantly. "Ima do whatever it is I gotta do to get *'us'* back on track but right now, you have to go back home"

"Why do you keep sayin that, what's wrong?" he asked in concern.

Heaven pulled out her phone, scrolled to a video and pressed play. His jaw dropped in disbelief because he really couldn't believe what he was seeing. It was a video of Rasheed sneaking into his room and leaving back out with a book he had taken off of the dresser. He played the video back and paused it on Rasheed's face. His eyes were wide with excitement and his smile full with greed. Rarri had brung him in with all love, wishing nothing but the best for him, so the betrayal cut deep.

Unknownq to Rasheed, the seven leather MCM poodles in Rarri's room had cameras in them.

"Yo grandpa came by the house the day after you, qq for a book he had left on yo dresser. When he stopped by to talk to me about a favor I needed. When he said it wasn't there, I decided the only way to see where it went was to check the cameras you told me you had put in the eyes of the dogs. I thought it could have been one of the workers or somethin but when I saw *'Rasheeqd'*, I couldn't believe it. it's dated the same day ya'll threw the party-"

"Ima kill cuh" he interrupted, feeling played. He remembered how Rasheed suggested they celebrate at his aunt's house because he wanted to go swimming in the pool. He had outsmarted him and he didn't like it not one bit.

Heaven exhaled in frustration and fingered her hair to the back.

"I don't know if that's possible."

"What?" Rarri asked in disbelief.

She looked at him seriously before answering.

"Rarri....I think he's your brother..."

He looked from the phone to her with a sour expression.

"My brother?"

"Yea...."

He shook his head.

"how is that?"

"After I saw the video, I put Carlos and Jose on him 24/7 to see what he was on. Mostly he stayed at the Chop shop or in traffic with everybody else. But, on a few occasions he would stop by a house in Calabasas for hours at a time. They doubled back to get pictures of who came in and out not thinkingq much of the woman. I noticed her though...Her name is Mary. She used to hoe for yo dad back in the day. Her and yo momma couldn't stand each other because instead of sharing a spot as planned, yo momma played her to the left and brung me in. God had a soft spot for Mary but one day he told us he caught her in the bathroom tryin to steal his nut out of the condom. He kept her close hopin she didn't get pregnant, but once she did, he sent her to the abortion clinic" Heaven shook her head in disappointment. "She walked in and never came back out. The first time I saw Rasheed, I noticed how much ya'll looked alike but I thought it was just a coincidence. Now I know the reason we never saw Mary again was because she never got that abortion."

'Ain't family a bitch' He couldn't help but to think about Sir Master's last words because they had been playing over and over in his head since he had heard them. Rarri put his back against the wall and rested his head back, thinking deeply.

"I killed Sir Master..." He said after a moment of silence.

"I know" she admitted. " I was about to do it but when I saw you sneakin in, I just pulled off. so yea, you're welcome."

He shook his relaxed head with a smile. Thankful for the charity kill. He debated on telling her what Sir Master told him.

"How you think I should handle this shit?"

She puffed out, thinking for a moment before she spoke again.

"They're throwin a party tomorrow night and I heard everybody is supposed to be there. I'll stay here with Wap while you do yo thang. He may be a thief and crafty ass nigga but he's still your brother so you can't kill him for that"

"Then, what should I do?" he asked...

She looked at him with a hint of playfulness in her eyes.

FORTY-THREE

THE CHOP SHOP WAS LIT. It was foreign cars parked up and down the block. You would have thought it was a concert instead of a house party. Rarri had to admit that this was as poppin as he had ever seen it before. Mothafuckas was everywhere. All of the bitches looked like strippers and hoes. All lifestyle, no theme. He saw plenty of familiar faces there too.

The rumors about him wasn't a secret so the people he walked by awed like he had risen from the dead. Their whispers didn't go unnoticed. Some, more farfetched than the others, but one thing he didn't come here for was to explain shit. So he just kept pushing and walked in like he owned the place cause, well, he literally did. As soon as people noticed it was him, they paraded with hugs, P-shakes and everything else.

"Where you been at, 'P'?" No love asked in excitement, happy to see him back. "The shop been brackin like a mothafucka. That nigga Sheed got it in music videos and all types of shit now."

"That's wassup" Rarri replied, scanning the crowd a bit. He looked up and saw Rasheed standing in the center of the twin staircase looking down at him with a proud smile. Rarri glared back in pure disgust which caused Rasheeds smile to fade.

The look in Rarri's eyes spoke a thousand words so Rasheed knew he had him figured out. He turned and disappeared down the hall with Rarri in full pursuit. He grabbed one of the candles that was in the hallway, opened Rarri's bedroom door, threw it on his bed then closed it back and continued to his destination.

"SHEED!" He yelled after him, angrily, then kicked in the first door he came across. "SHEED!!"

That room was empty, so he continued to the next and did the same. He was looking like a maniac and Rasheed's hiding pissed him off even more. "So you just gon run like a lil bitch?!"

You could see the veins in his neck and spittle fly from his mouth as he yelled. His anger had him thinking unclearly but then he snapped back to reality when he noticed that he kicked down the door to his own room and saw his bed on fire. He close it then stormed to Rasheed's room, put his hand on the doorknob and turned it. To his surprise, it was open. Rasheed stood in front of his desk with his back to Rarri. He closed the door behind him and locked it.

"It wasn't supposed to be like this. We was supposed to-" Rasheed started...

"Nigga, save that shit" Rarri cut him off. "I ain't come to listen to you talk. You been lyin long enough"

"You just came to kill me and not hear my side?" Rasheed asked.

"You my brother, I can't kill you" Rarri replied calmly, causing him to turn around in surprise. "But I am gon beat yo ass"

Rasheed noticed that Rarri didn't have a weapon in his hand and smiled to himself, then took off his jacket. "How'd you find out? Well, I guess that don't matter too much now." He added then squared up in a boxing stance. "Wassup"

Rarri ran and swung wildly at Rasheed's face but he blocked it with his left forearm then punched his little brother in the stomach with his right. That instantly knocked the wind out of him. He buckled over in pain, holding his stomach, trying his best to catch his breath. Rasheed bent down next to him, poked his lips out dramatically, inhaling and exhaling quickly like a pregnant woman takin breathing lessons.

"Breathe, lil bro, breathe" he mocked then pushed Rarri to the ground. "See, you a killa, not a fighter. Me, Ima lil bit of both I guess. You should see my trophies. Niggas never last long in the ring with me P. Mixed martial arts, kickboxin, Jujitsu. I got black belts in all three of those." Rasheed held up his fist, "So, you can't see me with these"

Rarri stood to his feet, held up his fist then charged him with a combination of punches, landing none. He blocked them all, then punched him in the jaw twice so quickly that Rarri didn't even see him swing. All he knew was that whatever he had did had him back on the ground and sitting on his ass. He bounced back up quickly, did the same and ended up right back in the same spot.

Rasheed laughed. "That's really all you got? Alright, come on. You tried, it's over, now let me help you up" He said, extending his hand but Rarri swatted it away.

"Fuck you!"

"Oh, so you want some more?" Rasheed backed up and got back in his fighting stance "Come on"

Rarri stood, squared up, then the both of them crept towards each other strategically. Rarri faked with his left, making Rasheed go for the block then came with a quick right and a faster left, landing a two punch combo.

"You ain't the only nigga that know how to fight. I got my knockouts from the set, stupid"

Rasheed put his hand to his mouth saw that he was bleeding, smiled, then rushed in and they both started locking, throwing blow for bow fuckin each other up. They touched almost every wall in the room and anything breakable was broken. Rarri slammed Rasheed's face into the T.V and Rasheed slammed him through a table. He thought that was going to be the end of it but Rarri was getting back up.

"All this over some fuckin books" Rasheed shouted tiredly feeling like they had been fighting for hours.

Rarri was just as tired, both of them bleeding and looking like Rocky Balboa after he got done fighting Drago. "It's not just some books" He looked at his brother from one knee. "It's our father's books, that he left for me."

"You?" Rasheed asked in disbelief. "I'm the first born. Those books belong to 'ME'" He added angrily, slamming his fist against his chest.

Rarri shook his head because he could see that Rasheed really believed that. Thinking back to everything Heaven had to told him about Rasheed's mother, Rarri knew she must have not had told him how he was conceived. 'She brainwashed him' He thought to himself as he looked at his brother standing there full of hate. Rarri knew right then and there that this wasn't Rasheed's fault, it was his mothers.

"Sheed, he never knew you was born. Yo momma stole you from a condom and ran off when he told her to get an abortion."

He looked hurt and for a split second it had broken him. He almost fell to the floor, but he caught himself and stood strong.

"You a lie..." He yelled then rushed Rarri with a kick sending him falling back down over the broken glass.

Rarri cut his hands getting back up. He clenched his fist in anger spilling blood to the floor. His mind was telling him to fight but his heart wouldn't let him. He loosened his grip and looked at his big brother, genuinely. "I'm not lyin bro. I swear" answered putting his bloody 'P' sign in the air. Rasheed looked at it, then at him in disgust "You ain't even got toes no more" He said, then hit Rarri in the jaw, sending him back to the floor.

Rarri tried to get back up but he was so dazed that he ended up falling back down. He clamped his teeth together making sure his jaw wasn't broke then flexed it wide to double check.

"You right...I don't got toes no more" He admitted as he tried getting up "But, I ain't 'just' a pimp"

"There you go, thinkin you better than everybody again" Rasheed kicked him in the ribs four times, making him fall flat down scraping the side of his face on the glass.

'AHHHH!!" Rarri screamed out. He was sure something had been broken. He held his side in agonizing pain. Rasheed punched him in the head with six hard hits then grabbed him by the back of his shirt and dragged him across the room. He leaned him against the wall then picked up his father's book from the floor and cocked it all the way back, ready to bring it down as hard as could. He had Rarri clenched by the front collar with his left hand for support.

"You still think you better than everybody?"

Rarri looked at him through his good eye, nodded and said "We both is"

His grip loosened and the door flew open.

"The shop on fire 'P' let's go" a hysterical Macky yelled after kickin the door in then his whole demeanor changed when he saw what was going on.

It was like everything was moving in slow motion and fast forward at the same time. Rarri and Rasheed instinctively looked to the doorway and seeing his boy on the floor looking like he had been hit by a car, Macky instinctively drew his signature .45 and pointed at Rasheed with nothing but murder on his mind.

"NOOO!" Rarri screamed.

'BOOM!'

Macky had shot Rasheed in his side, sending him falling to the floor, then ran to Rarri's aid and tried pulling him away but Rarri yanked himself free and crawled back to Rasheed

"Fuck cuh!" Macky yelled, then pointed his gun back at him for a kill shot, but Rarri covered him with his body for protection.

"He my Brother MACK! He my brother..." Rarri said then when he knew it was safe, he put Rasheed in his lap. Macky lowered his weapon and Rarri yelled for him to go and get help, not noticing the flames getting bigger in the doorway.

Macky went and closed it.

"We gon have to jump out the window"

"I-I-I couldn't. I couldn't... c-c-ouldn't crack the---the code" Rasheed stammered.

"What code?" Rarri asked.

His brother pointed to the book on the floor.

"Pass me that book, Macky" Rarri instructed his friend who was opening a window.

"A BOOK?!" he asked in shock. "YAAH, the house is on 'fuckin FIRE!"

"I know!" he yelled back in frustration, then calmed down. "I just need the book Mack. please."

Macky saw how serious he was, shook his head, grabbed the book then handed it to him.

"The crown" Rarri read the front then opened it quickly and began reading until the words ended. All the pages were blank, just as 'The Cheat Code' was, only these pages had no braille. Still, Rarri felt them anyway just to be sure, glad because he couldn't read it no how. By now, smoke was coming under the door.

"We gotta go cuh!" Macky yelled as he was literally halfway through the window.

Rarri's mind was racing a million miles per second but he was still stumped. He scanned through the blank pages again, just in case he missed something. "FUCK!" he swore to himself as tears fell from his eyes.

"Just g-g-go bro" Rasheed told him but Rarri just kept flipping through the book

"It's a riddle" He said, then went back to the last page with words and read out loud. "*I've given you pieces and I've given you clues, if you've made it this far, you will make it further. In dark times I will show you the light but good game always stays tight.*

From who you were to who you are and who you will become, the switch will change your life"

He read it once more and thought deeply as the smoke from the door grew thicker, repeating the key words.

"In dark times, in dark times, in dark times. I will show you the light. The switch will change your life..."

He quickly turned to Macky, "Turn the light off for me, Mack"

"Turn the light off? Cuh, I'm bout to *'jump'* nigga" He replied seriously as he was really about to do it, then swore to himself because he couldn't just leave his boy like that.

He climbed back in, ran to the light switch, turned it off then ran back to the window. Rarri and Rasheed's eyes grew wide because as soon as the light went off, the words on the page illuminated........"

Stay Tuned In For Rarri 3

Lastly

If you are locked up right now don't let your situation get the best out of you, get the best out of your situation.

Find something you are good at and seek ways to make it tangible . just because you are locked down doest mean you are dead. This is the perfect time to put into yourself because you are your best investment. People fagg off all the time but fuck them just don't fagg off on yourself by neglecting the gifts that you sre blessed with. I never even thought about being an author. To be honest I just picked up a pen and started writing out of boredom. I just wanted to create something I would enjoy reading but the people around kept punching me to finish it. Still it was more people speakin on a million reason why I couldn't do it.. I just looked at the ONE reason why I could.. I believe in me not what the next person think I should be . just because naysayers cant do somethin doesn't mean that you can't. Use everything nmatter good or bad as motivation to go harder. Fuck what the next person talkin about stay in your one lane. Strive to get to a point where your not worried about nobody to take care of you because you got your own Shit. You are the prixe so keep your head held high no matter what.

Once you understand the value of your worth nobody else seems to compare and there's no better feeling than that. There no doubt in my mind ima make it because even if I died right now and you prospered off of this then I still one by you being successful. We have to want to see each other win no matter where we from, our races or genders.. Don't none of that matters.. As long as we remain solid and real to the ones around us we are good. If You are a writer who trying to get out there look into publishing through Amazon. The shit is fuccin free so all you need is the basic shit to get your book out there. Its not impossible. If I did it you can too. Also hit up some of these magazine people for some promo. All they can do is say no or nothin at all😂. Grab a pen and do you thang. Stop playing!

Also if you need something to write in I have a notebook business where we sell notebooks that have book cover images on the front to make your work feel that much more real until you find the right cover for you story. We have covers for all genres of writers and sell through Amazon so you can receive it anywhere you are located. A's Journals on Amazon, tune in.

Facebook: fly bookz

Instagram: flyasbookz

Gmail:flyasbookz@gmail.com

Asanibandz88@gmail.com

Instagram: Asanibandz

Facebook: studd dula

Send a picture with you holding my books or notebooks and I will post it up.

Made in the USA
Las Vegas, NV
12 October 2023

78990617R00193